The Simon and Schuster
POCKET GUIDE TO

The Wines of
BORDEAUX

With an Introduction by
—HUGH JOHNSON—

AUX BORDELAIS

A Fireside Book
Published by Simon & Schuster, Inc.
New York

David Peppercorn's Pocket Guide to the Wines of Bordeaux was edited
and designed by Mitchell Beazley International Limited,
Artists House, 14-15 Manette Street, London W1V 5LB
Copyright © 1986 Mitchell Beazley Publishers
Text copyright © 1986 David Peppercorn
Maps copyright © 1986 Mitchell Beazley Publishers
All rights reserved including the right of reproduction
in whole or in part in any form

A Fireside Book
Published by Simon & Schuster, Inc.
Simon & Schuster Building
Rockefeller Center
1230 Avenue of the Americas
New York, New York 10020
FIRESIDE and colophon are registered trademarks
of Simon & Schuster, Inc.

1 2 3 4 5 6 7 8 9 10

ISBN: 0-671-63675-8
Library of Congress Cataloging in Publication Data
available upon request

The author and publishers will be grateful for any information which
will assist them in keeping future editions up to date. Although all
reasonable care has been taken in the preparation of this book neither
the publishers nor the author can accept any liability for any
consequences arising from the use thereof or from the information
contained herein.

Maps by Eugene Fleury
Typeset by Servis Filmsetting Ltd, Manchester, England
Reproduction by Gilchrist Bros. Ltd, Leeds, England
Printed and bound in Hong Kong by Mandarin Offset
International Ltd.

Editor	Elizabeth Hubbard
Designer	Sheila Volpe
Production	Androulla Pavlou
Senior Executive Editor	Chris Foulkes
Senior Executive Art Editor	Roger Walton

CONTENTS

INTRODUCTION

Access to the personal files of a top professional is surely the most that any serious amateur of wine could ask. The new generation of wine books represented by David Peppercorn's *Pocket Guide to the Wines of Bordeaux* and Serena Sutcliffe's companion volume on Burgundy amounts almost to such a privileged snoop.

The situation reports and critical opinions that form the basis of buying decisions are normally classified information. But wine literature has moved with quite startling speed from the phase of enthusiastic generalization to that of precise wine-by-wine commentary. In these two books it drops at least its sixth, if not its seventh, veil. Now we are allowed to know as much as the most experienced professionals.

David Peppercorn is one of the most perceptive and respected of that ancient aristocracy of Anglo-Saxon merchants whose speciality is the wine of Bordeaux. He inherited both skill and passion directly from his father, one of the great "claret men" of the previous generation. Indirectly, one might say, he inherited them from a long line of predecessors stretching right back to the *negotiator brittanicus* who was identified on the waterfront of Burdigala, Roman Bordeaux, 18 centuries ago.

Accumulated experience is a serious merchant's vital stock in trade. It allows him to watch the passing show with a sense of historical perspective, to interpret as well as observe. But to keep up with such a complex scene as Bordeaux demands above all

perpetual tastings and almost daily communication with the
market-place. Thousands of properties vary from one vintage to
another in their relative success or failure, while their older wines
develop – not always in predictable ways.

David Peppercorn combines these two essential elements – a
background of experience and a fund of knowledge constantly
kept up to date – as well as any merchant-turned-author has ever
done. It is a remarkable privilege to be able, as it were, to look
over his shoulder at the enthralling pageant of Bordeaux.

Hugh Johnson

HOW TO USE THIS BOOK

This book has three main sections: first, an introductory one
giving a general picture of the Bordeaux wine region and how it
works; second, a general A–Z of châteaux; third, a series of
château profiles arranged by appellation, with a short briefing
on each appellation. Out of the 4,000 or so châteaux in the
region, a careful selection has been made of some 750 properties,
ranging from the most illustrious growths to many lesser-known
crus that are worth seeking out. These include not only châteaux
but also some domaines and cooperatives.

To look up a name, turn first to the A–Z. If the name appears
only in the A–Z it will be followed by brief factual details such as
appellation, ownership, vineyard area and production figures. If
the château merits a profile, the A–Z entry will merely tell you its
appellation and the page on which the profile appears. If the
name is that of a secondary label you will be told which château it
belongs to. A star beside one of the A–Z entries indicates that,
although not profiled, the wine is above average in its class.

To save space, a number of abbreviations have been used.
Vineyard areas are expressed in hectares (shortened to ha), and
yields are given in hectolitres per hectare (hl/ha).

Where a company is the owner of a property, its name may be
preceded by a set of letters. These indicate types of company as
follows:

Ets	Etablissements	**SARL**	Société à
GAEC	Groupement		Responsibilité
	Agricole		Limité
	d'Exploitation en	**SC**	Société Civile
	Commun	**SCA**	Société Civile
GFA	Groupement Foncier		Agricole
	Agricole	**SCI**	Société Civile
SA	Société Anonyme		Immobilière

When grape varieties are referred to, the following abbreviations are used:

CF	Cabernet Franc	**Musc**	Muscadelle
Col	Colombard	**PV**	Petit Verdot
CS	Cabernet Sauvignon	**Sauv**	Sauvignon Blanc
Mal	Malbec	**Sém**	Sémillon
Mer	Merlot		

THE REGION
AND ITS WINES

Bordeaux occupies a pre-eminent place among the world's wine regions. Its special geographical situation enables it to produce more fine wines with more regularity than any other part of France, or any other country.

Nowhere else are the greatest wines made in such quantity (only Ausone and Pétrus are in really short supply). And if world-wide acclaim has driven the prices of the First Growths beyond the reach of most of us, there are a number of excellent wines at far more reasonable prices which can often rival the First Growths, especially when young. For if Bordeaux can claim nine Premiers Crus (eight red and one white), how many other remarkable and exceptional wines does it not make? Tot up the best of the classified Médocs (and some of the unclassified ones) and the best of the Graves and St-Emilion classified growths, to say nothing of the best Pomerols, and you arrive at a figure of around 100 growths that can or do produce great bottles of wine. An impressive roll call. This, of course, covers only red wines, but there are also great sweet white wines and good dry whites.

Of course, this small elite is only the tip of the iceberg. The Bordeaux bible, *Bordeaux et ses vins*, by Cocks and Féret, lists over 4,000 property names in its 1982 edition, while just over 21,000 growers made wine in the department of Gironde in 1984 (this includes *vin de table*) and over 81,000 hectares of vineyards were dedicated to the growing of vines with the right to an *appellation contrôlée*. Bordeaux wines are indeed within the reach of all today, and its most modest wines have never been better made.

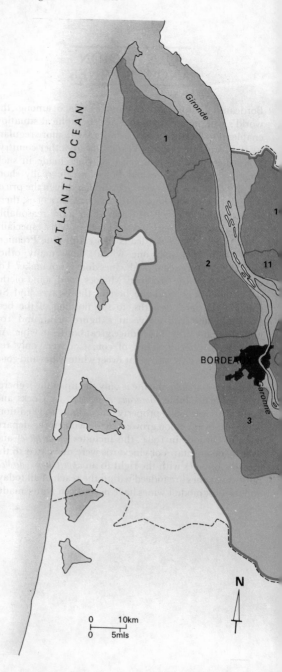

ATLANTIC OCEAN

Gironde

BORDEAUX

Garonne

1

2

11

1

3

N

| 0 | 10km |
| 0 | 5mls |

THE BORDEAUX REGION AND ITS WINE AREAS

1 Médoc
2 Haut-Médoc
3 Graves
4 Cérons
5 Sauternes and Barsac
6 Premières Côtes de Bordeaux
7 Loupiac
8 Ste-Croix-du-Mont
9 Côtes de Bordeaux-St-Macaire
10 Blayais
11 Bourgeais
12 Graves de Vayres
13 Entre-deux-Mers
14 Fronsac and Côtes de Canon-Fronsac
15 Pomerol
16 Lalande-de-Pomerol and Néac
17 St-Emilion
18 Montagne-, Lussac-, Parsac-, Puisseguin- and St-Georges-St-Emilion
19 Côtes de Castillon
20 Côtes de Francs
21 Ste-Foy-Bordeaux

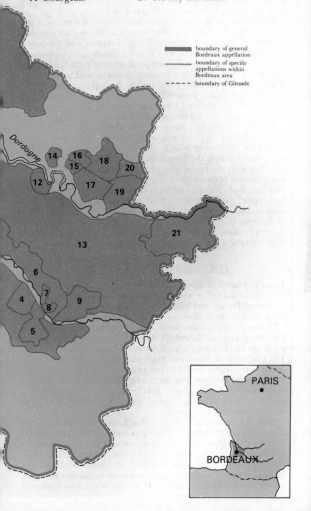

boundary of general Bordeaux appellation
boundary of specific appellations within Bordeaux area
boundary of Gironde

PARIS

BORDEAUX

GEOGRAPHY

Physically Bordeaux lies in the southwest of France, on the 45° latitude, with the often stormy waters of the Atlantic Ocean in the Bay of Biscay only a few miles away to the west, and with its vineyards spread out along the rivers Gironde, Garonne and Dordogne. Here the warming influence of the Gulf Stream is crucial – bear in mind that on the other side of the Atlantic the same latitude goes through Nova Scotia and Maine. The Gulf Stream and the Atlantic provide Bordeaux with hot summers, long mild autumns, often extending to the very end of October, relatively mild but wet winters, and mild springs. The consistency of the weather is emphasized by the way in which years of great cold (1709, 1740, 1820, 1956, 1985) or years of excessive rain (1930–32, 1965 and 1968) stand out.

The geology of the region is also important – not so much, it is now thought, for what the soils contain as for the drainage they provide. Going south from the Pointe de Grave and the ocean, the riverside land to the west of the Gironde and Garonne is basically gravel, that to the east predominantly sand, limestone and clay, in constantly changing patterns and proportions. There are exceptions, however, such as the important outcrops of gravel to be found in parts of Pomerol and the part of St-Emilion that adjoins it, and the limestone and clay under the gravel which gives Sauternes its special character.

The flat, gravelly ridges of the Médoc and Graves are protected from the Atlantic gales by the thick pine forests bordering the ocean which also decrease the rainfall. The presence of hills in the Premières Côtes and Entre-Deux-Mers, together with the rivers, also provides important differences in microclimate between those vineyards to the west of the Gironde and Garonne (Médoc and Graves) and those to the east of the Dordogne (the Libournais). One must also not forget the sheer distances involved as well. From the Pointe de Grave in the north to Langon in the south is 148km (92 miles), from the city of Bordeaux eastwards to Ste-Foy-la-Grande is 70km (44 miles), so that important climatic variations are hardly surprising.

HISTORICAL BACKGROUND

Three centuries of allegiance to the crown of England (1152–1453) gave Bordeaux a sense of unity as a region set apart from the rest of France and helped to orientate it firmly towards the Atlantic and the seafaring trade routes which this offered.

During these centuries the relative strengths and weaknesses of the sides ebbed and flowed. In the long term the development of sea trade was to have the most far-reaching consequences of all. The evolution of the city of Bordeaux, both as the commercial centre of the region and as its principal port, was natural enough in view of its position. But the development of Libourne as the main port on the Dordogne resulted from a deliberate act of policy by the English to expand trade by creating in 1270 an entirely new town and port.

After the inevitable trading set-back caused by the severance of the political ties between Bordeaux and England, it took some time for the region to recover, but, as it did, the value of the sea routes and the trading links built up through them became clear. Not only was trade with England, and soon Scotland and Ireland, restored on a lesser scale, but trade with other maritime powers, such as Holland and the Hanseatic ports, was developed.

Sea links were also important in establishing trade with Brittany, Normandy and Dunkirk. It was also quite logical that the lucrative West Indies business should have been built up and carried on through the port of Bordeaux. This brought considerable wealth to the city in the 18th century.

The 18th century also saw significant developments in the pattern of land ownership. The movement to build up important estates in the Médoc had begun in the previous century, but now it really took shape. This consolidation of land holdings in the hands of the so-called *noblesse de robe* (the legal and political aristocracy of Bordeaux) has had a vital influence in creating the château system which gives the Bordeaux vineyards their unique character. At the same time, a new and prosperous merchant class began to assert itself, first as courtiers (brokers) and négociants, and later as château proprietors.

This gave Bordeaux as a region a structure which was durable and resilient enough to withstand the vast social and political upheavals of the French revolutionary period (1789–96). Of course there were many and important changes in ownership. A British general even acquired a château and gave it his name, Palmer, after the final defeat of Napoleon (1815). But many châteaux changed ownership in name only, having been bought by relatives of exiles whose absence abroad led to their lands being forfeited, and the eventual return of these exiles, in many cases, saw a restoration of the status quo.

In the post-Napoleonic era the importance of the new merchant class, often enriched by commerce with the West Indies, greatly increased. Families such as the Bartons, Guestiers, and Johnstons became château proprietors as well as négociants. The growing success of the Médoc was crowned by the Paris Exhibition of 1855 for which the famous classification was prepared, covering only the red wines of the Médoc, with the sole exception of Haut-Brion, and the great sweet wines of Sauternes and Barsac.

In 1853 the Paris-Bordeaux railway was opened, and this was to have a vital impact on the opening of much of the French market to Bordeaux wines at a period of increasing prosperity. It was especially important for the development of St-Emilion, which had lagged behind Médoc until this time. Napoleon III had ushered in the Second Empire in 1851, and a period of new buoyancy enabled France increasingly to share in the fruits of the industrial revolution, which had been launched in Britain.

Parisian bankers like the Rothschilds (Lafite and Mouton) and the Pereires (Palmer) invested in properties in the Médoc. Even more important in the long run, the Libournais (St-Emilion, Pomerol and Fronsac) began to emerge from their long obscurity and make their mark. But just as the whole region seemed set on the greatest period of expansion and prosperity in its history, disaster struck. The period often called the Grande Belle Epoque was effectively ended in 1878 by the devastations of the disease phylloxera. Not until 1893 was there to be a large vintage of fine quality again.

It said much for the resources built up during the previous years, as well as the energy and determination of the large landowners who led the way in combating the disease, that Bordeaux recovered in the way it did. Once it had been discovered that grafting the original French vines on to disease-resistant American rootstocks was the only sure remedy, the reconstitution of the vineyards began. But an undertaking of this magnitude could not be accomplished overnight, nor without a great deal of cost and much experimentation.

The picture of what actually happened during these years is a complex one. The need to produce large quantities of serviceable wines quickly was met by planting on marginal lands not previously used for vines and on the Palus (riverside plain), where treatment by flooding and the sandy soil inhibited the spread of the disease. At the same time, the owners of quality vineyards fought with a good deal of success to preserve their ungrafted vines, realizing that fine wines needed mature vines. That is why many of the great vineyards of the Médoc, as well as some in St-Emilion and Pomerol such as Cheval Blanc, Figeac and La Conseillante, were able to continue making great vines during the years of transition.

But a new Belle Epoque was far from being just round the corner. After two great years in 1899 and 1900, there was to be no outstanding vintage again until 1920. Economically the years leading up to the First World War (1914–18) were depressed in Europe as a whole, and the Bordeaux trade did not experience the same degree of prosperity it had known in the 1850s, 1860s and 1870s. Although the 1920s were to produce some splendid vintages, economic conditions became steadily worse. The prices of the 1926 vintage collapsed, and the world slump soon followed. Poor vintages and a disastrous economic climate spelt ruin for many growers and merchants during the 1930s.

BORDEAUX SINCE 1945

It was against this background that Bordeaux celebrated peace in 1945 with a series of wonderful vintages, but it took some time for the region to repair the years of neglect and begin to rebuild its prosperity. It was not until the late 1950s that one could say with confidence that a new age was dawning, and that prices, and with them investment in vineyards and buildings, began to rise. The real prosperity of the 1960s culminated in the speculation and spiralling prices of 1971–73, which ended in a disaster precipitated by the oil crisis of 1974 and exacerbated by a thoroughly unhealthy market situation in Bordeaux itself. But, after only two years of disorder, the Bordeaux market recovered its equilibrium. Since then, progress, prosperity and good vintages have been the hallmark of the Bordeaux market.

TECHNICAL PROGRESS AND INNOVATION

The 1960s and 70s have been years of enormous technical progress. In the vineyards, the success of sprays in preventing rot have meant that not since 1968 has a Bordeaux vintage been harvested in an unhealthy condition. The vinification of these healthy grapes has also seen important improvements. The temperature at which wine is fermented is now much more carefully controlled than in the past. This means that even in very hot years, such as 1982 and 1983, very few wines become acetic, whereas in 1947 this misfortune was commonplace. The quality of dry white wines has improved almost beyond recognition with the use of fermentation carried out at around 18°C (64°F) and the practice of ageing in steel rather than wooden barrels.

Great improvements have been made among top growths, especially in the Médoc, where the properties are large, by making much more careful selections before the final *assemblage* for the *grand vin*. This has been one of Professor Emile Peynaud's many contributions to the improvements in quality which have been so widely achieved over the past 20 years.

Bordeaux tends to be rather more schizophrenic about a modernization which not everyone would hail as an improvement: the introduction of mechanical harvesters. Nowhere in France has their use spread more rapidly, and today more machines are employed in Gironde than in any other *vignoble* of France – 1,050 were in use by 1983. The large estates in Médoc and Entre-Deux-Mers are especially well adapted to their use, as the land is rather flat and the *cuviers* where the wine is vinified are usually adjacent to the vineyards. The major advantage of mechanical harvesting is its speed, enabling a much more precise decision to be made as to when the picking should begin, permitting the grapes to be harvested when perfectly ripe without running the risk that part of the harvest will be overripe or that the weather will break.

Many of the Crus Classés are still resisting the introduction of machines on the grounds that it would be detrimental to quality. One suspects that they are also concerned about the image created by the machine in the context of an expensive, high-quality product. The present indications are that, with the progress which has been made in adapting these machines to the French vineyards, excellent results can be obtained when grapes are in any case required to be de-stalked. For white wines, the cylindrical presses now in use can cope with the pressing of de-stalked white grapes, although the presence of stalks certainly helps to drain the *marc* (pulp left after pressing) better. Machines also leave unripe grapes unpicked, and in this respect make a better selection "on the vine" than would most pickers.

THE APPELLATIONS

The concept of appellations developed in France immediately after the First World War, and the final legislation giving effect to the system we now know was enacted in 1935. It meant that any wine of more than purely local fame was given the designation *Appellation d'Origine Contrôlée* (AOC), usually shortened to *Appellation Contrôlée* (AC). The original purpose was to protect the famous wine names of France from cheap imitations at a time of surplus production and low prices. It also spearheaded an important campaign to remove hybrid vines from French appellation vineyards. These are crosses between European vines and phylloxera-resistant American vines, as distinct from grafted vines or crosses between different European vines (e.g. Müller-Thurgau). These hybrids, which often carry over something of the odd "foxy" flavour to be found in American vines, were planted in many vineyards after the phylloxera as an alternative to grafting.

The principal things an appellation regulation does are:

1. To define the area entitled to a name (e.g. Médoc).
2. To list what grape varieties may be planted.
3. To lay down the density per hectare of vines to be planted, and how they shall be pruned.
4. To set minimum degrees of alcohol (and sometimes for white wines maximum degrees) and regulate chaptalization (addition of sugar to must to increase alcoholic degree in years of deficient ripeness).
5. To set maximum yields per hectare.
6. Since 1974 to insist on analyses and tastings before finished

wines may receive their appellation documents.
7. To require growers to make a declaration of their production
   after each vintage, and a declaration of the stocks they hold as
   at 31 August each year.

To administer this system and liaise with the syndicates of
growers in each appellation, the Institut National des Appellations d'Origine (INAO) was formed, and remains today the key
body for watching over and reforming the system.

In the Bordeaux region the definition of a particular area
entitled to an appellation of its own caused fewer problems than
in some other parts of France. But in the Libournais there was
much local controversy as to the use of the name St-Emilion. In
the 19th century its use was very widespread, as old copies of
Cocks and Féret bear witness. St-Emilion included not only
Pomerol and the communes to the north but also the area to the
east now known as the Côtes de Castillon. In 1921, the situation
was finally decided when the Tribunal of Libourne judged that
the name of St-Emilion should refer only to those parishes
contained within the ancient jurisdiction of the Jurade de St-
Emilion. But in 1936 the communes which had been refused the
right to sell their wines as St-Emilion were permitted to add the
name to their own, thus Montagne-St-Emilion, etc.

In the Médoc, the area north of St-Estèphe known as the Bas-
Médoc received the simple AC Médoc, while the best part
southwards as far as Blanquefort was made Haut-Médoc.
However, within the Haut-Médoc, the growers of the most
renowned villages sought, and eventually received, their own
appellations. A similar situation has recently arisen in Graves,
where the growers in the best parts of the northern Graves sought
to use the names of Pessac and Léognan instead of Graves. In the
event, a more common-sense compromise has been agreed – the
addition of the two names to that of Graves by the châteaux
concerned. One rather odd anomaly exists in Sauternes, where
the commune of Barsac, one of the five within the appellation,
also has its own AC, and growers here may call their wines Barsac
or Sauternes.

The control of what grape varieties may be planted ensures
that the traditional character of each wine is preserved and
prevents the use of inferior, and probably higher-yielding,
varieties. At the same time, of course, it prevents experimentation, not that this is something much sought after in Bordeaux.

The significance of the density with which vines are planted
may not at first be obvious. However, it has been shown that if
vines are planted more widely apart than is traditional in
Bordeaux they produce higher yields, and the character and
quality of the wine changes. A decree in 1974 fixed 2,000 vines
per hectare for the Bordeaux AC, and this compares with 5,000
to 10,000 for the Médoc ACs. Traditionally, 8,000 to 9,000 vines
are planted to the hectare in the Médoc, against 6,000 to the
hectare in St-Emilion.

The minimum degrees of alcohol are supposed to provide
some guarantee of quality and, unless they are achieved,
chaptalization (the addition of sugar) is illegal. But it is
interesting to note that the great clarets of the past were very low
in alcohol, often between 9% and 10% alcohol by volume, and
many have lasted superbly. Even as recently as the 1940s some
great wines scarcely reached 11%. Certainly, there is no call for a
Médoc to be more than 12% if it has to be chaptalized, or for a St-
Emilion to be more than 12.5%. In exceptional vintages it is, of

course, possible to produce wines of over 13% quite naturally in St-Emilion.

The relationship between quantity and quality has long been a vexed one. While it is clear that very high yields normally lead to lower quality, at what stage this occurs is not always easy to determine. Several points need to be made. The more effective control of disease, more use of fertilizers and the cloning of the most successful vines have all produced higher yields. The vintage of 1953 produced an average yield of 40.8hl/ha, and 1955 yielded 41.1, compared to 24 in 1949 and 25.7 in 1961. But 1970 produced 52.6, and 1973 achieved 55.3, which seemed remarkable by all historic standards. However, 1979 saw a figure of 62.9 reached, and the great 1982 vintage yielded 60. 1984, with its disastrous flowering of the Merlot, achieved only 36.9, but that should be compared with the figure of 17 in 1956 after that famous frost.

It is clear that the red grape varieties planted in Bordeaux are capable of producing fine wines from relatively high yields, certainly much higher than would have been thought possible a few years ago. In Burgundy, by contrast, the Pinot Noir's quality falls very significantly when yields rise over 50hl/ha in hillside vineyards. There were many examples of this in 1982. But in the same vintage in Bordeaux both the Merlot and the Cabernet Sauvignon produced magnificent wines of real concentration at this level of yield and higher. White wines are less susceptible to loss of quality from high yields, and in Bordeaux the best growths for dry wines tend to use the low-yielding Sémillon side by side with the high-yielding Sauvignon.

Bordeaux was the first major wine region in France to institute tastings before the granting of an appellation. St-Emilion had made this part of its new classification system, in itself the first classification to be tied to AC regulations, in 1955. In the Médoc tasting was introduced on a voluntary basis. After the major overhaul of the whole AC system in 1974 tastings became compulsory throughout the whole of France in the awarding of appellations. There is a certain cynicism about the tastings because it is said wines are rarely turned down. The panels consist of growers, courtiers (brokers) and négociants (merchants). The cask or vat samples have to represent an assemblage of all wines at a given property (including vin de presse and second-label wines) for which the appellation is required. So the quality of a sample is usually inferior to the quality which will go out under the château label, especially at the larger properties. Proprietors are often requested to resubmit samples because, at the early stage at which they are tasted, wines often show minor faults which subsequently disappear. My own experience of these tastings is that they are serious.

The declaration of stocks, which is another stipulation of the AC system, is more or less self-explanatory. It enables the authorities and the trade to know precisely how the last year's sales have gone and thus what there is to sell in the coming year. By adding together the stocks at 31 August with the declarations for the new vintage, the amount available for the coming sales campaign becomes clear. A comparison of the level of stocks from year to year also provides a valuable barometer of the health of the market and has an influence on price levels.

The overhaul of the AC system in 1974 was a far-reaching one which did much to remove the inflexibility of the old system and its insensitivity towards vintage variations. The essence of the new system revolves around three new concepts:

1. *Rendement de base* (basic permitted yield). This corresponds to the old maximum yields which were established in 1935 and had remained little changed since. For Bordeaux they were revised in 1984 (backdated to apply to the 1983 vintage), and most appellations were given higher allowances, sometimes by as much as 5hl/ha. But, as we shall see, under the new system, this *rendement de base* simply represents a norm and has less significance than previously.

2. *Rendement annuel* (annual yield). Now, each year, the growers in each appellation, through their syndicate, make a proposal to the INAO, bearing in mind the actual conditions of the year, as to what normal production levels should be. This figure may be above or below the *rendement de base*.

3. *Plafond limite de classement* (PLC). This is a fixed percentage (usually 20%), given in the decrees governing each appellation which, when applied to the *rendement annuel*, gives the maximum permitted yield for that particular year. If the *rendement annuel* allows a flexibility for the conditions of a particular year, the PLC allows for flexibility as between different vineyards and growers. To apply for this extra allowance, all the wines on the property must be offered for tasting, and anything over and above this limit has to go for distillation.

GRAPE VARIETIES

Today five grape varieties, three red and two white, dominate the vineyards of Bordeaux, but it was not always so. At the end of the 18th century, nine red and four white varieties were to be found in Médoc, but this was nothing compared with the 34 red and 29 white varieties which are recorded in the Libournais. The process of selection made rapid progress in the 19th century and was finally completed by the phylloxera crisis which, over a period of years, led to the replanting of all vineyards. Today the most important varieties are the following.

Red
Cabernet Sauvignon
This is the most important variety in Médoc and Graves, especially for the Grands Crus. It produces wine with a deep brilliant colour, a marked bouquet, often reminiscent of blackcurrants, and a flavour which is markedly tannic when young but which develops great finesse and complexity. This is a very hardy variety and it is notably resistant to *coulure* at the flowering and to grey rot before the harvest. It has a thick skin and is a late ripener. It does best on gravelly soils and is a relatively low yielder.

Cabernet Franc
This is an important secondary variety in both St-Emilion and Médoc. In St-Emilion it is known generally as the Bouchet. It produces very perfumed wines with less colour and tannin than the Cabernet Sauvignon, but in other respects it is very similar.

Merlot
The most important variety in St-Emilion and Pomerol, but it also has much importance in Médoc and Graves since it harmonizes so well with Cabernet Sauvignon. It produces wines which are deep in colour, less tannic and higher in alcohol than the Cabernet Sauvignon, supple and full-flavoured. It does well in the presence of clay, precisely where

the Cabernet Sauvignon does less well. It is an early ripener and generous yielder, but it is very susceptible to *coulure* during the flowering and to rot in wet weather. However, the new sprays have helped to overcome this last deficiency.

Malbec

Also known as Pressac in the Libournais and as Côt in Cahors. This variety was in the past particularly important in Fronsac, Pomerol and the Côtes de Bourg, as well as being represented in a minor role in most Médoc vineyards. Today, because of its flowering problems, its importance has seriously declined, and only in Bourg and Blaye does it remain as a significant element, although many châteaux in the Médoc, St-Emilion and Pomerol still have a few old Malbec vines left. This is a high-yielding, early-ripening variety, producing soft, delicate wines with good colour. It is especially useful for blending with more tannic varieties such as Cabernet Sauvignon.

Petit Verdot

This is used in small quantities in the Médoc, especially on the lighter soils of Margaux, but is of declining importance. It is late in ripening and produces highly coloured wines, high in alcohol and tannin, which add complexity to wines for long ageing.

White

Sémillon

This is the most distinctively Bordelais of the white varieties. Although it has suffered a decline as a result of the popularity of the Sauvignon it is now making something of a comeback. It is the most important component of all the great sweet wines, and provides complexity and ageing potential in dry Graves. Its distinctive and complex bouquet requires bottle age to develop in dry wines, and becomes richer and more honied with age. The wine is taut and firm at first, before becoming increasingly full-flavoured and complex with ageing. It blends very well with Sauvignon. Its susceptibility to *pourriture noble* (noble rot) is responsible for its success in making great dessert wines.

Sauvignon Blanc

This has been traditionally planted as a minor partner to the Sémillon in the sweet wine areas and as an equal component of the dry wines. In recent years it has been increasingly used on its own, especially in the Entre-Deux-Mers, to produce wines sold as Bordeaux Blanc Sauvignon. This variety, also widely planted in other parts of France, tends, when unblended, to have a character which is so strong that it obliterates regional characteristics, especially when complete ripeness is not obtained. However, in Bordeaux it can produce wines high in natural sugar and therefore in alcohol, with more finesse and style, especially when put into oak. The Pavillon Blanc of Château Margaux is an outstanding example of this. Sauvignon tends to be a lower and more erratic yielder than the Sémillon, so that where a vineyard is planted half and half with Sémillon, there will always be more Sémillon in the resulting blend.

Muscadelle

An extremely perfumed and aromatic variety that can be useful in small doses. It is particularly favoured in the Premières Côtes for producing sweet wines for early drinking, and as an adjunct to the Sémillon and Sauvignon.

The essence of winemaking in Bordeaux is to mix the different varieties in the right proportions for the soil in each particular vineyard and the style of wine the proprietor is trying to make. It is the small but important variations from château to château, coupled with soil and micro-climate differences, which give Bordeaux wines their remarkable variations and individuality. Thus, in the Médoc, where the Cabernet Sauvignon dominates, some proprietors will use Merlot as their second variety, with very little Cabernet Franc; others will use less Merlot and more Cabernet Franc. In St-Emilion and Pomerol, where Merlot is dominant, some proprietors have 80% Merlot, while others plant it half and half with Cabernet Franc or mix it with Cabernet Franc and Cabernet Sauvignon in a ratio of one third each – in fact you will find every conceivable variation in the proportions.

CHATEAUX

The château system has been a crucial factor in building the prestige of the great Bordeaux wines. In the Médoc, the putting together of many small farms in the 18th century enabled large estates to be formed, capable of producing sufficient quantities of wine to create a wide reputation on many markets. The First Growths led the way in England in the early years of the 18th century; the others followed on, creating a unique image of excellence for Bordeaux.

In the Médoc, the château names have in effect become marques, whose proprietors can increase the size of their vineyards at will, provided they remain in the same appellation. Nobody here controls today the extent of an individual vineyard. Only the reputation of the wine and its consistent quality counts. But in St-Emilion, where the 1954 classification system is under the control of the INAO, vineyards of classified wines cannot be expanded at will, and when Beau-Séjour-Bécot took over two other properties and incorporated their production into its Premier Grand Cru Classé wine, it lost its status in the 1985 revision of the classification.

The very success of the château system, however, has produced its own problems. It is difficult for the consumer to remember the names of more than a handful of châteaux, let alone the thousands that exist in the whole region. But because the consumer knows that good Bordeaux wines come from châteaux, it is hard to create successful brands, which cannot of their nature have a château name. It is not without significance that the most successful brand of claret by far is Mouton-Cadet, precisely because most people believe, erroneously, that it is directly connected with the famous Château Mouton-Rothschild. Even the Caves-Coopératives now sell many of their wines under château names.

COOPERATIVES

Cooperatives are of increasing importance in Bordeaux, and their role is changing. Initially much of the wine they sold went to négociants for their generic blends and brands. Increasingly, however, they are vinifying the wines of their best members separately and marketing them under their château labels, on which they have the right to put "*mis à la propriété*". In addition they are creating their own brands and selling these and some of their château wines directly to wholesalers in France and to

importers in foreign markets, rather than through the traditional
Bordeaux trade, although the latter remains a significant part of
their business. The most important cooperative in Médoc is at
Bégadan, with 170 members producing some 20,000hl of Médoc
AC. In St-Emilion the Union de Producteurs has 330 members
producing some 50,000hl, including over 11,000hl of St-Emilion
Grand Cru, the best of it aged in casks, of which they buy 600 new
ones each year. In the Haut-Médoc, the most important
cooperative is at St-Estèphe. It has 200 members and produces
some 18,000hl of this important AC, nearly one third of the total
production of the appellation.

NÉGOCIANTS

Traditionally, the Bordeaux trade has been carried on by the
négociants. In Bordeaux itself this has centred on the Quai des
Chartrons, conveniently placed for the docks. Négociants not
only distributed Bordeaux wines in France and on export
markets, they also effectively acted as bankers for the château
proprietors, buying their wines when they were a few months
old, then either taking them into their own cellars, where they
would be looked after until ready for bottling, or keeping them at
the château for château-bottling. They also kept substantial
bottle stocks and could always supply mature wines ready for
drinking or old vintages for special occasions.

Inflation and high interest rates, however, have provided a
challenge to which the négociants have not found an answer.
None has been able to achieve the size and financial muscle to
meet the problems now posed while retaining their traditional
role, which has inevitably contracted. Far more wines are now
château-bottled, and far more stock is now held and financed at
the property than ever before. Many firms now work on
minimum stocks or act purely as brokers, not buying wines until
they have sold them, which puts them at the mercy of the
notoriously volatile Bordeaux market. The courtiers themselves
still have an important role to play as the link between the
growers and the négociants; largely because there are so many
growers, the bigger merchants in particular simply could not
select from the range of wines they need to.

The following are the leading négociant houses today:

B. d'Arfeuille A small, well-respected family firm in Libourne
who are also proprietors (Châteaux La Pointe, Pomerol, and La
Serre, Grand Cru Classé, St-Emilion). They naturally specialize
in Libournais wines, but also cover the full range of other
Bordeaux districts.

La Baronnie (formerly **La Bergerie**). The commercial arm of
Baron Philippe de Rothschild's interests. Apart from selling their
property wines, Mouton-Baronne-Philippe and Clerc-Milon,
the principal business is Mouton Cadet and its associated brands.
(Mouton-Rothschild is sold via the Bordeaux market, and not
exclusively through La Baronnie.) The firm is very strong on
export markets.

Barton & Guestier. This famous old concern is now part of
Seagrams and is only a pale reflection of the firm it used to be,
largely concentrating on brands sold on the US market.

Borie-Manoux. A dynamic family firm with some important
properties as a basis for their quality business (Châteaux
Batailley, Trottevieille, Beausite etc.). Their wines are well
distributed on export markets as well as in France.

Calvet. Once one of the great names of Bordeaux, now only a shadow of their former selves, they were recently sold to British brewers Whitbreads. Now mostly selling generic brands.

Castel Frères. A large firm specializing in cheap wines, especially its *vin de table* marque, Castelvin. They have purchased and restored the extensive buildings of the cooperative in Arcins where they vinify the production of a number of small properties of the appellations Margaux, Haut-Médoc, Médoc and Bordeaux Supérieur. Most of the firm's business is concentrated in France.

Cordier. One of the leading firms in Bordeaux, who are also important proprietors (Châteaux Gruaud Larose, Talbot, Meyney, Lafaurie-Peyraguey, Clos de Jacobins – as well as managing Cantemerle). The Cordier family sold control of the company in 1984 to an important financial group whose other interests include the Domaines de Salins du Midi. The Cordier properties are sold by them on an exclusive basis and not through the market, so they specialize in selling a very limited range of their own exclusivities and generic brands. Over half their business is export.

Edmond Coste. This family firm operating from Langon in the Graves has become well known, under the directorship of Pierre Coste, for its advocacy of wines vinified to be drunk young. Coste works very closely with a number of growers in his region, and his white wines were among the first to set the trend for low-temperature fermented wines. His reds are soft and fruity, but sometimes lack regional characteristics as a result of this vinification.

Cruse. Another household name which no longer holds its former position. The family sold out during the 1974 crisis to Société des Vins de France. Brands are important, but some château wines are still offered.

CVBG (Consortium Vinicole de Bordeaux et de Gironde). This group includes Dourthe and Kressmann, and the wines are marketed under these old company names. In 1983 the families sold out to a Dutch company. These companies have a good reputation and sell a wide range of wines, many on an exclusive basis. Château Maucaillou belongs to the Dourthe family while they manage Château Belgrave, 5ème Cru Classé. The Kressmanns own the classified Graves Château La Tour-Martillac.

Dulong Frères & Fils. A family business situated at Floirac just across the bridge from Bordeaux. They enjoy a good reputation for their Petits Châteaux and Cru Bourgeois exported to the UK and the USA.

Louis Eschenauer. This was one of the first of the old Chartronnais firms to be sold, this time to John Holt of Liverpool (now part of Lonrho) in 1959. They own Châteaux Rausan-Ségla and Smith-Haut-Lafitte.

Gilbey de Loudenne. This is part of IDV, the wine and spirit division of Grand Metropolitan, the international hotel and leisure group. They market Château Giscours and Château de Pez world-wide, as well as a small portfolio of brands headed by La Cour Pavillon. An export-oriented company.

Nathaniel Johnston. Formed in 1734 and still run by the same family. If they no longer own great châteaux like Ducru-Beaucaillou, they still specialize in selling a wide range of Bordeaux's leading growths, especially for export.

J. Lebègue & Cie. The emphasis here is on bulk wines, both AC and *vin de table*, much of it for export.

Alexis Lichine & Cie. There is now no connection at all between Alexis Lichine himself and the company which bears his name and which belongs to the British brewers Bass Charrington. This is an important company selling a wide range of wines and operating widely in export markets. Château Lascombes, also belonging to Bass, is their flagship, and is marketed by them on an exclusive basis.

A. de Luze & Fils. This old family firm was sold to a British paper group during the oil crisis, but now belongs to Rémy Martin of Cognac. The business is still run along fairly traditional lines with the emphasis on quality wines.

Mähler-Besse. A family firm still firmly rooted in its Dutch origins. Part owner of Château Palmer.

Yvon Mau & Fils. A firm specializing in generic wines and Petits Châteaux and situated near La Réole in Entre-Deux-Mers.

Mestrezat SA. A house specializing in a wide range of wines mostly château-bottled. They part own, or participate in the management of, Grand-Puy-Ducasse, Chasse-Spleen, and Rayne-Vigneau, as well as several lesser *crus*.

A. Moueix. Armand Moueix's business, run from Château Taillefer in Pomerol, may not have the glamour of his cousin's firm in Libourne, but this is a serious quality house nevertheless. It is also firmly based on properties, of which the two Grands Crus Classés of St-Emilion, Châteaux La-Tour-du-Pin-Figeac and Fonplégade, are the best. Very much Libournais specialists, their association with Schröder & Schÿler has enabled them to present a more comprehensive range for export.

J.P. Moueix. Jean-Pierre Moueix is a legend in his own lifetime. No one has done more to carry the fame of Libournais wines into the US and UK markets and raise their prestige world-wide. Now Christian, his son, and Jean-Jacques, his nephew, are there to carry on the tradition, and the old Bordeaux house of Duclot has been transformed into Moueix-Export, with a classic range of Médocs, Graves and Sauternes to complement the St-Emilions and Pomerols. They have the ownership or exclusive distribution of many châteaux, headed by Pétrus, Trotanoy, La Fleur Pétrus and Magdelaine.

Les Fils de Marcel Quancard. A family firm, based at La Grave-d'Ambarès in Entre-Deux-Mers, which has grown considerably in the past 20 years. They own several properties, including Château Terrefort, and offer a wide range of Petits Châteaux and brands.

De Rivoyre & Diprovin. Not an easy name to trip off the Anglo-Saxon tongue so, for export, the names Louis Dubroca and Rineau are used. Specializes in a large selection of Petits Châteaux and Cru Bourgeois, as well as the big names *en primeur*. Has a substantial business in France as well as exporting to the UK and USA.

Schröder & Schÿler. A famous old business founded in 1739 and still with Schÿlers working in the company. A recent association with A. Moueix of Château Taillefer, Pomerol, has given them more strength in Libournais wines. Their main markets are still their traditional ones of Scandinavia and Holland. They are proprietors of Château Kirwan.

SDVF (Société de Distribution des Vins Fins). Founded in 1973 by M. Hernandez at a time when many firms were in trouble. He bought large stocks of Crus Classés at low prices when no one else wanted them – and has never looked back.

Maison Sichel. This well-respected family firm has a share of Château Palmer, and its head, Peter A. Sichel, owns and lives at Château D'Angludet. Since they separated from H. Sichel of

Mainz and London, all Sichel brands in Germany, the UK, Eire and the USA (where Shieffelin own the rights) have passed out of their hands. On these markets they sell as Gallaire, although in the UK Peter A. Sichel trades under his own name. H. Sichel have their own company in Bordeaux which furnishes the wines for the Sichel brands in Germany, the UK, Eire and the USA.

GRAND VIN DE SAUTERNES — 1

APPELLATION SAUTERNES CONTROLÉE — 2

CHÂTEAU RABAUD-PROMIS — 3

PREMIER CRU CLASSÉ — 4
DEPUIS 1855

1979 — 5   75cl — 6

MIS EN BOUTEILLE AU CHATEAU — 7

G.F.A. DU CHÂTEAU RABAUD-PROMIS PROPRIÉTAIRE A BOMMES 33210 LANGON (FRANCE) — 8

PRODUIT DE FRANCE

Understanding a Bordeaux label

1. Almost every Bordeaux wine describes itself as a "Grand Vin", whether it is a Cru Classé or a simple Bordeaux rouge.

2. It is a legal requirement that the appellation be indicated. The name has to appear between the words "Appellation" and "Contrôlée".

3. The majority of Bordeaux wines are sold under a château name. In addition, many wines that are sent to be vinified at *caves coopératives*, but kept separate, are allowed to use their property names.

4. Classification. The wines of Sauternes and Barsac were classified in 1855 at the same time as those of the Médoc. More recently there have been classifications for St-Emilion and Graves.

5. Year of vintage.

6. This is the standard bottle size in the EEC.

7. "Bottled at the château". Until a few years ago the majority of Bordeaux wines were bottled either in the Bordeaux

cellars of négociants or abroad in such places as London and Brussels. Château-bottling became obligatory for all Crus Classés in the early 1970s. The words *mis en bouteille à la propriété* indicate that the wine has been bottled by the *cave coopérative* where it was made.

   8. Name and address of producer.

CLASSIFICATIONS

The Médoc First Growths had emerged as such in the 18th century and, by the early 19th century, classifications were being made covering quite a range of Médocs and some Graves. They were essentially based on market prices and were produced by courtiers and négociants as guides for their customers.

When the newly fledged Second Empire was preparing its answer to London's Great Exhibition of 1851 it was decided to show a range of Bordeaux wines, and the question arose as to which châteaux should represent the region. A commission of courtiers was given the task, and the result was the Classification of 1855 encompassing the red wines of Médoc plus Château Haut-Brion, and the great sweet wines of Sauternes. It was rather an accident of history that this particular list should have become enshrined as an immutable and permanent order of merit, something its authors certainly never intended. When, in 1867, a group of St-Emilions was shown at a subsequent Paris Exhibition, no such permanent value was accorded to the list.

There have been various attempts to up-date the 1855 classification, but the vested interests opposed to it seem more powerful than those who would like to see change. I will indicate under the individual entries which growths I consider at the present time to be superior or otherwise to their classification. The only official change was the elevation of Mouton-Rothschild to the status of First Growth in 1973, recognizing a position it had in reality long held. It has to be remembered that there is no control over the vineyards of any châteaux contained in this list. Some have remained virtually unchanged since 1855, while others have expanded or contracted.

1855 Classification of the Médoc

This is essentially the original 1855 list. Apart from the promotion of Mouton-Rothschild to Premier Cru in 1973 there have been no fundamental changes, except that certain *crus* have disappeared, while others have been divided or have changed their names. The list encompasses the great red wines of the Médoc, the sole exception being the inclusion of Haut-Brion in the Graves.

Premiers Crus			
Lafite-Rothschild	Pauillac	Lascombes	Margaux
Margaux	Margaux	Brane-Cantenac	Cantenac
Latour	Pauillac	Pichon-Longueville-	
Haut-Brion	Pessac	Baron	Pauillac
	(Graves)	Pichon-Longueville-	
Mouton-Rothschild	Pauillac	Comtesse	Pauillac
		Ducru-Beaucaillou	St-Julien
Deuxièmes Crus		Cos d'Estournel	St-Estèphe
Rausan-Ségla	Margaux	Montrose	St-Estèphe
Rauzan-Gassies	Margaux		
Léoville-Las-Cases	St-Julien	*Troisièmes Crus*	
Léoville Poyferré	St-Julien	Kirwan	Cantenac
Léoville-Barton	St-Julien	d'Issan	Cantenac
Durfort-Vivens	Margaux	Lagrange	St-Julien
Gruaud-Larose	St-Julien	Langoa-Barton	St-Julien

		Cinquièmes Crus	
Giscours	Labarde		
Malescot-St-		Pontet-Canet	Pauillac
Exupéry	Margaux	Batailley	Pauillac
Boyd-Cantenac	Cantenac	Haut-Batailley	Pauillac
Cantenac-Brown	Cantenac	Grand-Puy-	
Palmer	Cantenac	Lacoste	Pauillac
la Lagune	Ludon	Grand-Puy-	
Desmirail	Margaux	Ducasse	Pauillac
Calon-Ségur	St-Estèphe	Lynch-Bages	Pauillac
Ferrière	Margaux	Lynch-Moussas	Pauillac
Marquis-d'Alesme-		Dauzac	Labarde
Becker	Margaux	Mouton-Baronne-	
		Philippe	Pauillac
Quatrièmes Crus		du Tertre	Arsac
St-Pierre	St-Julien	Haut-Bages-Libéral	Pauillac
Talbot	St-Julien	Pédesclaux	Pauillac
Branaire-Ducru	St-Julien	Belgrave	St-Laurent
Duhart-Milon	Pauillac	Camensac	St-Laurent
Pouget	Cantenac	Cos-Labory	St-Estèphe
La Tour-Carnet	St-Laurent	Clerc-Milon	Pauillac
Lafon-Rochet	St-Estèphe	Croizet-Bages	Pauillac
Beychevelle	St-Julien	Cantemerle	Macau
Prieuré-Lichine	Cantenac		
Marquis-de-Terme	Margaux		

1855 Classification of the Sauternes

Again, the original list, apart from divisions and changes of name.

Grand Premier Cru		**Deuxièmes Crus**	
Yquem	Sauternes	de Myrat	Barsac
Premiers Crus		Doisy-Daëne	Barsac
la Tour-Blanche	Bommes	Doisy-Dubroca	Barsac
Lafaurie-Peyraguey	Bommes	Doisy-Védrines	Barsac
Clos Haut-		d'Arche	Sauternes
Peyraguey	Bommes	Filhot	Sauternes
Rayne-Vigneau	Bommes	Broustet	Barsac
Suduiraut	Preignac	Nairac	Barsac
Coutet	Barsac	Caillou	Barsac
Climens	Barsac	Suau	Barsac
Guiraud	Sauternes	de Malle	Preignac
Rieussec	Fargues	Romer	Fargues
Rabaud-Promis	Bommes	Lamothe	Sauternes
Sigalas-Rabaud	Bommes		

After the Second World War, interest in classifications revived, and both Graves and St-Emilion began to pursue the matter with the INAO. The Graves classification, which was a great deal simpler to agree, came out first in 1953, encompassing only red wines, and this was revised in 1959 to include white wines as well. With such a small number of wines actually classified, there is, not surprisingly, no attempt to place the wines in different categories, with the result that the wines vary in quality considerably, from Haut-Brion with its Premier Cru status, to wines that sell at prices of Médoc Fifth Growths or top Crus Bourgeois. Again, I shall assess the standing of each wine under its individual entry.

Classed growths of the Graves

Red Wines

Bouscaut	Cadaujac	La Tour-Martillac	Martillac
Haut-Bailly	Léognan	Smith-Haut-Lafitte	Martillac
Carbonnieux	Léognan	Haut-Brion	Pessac
Domaine de		la Mission-Haut-	
Chevalier	Léognan	Brion	Talence
Fieuzal	Léognan	Pape-Clément	Pessac
Olivier	Léognan	Latour-Haut-Brion	Talence
Malartic-Lagravière	Léognan		

White Wines

Bouscaut	Cadaujac	Malartic-Lagravière	Léognan
Carbonnieux	Léognan	la Tour-Martillac	Martillac
Domaine de		Laville-Haut-Brion	Talence
Chevalier	Léognan	Couhins	Villenave
Olivier	Léognan		d'Ornon

St-Emilion had long been in a chaotic state, posing special problems for the consumer. A large number of *crus* described themselves as Premiers Crus; the properties are small, for the most part, and many of the names are similar – they also have a way of changing more often than elsewhere. Although there are over 5,000ha now under vine in the St-Emilion appellation, only five domaines are of more than 25ha in size, and then there are only 28 properties with between 12 and 25ha, covering 483ha. The classification divides the châteaux of the region into two categories – Premiers Grands Crus Classés and Grands Crus Classés. With the Premiers, Ausone and Cheval Blanc are singled out as category A, the rest as B. The first list was published in 1955, comprising 12 Premiers Grands Crus and 63 Grands Crus. In 1969, at the first revision, the Grands Crus were increased to 71, while in 1985 a second revision reduced the Premiers Crus to 11, and the Grand Crus to 63.

The 1985 St-Emilion classification

Premiers Grands Crus Classés

(A) Ausone	Fonroque
Cheval-Blanc	Franc-Mayne
(B) Beauséjour	Grand-Barrail-
(Duffau-Lagarrosse)	Lamarzelle-Figeac
Belair	Grand-Corbin-Despagne
Canon	Grand-Corbin
Clos Fourtet	Grand-Mayne
Figeac	Grand-Pontet
la Gaffelière	Guadet-Saint-Julien
Magdelaine	Haut Corbin
Pavie	Haut Sarpe
Trottevieille	Laniote

Grands Crus Classés

l'Angelus	Larcis-Ducasse
l'Arrosée	Lamarzelle
Balestard la Tonnelle	Larmande
Beau-Séjour-Bécot	Laroze
Bellevue	Matras
Bergat	Mauvezin
Berliquet	Moulin-du-Cadet
Cadet-Piola	l'Oratoire
Canon-la-Gaffelière	Pavie-Decesse
Cap de Mourlin	Pavie-Macquin
le Chatelet	Pavillon-Cadet
Chauvin	Petit-Faurie de Soutard
Clos des Jacobins	le Prieuré
Clos la Madeleine	Ripeau
Clos de l'Oratoire	Sansonnet
Clos Saint Martin	Saint-Georges-Côte-Pavie
la Clotte	la Serre
la Clusière	Soutard
Corbin	Tertre-Daugay
Corbin-Michotte	la Tour-du-Pin-Figeac
Couvent des Jacobins	(Giraud-Bélivier)
Croque-Michotte	la Tour-du-Pin-Figeac
Curé-Bon la Madeleine	(Moueix)
Dassault	la Tour-Figeac
la Dominique	Trimoulet
Faurie de Souchard	Troplong-Mondot
Fonplegade	Villemaurine
	Yon-Figeac

The Crus Bourgeois of the Médoc were originally classified in 1920, but by 1962 there were only 94 members compared with 444 properties which existed in 1932. Today there are over 200 *crus* claiming to be Crus Bourgeois, and of these 150 belong to the Syndicat. It issued its first *classement* in 1966, and a revision in 1978. This divided the members into Grands Bourgeois Exceptionnels, Grand Bourgeois, and Bourgeois. But unfortunately EEC regulations at present permit only the words "Cru Bourgeois" to appear on a label. The distinctions made in 1978 are useful, however, because of the criteria used.

Cru Bourgeois must have a minimum of seven hectares, the wine must be made on the property (not at a cooperative), and the Syndicat must be satisfied that the wine is of good quality. There are 68 in this category.

In the case of **Cru Grand Bourgeois**, on top of the above rules the wine must be matured in cask. There are 41 such *crus*.

Cru Grand Bourgeois Exceptionnel is the tightest category. In addition to the requirements for the above categories, these *crus* must be in the communes of the Haut-Médoc, the area covered by the Crus Classés, and the wine must be château-bottled. There are 18 of these (indicated by the letter *E*).

1978 Classification of Crus Bourgeois of the Médoc and Haut-Médoc

The château name is followed by that of the commune.

Grand Bourgeois

Agassac	Ludon E	Malleret	Le-Pian
Andron-Blanquet	St-Estèphe E	Marbuzet	St-Estèphe E
Beaumont	Cussac	Meyney	St-Estèphe E
Beausite	St-Estèphe E	Morin	St-Estèphe
Bel-Orme	St-Seurin-de-	Moulin-à-Vent	Moulis
	Cadourne	Le Meynieu	Vertheuil
Brillette	Moulis	Martinens	Margaux
Capbern	St-Estèphe E	les Ormes-Sorbet	Couquèques
La Cardonne	Blaignan	les Ormes-de-Pez	St-Estèphe
Caronne-Ste-		Patache d'Aux	Bégadan
Gemme	St-Laurent E	Paveil-de-Luze	Soussans
Chasse-Spleen	Moulis E	Peyrabon	St-Sauveur
Cissac	Cissac E	Phélan-Ségur	St-Estèphe E
Citran	Avensan E	Pontoise-	St-Seurin-
Colombier-		Cabarrus	de-Cadourne
Monpelou	Pauillac	Potensac	Potensac
Coufran	St-Seurin-	Poujeaux	Moulis E
	de-Cadourne	La Rose-	
Coutelin-Merville	St-Estèphe	Trintaudon	St-Laurent
Le Crock	St-Estèphe E	Reysson	Vertheuil
Duplessis		Ségur	Parempuyre
(Hauchecorne)	Moulis	Sigognac	St-Yzans
Dutruch-		Sociando-Mallet	St-Seurin-
Grand-Poujeau	Moulis E		de-Cadourne
Fontesteau	St-Sauveur	du Taillan	Le Taillan
Fourcas-Dupré	Listrac E	la Tour-de-By	Bégadan
Fourcas-Hosten	Listrac E	la Tour-du-	
La-Fleur-Milon	Pauillac	Haut-Moulin	Cussac
Du Glana	St-Julien E	Tronquoy-	
Greysac	Bégadan	Lalande	St-Estèphe
Hanteillan	Cissac	Verdignan	St-Seurin-
Haut-Marbuzet	St-Estèphe E		de-Cadourne
Lafon	Listrac		
de Lamarque	Lamarque	**Bourgeois**	
Lamothe	Cissac	Aney	Cussac
Laujac	Bégadan	Balac	St-Laurent-
Liversan	St-Sauveur		de-Médoc
Loudenne	St-Yzans	Bellerive	Valeyrac
Mac-Carthy	St-Estèphe	Bellerose	Pauillac

La Bécade	Listrac	Landon	Bégadan
Bonneau-Livran	St-Seurin-de-Cadourne	Crû Lassalle	Potensac
le Boscq	St-Christoly	Lartigue-de-Brochon	St-Seurin-de-Cadourne
le Breuil	Cissac	Le Landat	Cissac
la Bridane	St-Julien	Lestage	Listrac
de By	Bégadan	Mac-Carthy-Moula	St-Estèphe
Castéra	St-Germain-d'Esteuil	Monthil	Bégadan
Chambert-Marbuzet	St-Estèphe	Moulin Rouge	Cussac
Cap-Leon-Veyrin	Listrac	Panigon	Civrac
Carcanieux	Queyrac	Pibran	Pauillac
la Clare	Bégadan	Plantey-de-la-Croix	St-Seurin-de-Cadourne
la Closerie	Moulis	Pontet	Blaignan
Duplessis-Fabre	Moulis	Ramage-la-Bâtisse	St-Sauveur
Fonréaud	Listrac	la Roque-de-By	Bégadan
Fonpiqueyre	St-Sauveur	de la Rose-Maréchale	St-Seurin-de-Cadourne
Fort Vauban	Cussac	St-Bonnet	St-Christoly
la France	Blaignan	Saransot	Listrac
Gallais Bellevue	Potensac	Soudars	Avensan
Grand-Duroc-Milon	Pauillac	Tayac	Soussans
Grand-Moulin	St-Seurin-de-Cadourne	la Tour-Blanche	St-Christoly
Haut-Bages-Monpelou	Pauillac	la Tour-du-Mirail	Cissac
Haut-Canteloup	Couquèques	la Tour-Haut-Caussan	Blaignan
Haut-Garin	Bégadan	la Tour-St-Bonnet	St-Christoly
Haut-Padarnac	Pauillac	la Tour St-Joseph	Cissac
Houbanon	Prignac	des Tourelles	Blaignan
Hourtin-Ducasse	St-Sauveur	Vieux Robin	Bégadan
de Labat	St-Laurent		
Lamothe-de-Bergeron	Cussac		

Vineyards at present being reconstituted

Les Bertins	Valeyrac	Lavalière	St-Christoly
Clarke	Listrac	Romefort	Cussac
Larivière	Blaignan	Vernous	Lesparre

The following properties have joined the Syndicate of Bourgeois Growths of the Médoc since 1978 but are at present not classified because of EEC regulations.

Anthonic	Moulis	Maucaillou	Moulis
Bellevue	Valeyrac	Maucamps	Macau
Les Bertins	Valeyrac	Monbrison	Arsac
Bonneau	Avensan	Moulin-de-la-Roque	Bégadan
Bourdieu	Vertheuil	Moulin Riche	St-Julien
Bournac	Civrac	Moulis	Moulis
Cailloux-de-By	Bégadan	Pey-Martin	Ordonnac
Canuet	Margaux	Peyredon-Lagravette	Medrac-Listrac
Charmail	St-Seurin	Puy-Castéra	Cissac
l'Estruelle	St-Yzans	Domaine de la Ronceray	St-Estèphe
Goudy-la-Cardonne	Ordonnac	St-Paul	St-Seurin
Grivière	Blaignan	St-Roch	St-Estèphe
Hauterive	St-Germain-d'Esteuil	Sestignan	Jau Dignac-Loirac
Haut Logat	Cissac	Terrey-Gros-Cailloux	St-Julien
Lalande	Listrac	Tour-du-Roc	Arcins
Lestage Simon	St-Seurin	Tourteran	St-Sauveur
Liouner	Listrac	Vieux-Robin	Bégadan
Magnol Dehez	Blanquefort		
Malescasse	Lamarque		
Malmaison	Listrac		
Martinens	Cantenac		

WHAT HAPPENS IN THE VINEYARD

Good wine begins with good grapes, and good grapes in turn depend on good viticulture and the weather. A leading proprietor said to me recently that, after the enormous progress made in the past 20 years in wine-making, there was not much more to be done in this respect, but there were still improvements possible in viticulture.

If we start with a new vine, the first important decision to be taken is what American rootstock to use and which clone of the European vine to select. Different varieties perform better in different soils. For instance, much work has been done in recent years by the Station de Recherches Viticoles du Sud-Ouest to discover rootstocks that are resistant to chlorosis in limestone soils. Furthermore, some varieties do better than others in poorly-drained, humid soils as against dry, well-drained ones. Less work has been done on the cloning of vines here than in Burgundy, to say nothing of Germany.

The yearly pattern of work in the vineyards roughly proceeds as follows:

January. The work of the *taille* (pruning), begun in December, continues. New stakes are put in place and secured, and the pruned canes are attached to the vines.

February. The pruning continues, together with the cleaning up of the vineyard, gathering of the bundled canes, and so on. The first treatment of the vines against excoriose (a fungus which attacks the wood), esca (another fungus, also called black measles), and red and yellow spider (which would later attack the young leaves).

March. The first buds normally break in late March, between the 20th and 30th of the month. The first ploughing removes the earth from around the foot of the vine in order to aerate it after the winter.

April. Winter has finished and spring begins. This is when any dead vines are replaced and the first hoeing takes place. The vines may be dusted with sulphur against oidium and sprayed with a copper-sulphate solution against mildew.

May. The work begun in the previous month continues, according to weather conditions, as do the treatments against disease. The first pinching back of the young shoots is carried out, to limit the growth of the vine and direct it toward the production of grapes, and stray shoots from the base of the vine are cut back.

June This is classically the month of the flowering. In the 10 years 1975–84, the earliest flowering began on 26 May (1982) and the latest on 15 June (1977). Most typically it happens between the 2nd and 10th of the month. This gives the approximate timing for the vintage, which normally occurs 100 to 110 days after the flowering. Ploughing now continues, the new shoots are tied up, and the length of the new growth permits it to be put between the second and third row of wines, but not attached to them.

July. The soil is now ploughed away from the vines again, so there is a mound of soil running between each row of vines, and weeds are hoed. Treatment continues according to the conditions. The *véraison* (the changing of the colour of the grapes, the most important indication of ripening between the flowering and the vintage) can begin in late July. This happened in 1982, 1981, 1976 and 1975.

August. A quiet period when many vignerons go on holiday. But this can be a crucial time for treating the vines if the weather is damp and humid, especially against premature rot. If the *véraison* (appearance of the grapes) has not occurred in July it usually is to be observed in the first week of August, but in 1980 it did not occur until the 18th.

September. The preferred month for beginning the vintage. In the past 10 years, the vintage began in this month in half of them: 1983, 1982, 1981, 1976 and 1975. In the weeks before the harvest the last preventative treatments are carried out, but the vigneron hopes to be able to concentrate his effort in preparing for the vintage in the *cuvier*.

October. The month of the vintage and hence the key month in the viticultural calendar. Even if the vintage began in September, most of it will take place and be completed in October (except for 1982 and 1976). Sometimes the vintage in Sauternes will go on until the end of the month.

November. Now that the harvest is over, the plough returns to the vineyard to earth up the vines for the winter, and the manuring takes place.

December. The pruning begins. First the foliage is cut back to make the work of pruning easier and the cuttings are bundled up and burnt. Any vines that have been damaged or have died during the year are noted for replacement next year. The work goes on.

MAKING WINE

Red wine

Thirty years ago it was almost true to say that in most years the great red Bordeaux made themselves. They are still not complicated wines to make, but the art has been refined, at least at most properties.

The process is as follows:

1. The grapes arrive in the *cuvier* and are moved via an Archimedean screw mechanism to the *fouloir-égrappoir*, which crushes and de-stalks the grapes. The word "crush" is perhaps an exaggeration of what actually happens; this machine breaks the skins rather than crushing the grapes, as can be clearly seen when the pulp is then pumped into the fermenting vat. Mechanically-harvested grapes do not, of course, need to be de-stemmed. There has been much refinement of the basic *fouloir-égrappoir* in recent years to make the process gentler and ensure that no tannins from the stalks are released into the pulp.

2. The traditional fermentation *cuve* (vat) in Bordeaux is wooden, and the top is often reached by a wooden gallery for ease of access. Many of these old *cuves* are still in use, but are steadily being replaced by stainless steel, metal lined with enamel, or concrete lined with enamel. The advantages of the new *cuves* are that: (a) they are easier to clean; (b) they make it easier to control the temperature of the fermentation; (c) they are often of smaller size to assist selection and temperature control. The fermentation usually lasts from five to ten days, and the object is to ferment at between 28°–30°C (82°–86°F), instead of allowing the temperature to rise to 34°C (93°F) as formerly.

3. After the fermentation has been in progress a few hours, the solid matter, mostly skins, rises to the top of the vat to form what is known as the cap. At regular intervals the fermenting must is pumped over the top of the cap to keep it moist, keep its temperature down and extract colour. A variation on this classic system is the submerged cap. This is a method whereby the cap is prevented by a mesh from rising to the top of the *cuve*.

4. In Bordeaux, natural yeasts are usually allowed to do their work. Normally there is an abundance of them, and results have usually proved satisfactory. Only when the grapes are unhealthy (affected by rot) can problems arise, and this is now rare.

5. The temperature is controlled by a variety of means. The most traditional in Bordeaux is a contraption that looks like a milk cooler. The must passes through a coil while cold water runs over the outside of the coil. With stainless steel vats, either the cold water can run down the exterior sides, or interior coils can be used, as they can be on other types of vat. All this is a long way from throwing blocks of ice into vats, a system still in use in 1961 in many cellars.

6. Chaptalization is now much more frequent in Bordeaux where, prior to 1962, it was almost unknown and illegal. Most Médocs are now chaptalized to 12% and St-Emilions and Pomerols to 12.5%, except, of course, in the best years when the natural degrees are quite sufficient. The sugar is normally added at the beginning of fermentation after the composition of the must has been carefully checked.

7. The progress of the fermentation, showing the fall in density and the temperature, is normally kept on a chart on each vat and checked every few hours. When no sugar remains to ferment, the wine (as it has now become) is either drawn off or left to macerate for some days in the presence of the skins. In the past this often continued for several weeks, but now the view is that most of the colour extraction takes place during fermentation owing to the high temperatures, and that afterwards the improvement to colour is minimal but tannins are still extracted, which may not always be desirable. Bacterial infections are also possible, so many wine-makers now like to draw the wine off once it is finished.

8. After the new wine has been drawn off, the remaining solid matter (mostly what was contained in the cap) is removed from the vat and pressed. The result is what is known as *vin de presse*. The first *vin de presse* is usually of superior quality and will later be added back to the finished wine at the *assemblage*. The result of the second pressing is not normally of sufficient quality to be included in the final *assemblage*. These two *vins de presse* between them account for about 15% of the wine produced. While *vin de presse* is not usually a desirable element in ordinary wines made for early consumption, it is richer in all its elements than the free-run wine, except in alcoholic degree, and so adds an important element in fine wines intended for long maturation and keeping.

9. The next stage is known as malolactic fermentation. Ideally, this should follow immediately after the alcoholic fermentation. It is the process by which the astringent malic acid is converted into the more supple lactic acid, and in the process the total acidity is also diminished. Some properties like this to take place in *cuve*, others put the wine straight in cask. This secondary fermentation passes most easily at 20°–25°C (68°–77°F), so the emphasis is on completing it before the weather turns really cold, since the large *cuviers* of Bordeaux are hard to heat in comparison with the small cellars of Burgundy. If vats are equipped with an internal cooling system this can also be used to warm them to facilitate the malolactic fermentation. Until this is finished the wine is not truly stable, and it is also vulnerable to bacterial infections. In the past, it was often observed that the wine would begin "working" in the spring, at the time when the vine began to push out its first buds. This was, in reality, carbon dioxide released when the malolactic fermentation began again, the warm weather permitting the bacteria to become active once more. But it is preferable to finish the process in the autumn rather than leaving the wine unstable through the winter.

Most, but not all, properties leave the new wine in *cuve* until the final selection or *assemblage* has been made. This usually happens in January, sometimes later, depending on the year. All the *cuves* are tasted and decisions taken as to what will go into the Grand Vin (the main château label) and what should be eliminated in order to maintain the quality and reputation of the château. Sometimes there is a second label (such as Pavillon Rouge of Château Margaux, Réserve de la Comtesse of Pichon-Lalande, Clos du Marquis of Léoville-Lascases), but most of the rejected wine is usually sold under a simple generic label. This only applies to large properties and, therefore, mostly to the Médoc.

One of the less publicized but important decisions taken at this time is the addition of *vin de presse*. This gives the wine more tannin and extracts, and provides an important element in wines of quality, intended for ageing.

All the best Bordeaux châteaux mature their wines in oak casks of 225 litres, the finest using 100% new casks each year. But the wine has to have the power and composition to withstand such handling and, apart from the First Growths, most Crus Classés use around one third new wood each year. While wooden barrels are an important factor in giving complexity and "finish" to a wine, they must be in good condition and not, in any case, more than about five years old. In the past, many lesser *crus*, which could not afford to buy new casks regularly, spoilt their wines by keeping them in old casks, which can easily taint the wine, making it seem mouldy or just not clean. It is better to keep the wine in vat rather than do this, and this is the policy of many lesser *crus* today, with resulting benefit to the wine. Bottling dates vary according to the style and quality of the wine. The old system for the First Growths was to bottle only after the third winter in cask, that is in the spring of the third year. Now, most wines are bottled either after the vintage in the second year (at latest) or several months earlier in the late spring or summer of the second year (most commonly).

Dry white wines

Over the past few years in Bordeaux the preparation of these wines has changed much more radically than in the case of the reds. The use of stainless steel, horizontal presses and low-temperature fermentation have really revolutionized the style and quality of dry wines. In the past, Bordeaux made a few superb Graves, but much of its white wine production was over-sulphured, heavy and dull. Now the wines are fruity and perfumed, fresh and clean.

The basic process is as follows:

1. The grapes are fed into a horizontal press as they come from the vineyard, stalks and all (except, of course, when mechanically harvested). The pressing must be very gentle, and the *marc* (solid cake or pomace of skins and other solid matter) is continuously broken up by chains inside the press, which rotates at the same time as the grapes are squeezed by the action of the press.

2. The juice runs from the press and is collected in a stainless

steel *cuve*. This will often nowadays be chilled and held as grape juice to precipitate its solids over a period of 12 to 24 hours. This process is known as *débourbage*. Some of the best Graves vignerons run the must straight into new barrels, which are often kept in an air-conditioned *chais*. The must is lightly sulphured to guard against oxidation.

3. Fermentation then takes place after the must has been racked off its solids after the *débourbage*, either into another *cuve* or into a barrel. Fermentation is now usually controlled at between 15°–20°C (59°–68°F).

4. Again, as with reds, whites in Bordeaux normally undergo a malolactic fermentation.

5. As soon as the wine is finished, it is clarified to avoid picking up any undesirable odours. This is usually done by filtration, or in large cellars by centrifuge.

6. Since the object nowadays is to prevent oxidation, wines spend much less time in pre-bottle maturation. Only the finest Graves spend more than a few months in cask; most wines are kept in *cuve* and bottled in the spring, some six months after the vintage, to conserve their freshness and fruit.

Sweet white wines

Because of the state of grapes affected by *pourriture noble* (noble rot or *Botrytis cinerea* to give the scientific name), both the vintaging and vinifying of grapes for sweet wines pose special problems. The vintaging cannot be done as for dry wines, because the over-ripeness of the grapes, leading to infection by *Botrytis cinerea*, does not occur uniformly, either in the vineyard or even in single bunches. This means that the workers go through a vineyard several times (four to six times in the best properties) selecting the best grapes from each bunch, and that only skilled local labour can be used. Such grapes obviously cannot be mechanically harvested.

Botrytis cinerea itself is a fungus which, when it attacks overripe grapes, dehydrates them thus concentrating their sugar content. Mild humid conditions, typical of a Bordeaux autumn, are required for this infection to thrive. If conditions are too dry, the fungus will not attack even very ripe grapes. This happened in 1978. On the other hand, if it rains at the wrong moment the vintage can be ruined, or only a small part of it will be any good. For these reasons there are far fewer successful vintages in Sauternes than in the neighbouring Graves.

The process of vinification is as follows:

1. Because of the condition of the grapes, they are not crushed in a separate operation, but go straight into the press. The pressing is slow and difficult because the grapes are so rich in sugar (20°–25° baumé – 360 to 450 grams per litre). Three pressings are usually made in Sauternes.

2. A *débourbage* is not usual because of the danger of sulphur dioxide combining and because a must so rich in sugar and bacteria is very susceptible to oxidation. The best solution is to centrifuge and then chill the must before beginning the fermentation, which can still be in barrel but is now more usually and safely in *cuve*.

3. The fermentation is slow and often continues for many weeks. It must be followed very carefully in order to obtain a balanced wine. Thus, a wine with 12.5% alcohol is well balanced with 30 to 35 grams of sugar per litre but not with 50. This sort of result would be typical of wines made in the Premières Côtes. But a wine with 14% alcohol needs 60 to 70 grams to be balanced.

Although the yeasts become tired and "blocked" when the level of alcohol rises to around 14%, the wine will still not be permanently stable, and must therefore be stabilized by the addition of sulphur dioxide. This is often assisted by filtration and chilling. Wines with less sugar must, in any case, be stopped in this way in order to ensure a balanced wine.

4. The *élevage* (literally raising the wine, as one would children or cattle) then proceeds in much the same way as for dry wines, except that the best sweet wines seem to benefit from maturing in cask, and the process is more lengthy, often two to two and a half years before bottling. Selection as between *cuves* and even casks is also most important when seeking to obtain really fine Sauternes, or indeed Loupiac or Ste-Croix-du-Mont.

VINTAGES

In temperate climates vintages are always important. Although there are fewer poor vintages than there used to be in Bordeaux, it is still important to know how the vintages vary, because this can tell you broadly which wines should be laid down and which can be drunk early, in the broadest terms. But each year has its distinctive character. Indeed the finer the year, the stronger the vintage character, and the more pronounced the character of each *cru*.

1985

At the time of going to press the prospects for the 1985 vintage are encouraging. Following a good flowering, a fine summer and an exceptionally hot September, the harvest was plentiful, and the wines should be above average.

1984

Weather and general assessment. A cold wet May seems to have been responsible for the worst *coulure* (failure of flowers to set) in the Merlot in living memory. Then rain and storms in late September gave way to perfect October weather for vintaging. A very mixed vintage, too early for a final assessment.

Médoc and Graves. Average yields produced wines of generally better quality than expected, nearer to 1981 than 80. But selection is all-important. Outside a few leading *crus*, the wines are short on the palate.

St-Emilion and Pomerol. A very small crop of rather average wines which initially seem to lack character and can appear mean.

Dry whites. Excellent quality, normal yield. The wines have more delicacy and are lighter than the 1983s.

Sweet whites. The potential for quality was reduced by the wet weather at the end of September, but some fine wines were made.

1983

Weather and general assessment. After a wet spring the weather for the flowering in June was perfect, and the result promised a large vintage to begin around 25 September. The first part of September caused anxiety, with too much rain, but from 18 September until 16 October the weather was ideal for the vintage. A very fine year, not quite as consistent as 1982, but producing classic wines with depth and character.

Médoc and Graves. Another large vintage, quality not so regular as in 1982 but very fine at Crus Classés level with some very stylish wines. Another year for laying down.

St-Emilion and Pomerol. A high yield with some outstanding wines, but again more variation than in 1982. Laying-down wines.

Lesser reds. The best wines have vigour, fruit and charm and should provide very useful drinking over the next five years.

Dry whites. Wines have more acidity and style than the 1982s. Very good.

Sweet wines. A great year, probably the best since 1976. Very luscious wines, but well balanced.

1982

Weather and general assessment. A classic hot year, with a large yield; but sustained warm weather led to perfect ripeness. Certainly the most outstanding vintage since 1961. The wines have a very special vintage character.

Médoc and Graves. Produced wines of exceptional concentration and power, with plenty of fruit to cover the high tannin levels. An exceptional year, the most individual since 1961.

St-Emilion and Pomerol. Produced wines of exceptional opulence and power, reminiscent of 1947. As in 1947, some of the top wines could be remarkable drinking early on (1987–88).

Lesser reds. At this level, there is consistency, allied to exceptional attractiveness and relatively early development. These wines will win a lot of friends for Bordeaux in the next few years.

Dry whites. These wines have charm but are short of acidity. For early drinking in the main.

Sweet whites. The dry hot weather delayed the noble rot, and then the rain in October started too early, resulting in medium-weight wines which are no more than good.

1981

Weather and general assessment. Good weather right through the growing period, but some rain during the vintage. Wines have more breed but less body than in 1979.

Médoc and Graves. Classic wines, with length and finish. Not as powerful as the 1979s nor as firm as the 1978s but with all the breed of a really fine year.

St-Emilion and Pomerol. The wines have elegance and style; at the same time the best are full and luscious in flavour, although many are rather light, developing fairly quickly.

Lesser reds. Charming wines for drinking in 1986–88.

Dry whites. Elegant wines of medium weight. All but the top wines are for early drinking.

Sweet wines. The best wines are finely perfumed and luscious, better than the 1982s.

1980

Weather and general assessment. The coldest June since 1946 caused prolonged flowering and widespread *coulure*. A very cold July was followed by a warm August and September. For many châteaux, this was the latest harvest since 1922, with the smallest crop since 1969, mainly due to a very small harvest of white wines. A very useful vintage of early-developing stylish wines.

Médoc and Graves. Very attractive wines for early drinking, now mostly at their best but with the balance to remain good for some years. The selection carried out by the leading châteaux produced dividends. A good follow to 1976.

St-Emilion and Pomerol. More variable than Médoc but, since the Merlot ripened better than the Cabernet Sauvignon, these areas produced many supple, fruity wines for early drinking.

Lesser reds. Very variable at this level. These wines should be drunk without delay.

Dry whites. Light, pleasant wines that should have been drunk by now for the most part.

Sweet whites. The wines are rather light, but the best have a pleasant fruitiness and charm without real lusciousness.

1979
Weather and general assessment. A late flowering in warm, sunny conditions led to an excellent setting and the prospect of a large vintage. There was a setback in August with cold, wet weather, but better conditions in September enabled a large crop to be gathered. The wines have great depth of fruit and vigour, lots of charm, but are slightly lacking in backbone and breed.

Médoc and Graves. The wines have a marked vintage character, rich and dense in texture, softer and quicker developing than the 1978s, but perhaps with less breed. They promise to give great pleasure for some years to come.

St-Emilion and Pomerol. The exceptional ripeness of the Merlot produced much more luscious, dense and opulent wines than in 1978. This is the sort of year that brings out the best in these districts. Many wines are already delightful but should also last.

Lesser reds. Pleasing, robust wines for enjoying up till 1987/88. Lots of good wines at this level.

Dry whites. Very stylish wines, with fruit and breed. Mostly at their peak now, but the best Graves will last for some years.

Sweet whites. Vies with 1981 as the best vintage between 1976 and 1983. Luscious, fruity wines with style. Developing well.

1978
Weather and general assessment. A year of contrasts. The wettest March since 1870, then exceptionally dry weather in July, August and September. The vintage – of average size – was late, but, thanks to a dry October, vintaged in ideal conditions. These are classic, long-term developing wines, which many will prefer to 1975 because of their harmonious balance.

Médoc and Graves. Although not a year of perfect ripeness, the wines have great character and finesse. Their considerable tannin, well blended with fruit and richness, promise a long development. They are more harmonious than the 1975s and will be ready earlier.

St-Emilion and Pomerol. At first these wines seem to lack the power and richness of the Médocs, but they have developed very attractively. Some wines are rather lean, but most are decidedly stylish. Not such typical wines as the 1979s.

Lesser reds. Consistently sound wines at this level, but some are now getting a little dry.

Dry whites. A fine year, with the best Graves needing longer to develop than the 1979s. Lesser wines should be drunk soon.

Sweet whites. A freak year, with perfect ripeness but almost no noble rot, so the wines lack classic character.

1977
Weather and general assessment. Frost at the end of March caused serious damage, especially in Pomerol and St-Emilion. A cold summer threatened disaster on a scale far exceeding 1972. Then came the driest September, with the most hours of sunshine (not the highest temperatures) for 100 years. Some useful commercial wines, but they tend to lack appellation character.

Médoc and Graves. Many light, pleasing wines, but mostly lacking a real character of appellation or *cru*. Mostly at their best by now and should be drunk while the fruit lasts.

St-Emilion and Pomerol. Small wines, not without charm, but lacking individuality. Should be drunk soon.

Lesser reds. Some pleasing, light wines, but they should have been drunk by now.

Dry whites. A few Graves are stylish and pleasing.

Sweet whites. A year to forget.

1976

Weather and general assessment. An unusual year, with very dry, hot weather from April to the end of August. By then, conditions resembled 1921, 47 and 49. The vintage began early (13 September), but there was considerable rain during the month, which diluted the musts. The thick skins and very small, concentrated berries would have produced something even more tannic and rich than 1975, had it not been for the rain. As it was, this mixture of tannin and concentrated fruit, diluted with rain water, produced wines which vary considerably. Some are deeply coloured, rich and fruity. In others tannin and fruit seem to have separated. It has also affected the whole development cycle of the wines, which has been relatively rapid.

Médoc and Graves. The best wines are supple, powerful and attractive, but there are also disappointments. The wines have developed well and are by now mostly at their best. Whether they will make old bones is hard to say.

St-Emilion and Pomerol. Overripeness and diluted colours are a feature here. Many wines suffer from low acidity and have aged rapidly. A few have more structure and are delicious now.

Lesser reds. These wines were delicous when three to five years old, but most are now looking tired and dry.

Dry whites. These wines were low in acidity and needed to be drunk early. But some top Graves are rich and fine, still improving.

Sweet whites. A great vintage, with luscious wines which are more elegant and stylish than the 1975s.

1975

Weather and general assessment. Excellent flowering was followed by a very dry, hot summer. Some rain in September was just what was needed. A year of moderate yields, good alcoholic degrees and thick skins resulted in very tannic, slow-developing wines. They lack the balance and charm of the 1961s, which some optimists believed them to resemble at an early stage.

Médoc and Graves. It is still hard to say just how good these wines are going to be. Some seem to be too tannic and dry, others have splendid concentration and power. Still a year to watch.

St-Emilion and Pomerol. As often happens in a very tannic year, the best wines seem better balanced than in the Médoc. Here the emphasis is on ripeness and opulence and there are many successful wines.

Lesser reds. The denseness and tannin suggested a long evolution, even at this level, but many wines are now tough and too dry.

Dry whites. The best Graves are concentrated and powerful but lack the elegance of the 1976s.

Sweet whites. Many wines have too much botrytis and are too alcoholic, resulting in clumsy, tarry wines which are ageing rapidly (Yquem, Climens, Coutet and Doisy-Daene are notable exceptions).

1974

Weather and general assessment. A good flowering ensured a large vintage. A fine summer promised good quality, but a cold, wet September changed all that. These are austere, charmless wines for the most part, which lack any real appellation or *cru* character.

Médoc and Graves. The wines have a good colour but little else to recommend them. Léoville Barton was a honourable exception.

St-Emilion and Pomerol. The wines are as dreary here as in the Médoc, but Figeac is an exception.

Dry whites. Some pleasant Graves survive and could provide a few nice surprises.

Sweet whites. A year to forget.

1973

Weather and general assessment. Good flowering conditions ensured a large crop, but the summer alternated between hot and sunny (August) and very wet (July and the second half of September). A good October enabled the vintage to be gathered in good conditions. A big commercial vintage, with a wide spectrum of qualities. The best wines have lots of unaffected charm.

Médoc and Graves. Very attractive early-developing wines. The majority should have been drunk by now, but some are holding up surprisingly well.

St-Emilion and Pomerol. Rather overblown wines which had great charm but were short-lived, with a few exceptions.

Lesser reds. Uneven once their early charm had faded. Should have been drunk.

Dry whites. Some stylish Graves have lasted well, but most should have been drunk some time ago.

Sweet whites. Pleasant but moderate wines, on the light side.

1972

Weather and general assessment. A cold spring led to a late and protracted flowering; then a poor summer, with more than its share of rain in August, resulted in a very late harvest and unripe grapes. The year is more remembered for its high prices that triggered off the collapse of the market than for its mean, dull wines which are best forgotten.

1971

Weather and general assessment. A cold, wet spring caused a poor flowering and a correspondingly small crop. Then the summer turned warm and sunny with just the right amount of rain. This provided the complete contrast to the previous vintage, the sprinter against the long-distance runner.

Médoc and Graves. Very flattering, charming wines which developed quickly and have been at their peak since the late 1970s. With their low acidities, they now need drinking, and some have already turned the corner.

St-Emilion and Pomerol. Some great successes here, with rich, luscious but rather overblown wines. They should be drunk up, except for a few Pomerols.

Dry whites. Very perfumed, elegant Graves at the top level and lasting well.

Sweet whites. A great classic Sauternes year, combining richness with elegance, usually better than the 1970.

1970

Weather and general assessment. Ideal growing conditions produced the rare combination of quantity and perfect ripeness. For the first time the new plantings of the 1960s yielded quality wines, and 1970 marked the beginning of the great switch from white to red wines and heralded the large yields of the 1970s and 80s. This was the largest quality year since 1934. This fine vintage has been slow to develop but worth drinking for.

Médoc and Graves. These wines have taken much longer to develop than expected, due perhaps to a lack of maturity in parts of the vineyards at this period. Nevertheless, these are classic long-distance wines, well structured, with breed and fruit to match the tannin. They are now beginning to become enjoyable to drink, especially the Margaux, St-Juliens and Graves.

St-Emilion and Pomerol. Also slow to evolve, but they have more charm now than many Médocs and can mostly be drunk with pleasure. But the power and the structure of these wines also promise a long life.

Dry whites. The best Graves are rich and solid and are still holding well.

Sweet whites. Big luscious wines, with less style for the most part than 1971. Long-lasting wines.

1969

Weather and general assessment. A poor spring and flowering ensured a small crop. There was rain in early September, but then conditions turned fine for the vintage. The growers persuaded themselves and others that the wines would be "useful", but the bottom fell out of them during the second winter. Then, even with some assistance from 1970, the wines were never better than dull and meagre. Now to be avoided, except for some plesant honourable Sauternes.

1968

Weather and general assessment. The last great year of rot in Bordeaux. Just a bad summer (August the coldest and wettest for 20 years), so that fine weather in October could not save matters. A few wines were pleasant when young, if light and short, but they are dead and buried now – or should be!

1967

Weather and general assessment. A good flowering, July and August hot and dry, then three weeks of wet and cold conditions in September, with the final week hot. Mixed conditions during the vintage, good weather punctuated by heavy rain. This was the largest harvest of red AC wines of the decade, but the quality was uneven, and many wines have a characteristic bitterness at the finish.

Médoc and Graves. A few pleasant surprises still, but most wines are now going dry and were better a few years ago. Drink up!

St-Emilion and Pomerol. In general, superior to Médoc and Graves. The wines have more charm, with Pomerol leading the way and the St-Emilion Côtes, generally superior to the Graves. But these wines are mostly fading now and should be drunk.

Sweet whites. A great year for Sauternes, much better than 1966. The wines have great fruit and style and are still fresh. A long-lived classic vintage.

1966

Weather and general assessment. After a good flowering the summer was cool and dry, and it was not until September that there was any real heat, emphasizing once again that the quality of the vintage is made in September. Harvesting conditions were ideal, and there was no rot. After 1961, this was the best vintage of the decade and a very consistent one.

Médoc and Graves. Very classic wines, with structure, length and great style. After a long period of gestation, these wines are really coming into their own and should continue to give enjoyment for many years to come.

St-Emilion and Pomerol. There was a tendency to say that the 1967s were better here, but I have found the 1966s have remained fresher, even when they seemed lighter. Wines of great charm and style, with some outstanding bottles. Mostly at their best now.

Sweet whites. These wines have less sugar and style than the 1967s and look older.

1965
Weather and general assessment. An appalling summer of heavy rains, with a wet, humid September, leading to grapes that were both unripe and rotten. The worst of the three bad years of the 1960s. The wines were thin and nondescript.

1964
Weather and general assessment. Very good flowering conditions were followed by a hot, dry summer so that, when the vintage began (21 September), expectations were high. Unfortunately torrential rains fell from 8 to 17 October, and a number of leading Médoc châteaux were seriously affected. So this was a vintage of very varied fortunes. Both 1962 and 1966 provided more consistent wines.

Médoc and Graves. Graves, St-Julien, Margaux and those Pauillacs which were picked early fared best. Such wines are generous and supple, if a little lacking in backbone. The wines affected by rain are thin and washed out and should be avoided.

St-Emilion and Pomerol. Wines of real concentration, powerful, full of fruit and richness, the best of which are keeping well. In spite of their extra weight, many seem to lack the staying power of 1966 or 1961.

Sweet whites. The October rain ruined the Sauternes harvest, and few decent wines were made.

1963
Weather and general assessment. A cold, wet summer led to widespread rot and a lack of ripeness, although conditions during the harvest were good. The wines had a curious orange colour and the smell of rot. A year best forgotten.

1962
Weather and general assessment. A late flowering in good conditions, a moderate summer interspersed with rain, then a hot Indian summer in September and good harvest conditions in October saved the vintage. A year overshadowed by 1961, but with a large crop of consistent, sound, attractive wines.

Médoc and Graves. These wines have developed real depth and complexity in their maturity. Classic wines for enjoying now, although there is some mileage left in the top wines.

St-Emilion and Pomerol. Lovely, mature wines, some now showing their age. Should be enjoyed now.

Sweet whites. An excellent vintage for Sauternes, the wines are well balanced and elegant, at their peak now.

1961
Weather and general assessment. Cold, wet weather during the flowering ensured that this would be a small crop, then drought conditions further reduced yields. The result: a small crop of wines, high in extract and alcohol, which have developed into the outstanding year since the Second World War, with no rival since until the 1982s.

Médoc and Graves. These wines continue to gain in complexity with age. They have plenty of tannin matched by fruit and richness and are marvellously harmonious. They still seem to have a long life ahead.

St-Emilion and Pomerol. Some châteaux were still suffering from the effect of the 1956 frost, but the best wines are opulent and almost opaque. More advanced than the Médocs, they are now at their best.

Sweet whites. Some wines are over botrytized and seem top heavy. Others are superbly balanced like the 1962s.

Older vintages still drinking well

1959. Wines have a very roasted character. Some are not far behind 1961 but most lack their harmony.

1955. Some still remarkably fresh, solid and more interesting than a few years ago.

1953. Delightful wines, now lightening and fading.

1952. Mixed fortunes, but the best are concentrated and classic.

WHAT MAKES GREAT BORDEAUX

The following is a list, with brief notes, of the main factors that determine the quality of a great Bordeaux wine.

Red

Vineyard
Well-drained, relatively poor soil, high in gravel (Médoc and Graves), limestone (St-Emilion Côtes), gravel and sand (St-Emilion Graves) or gravel and clay (Pomerol).

Grape varieties
Cabernet Sauvignon, Cabernet Franc and Merlot.

Mature healthy grapes
The right balance of sugar and acidity, no rot.

Careful vinification
No extraction of acids from the stalks. Fermentation at 28°–30°C (82°–86°F).

Careful selection
Rejection of any sub-standard *cuves* (young vines, grapes from an inferior part of the vineyard, *cuves* affected by rain or rot).

Addition of vin de presse
This adds colour and extracts and so provides additional elements to assist ageing.

Use of new barrels
The percentage of new barrels should be correct for the weight of the wine; it ranges from 100% to 30%.

Bottling at the right time
After 18–24 months, depending on the wine's tannin and power.

Sweet white

Vineyard
Well-drained, poor soil, characterized by the presence of clay with gravel and limestone.

Grape varieties
Sémillon and Sauvignon.

Overripe grapes affected by noble rot
This must be carefully controlled by selection. Too little botrytis and the wine lacks character; too much, and the wine becomes clumsy.

Selection in the vineyard
The pickers must go through the vineyard from three to six times to select overripe and botrytized grapes.

Slow and long fermentation in cask
The ideal temperature is normally about 20°C (68°F). Because of this and the high concentration of sugar, the fermentation usually lasts two to five weeks.

Cask ageing
The best *crus* still keep their wines two to three years in cask. A proportion of the casks are new.

Selection for bottling
Selection is made between pressings (the third is usually the best) and between casks.

A–Z OF CHATEAUX

This A–Z is both an index to the profile section (profiled names are shown in colour) and a directory of some 400 châteaux that are not profiled. In the case of the latter, certain basic information is contained in the A–Z entries. Where possible, the following details are given, and in the corresponding order: château name, appellation, classification (if any), owner (see page 4 for types of company), size of vineyard in hectares, colour of wine (R or W for red or white), and average number of cases produced annually. If a star appears after the name it means that the wine concerned is one that, although not profiled, is above average and worth investigating. The initials S.l. indicate that the wine is a second label. A.l. indicates an alternative label. The appellations are abbreviated as follows.

Name	Abbreviation
Barsac	Bars.
Blaye	Bl.
Bourg	Bg.
Bordeaux	Bord.
Bordeaux Supérieur	Bord. Sup.
Canon-Fronsac	C-Fron.
Côtes de Castillon	Cast.
Entre-Deux-Mers	E-D-M
Fronsac	Fron.
Graves	Gr.
Haut-Médoc	H-Méd.
Lalande-de-Pomerol	L-de-Pom.
Listrac	Listr.
Loupiac	Loup.
Lussac-St-Emilion	L-St-Em.
Margaux	Marg.
Médoc	Méd.
Montagne-St-Emilion	M-St-Em.
Moulis	Moul.
Pauillac	Pau.
Pomerol	Pom.
Premières Côtes de Bordeaux	Prem. Côtes.
Puisseguin-St-Emilion	P-St-Em.
Ste-Croix-du-Mont	Ste-Cr.
St-Emilion	St-Em.
St-Estèphe	St-Est.
Sauternes	Saut.

This is not a comprehensive list of Bordeaux châteaux, but aims to give as broad and useful a selection as possible within the limits of the space available.

d'Agassac, p.82
de l'Amiral. S.l. of Labégorce-Zédé
Andron-Blanquet, p.76
Aney. H-Méd. CB. Raimond Père & Fils. 20ha. R.10,000
L'Angelus, p.112
d'Angludet, p.53
des Annereaux, p.136
Anthonic, p.60
d'Archambeau, p.94
d'Arche, p.104

d'Arche-Lafaurie. S.l. of d'Arche. Not used since 1981
d'Arcins. H-Méd. CB 1932. SC. 70ha. R.37,500
Arnaud-Jouan. Prem. Côtes. M.Darriet. R.3,000. W.18,000
Arnauld. H-Méd. CB 1932. M.Roggy. 15ha. R.7,500
Arricaud. Gr. A.J.Bouyx. 28ha. R.3,000. W.8,000.
L'Arrosée, p.112
d'Arsac, p.82

de Clotte. Côtes de Cast. Mme
J.Guerret-Denies.15ha. R.8,000.
See p.142

La Clotte, p.116

La Clusière, p.116

Colombier-Monpelou, p.70

La Commanderie.St-Est., p.77

La Commanderie. Pom. F. &
Mlle M.H. Dé. 5.8ha. R.2,500

de la Commanderie.* L-de-
Pom. Dr. H.-R.Lafon. 19ha.R.
R.8,000

Connétable Talbot. S.l. of
Talbot

La Conseillante, p.130

Corbin, p.116

Corbin-Michotte, p.117

Cordat, Clos. S.l. of Monbrison

Cormeil-Figeac, p.117

Cos-d'Estournel, p.77

Cos-Labory, p.78

de la Coste. S.l. of Paveil de
Luze

Côte-Baleau, p.117

Coucheroy. S.l. of La Louvière

Coufran, p.85

Couhins, p.96

Couhins-Lurton, p.96

Coulac. Ste-Cr. G.Despujols.
7ha. W.3,000

La Cour-Pavillon. Bord. Brand
of Gilbey de Loudenne. R. & W.

de Courbon, Gr. J. Sanders.
6.5ha. W.3,000

la Couronne, p.70

de Courteillac. E-D-M. Baron
du Foussat. 30ha. R.6,000.
W.8,000

La Couspaude, p.117

Coustolle, p.139

Coutelin-Merville, p.78

Coutet, Gr., p.97

Coutet, St-Ém., p.117

Coutet, Saut., p.105

Le Couvent, p.117

Couvent-des-Jacobins, p.117

Crabitey.* Gr. SC. 18ha.
R.3,000. W.400

Le Crock, p.78

La Croix, Pom., p.130

La Croix. S.l. of Ducru-
Beaucaillou, p.66

La Croix-Blanche. S.l. of des
Tours

La Croix du Casse.* Pom. SC.
9ha. R.4,500

La Croix-de-Gay, p.131

La Croix-Landon.. Méd.
J.P.Laforgue. 9ha. R.4,000

Le Croix de Mazerat. S.l. of
Beauséjour (Duffau-Lagarosse)

La Croix de Millorit. Bg.
A.Jambert. 17ha. R.7,500

La Croix de Pez.* St-Est. Guy
Guyonnard. 7ha. R.2,750

La-Croix-St-André. L-de-Pom.
M.Carayon. 15ha. R.6,000

La Croix-St-Georges. Pom. J.-
F. Janoueix. 4ha. R.1,800.

Adjoining and under same
ownership as La Croix, p.130

La Croix-Toulifaut. Pom. J.-F.
Janoueix. 1.5ha. R.800.

Croizet-Bages, p.71

Croque-Michotte, p.118

du Cros.* Loup. M.Boyer. 38ha.
W.3,500

Cru St-Marc. S.l. of La Tour-
Blanche

du Cruzeau, p.97

de Cugat. E-D-M. B.Meyer.
25ha. R.11,500. W.4,500

Curé-Bon-La-Madeleine, p.118

Cure-Bourse, Domaine de. S.l.
of Durfort-Vivens

Dalem, p.139

La Dame-Blanche. White wine
of du Taillan

Dassault, p.118

Le Dauphin-Château-Guiraud.
S.l. of Guiraud, p.106

Le Dauphin-de-Lalague. S.l. of
Guiraud

de la Dauphine, p.138

Dauphiné-Rondillon. Loup.
J.Darriet. W.10,000

Dauzac, p.55

Desmirail, p.55

Despagnet.* St-Em. P.Faure.
8ha. R.4,400

Deyrem-Valentin, p.55

Dillon, p.85

Doisy-Daëne, p.105

Doisy-Dubroca, p.105

Doisy-Védrines, p.105

Domaine des Douves. S.l. of
Beauregard

La Dominique, p.118

Doms.* Gr. M.Duvigneau &
L.Parage. 22ha. R.3,000. W.3,500

Dubory. S.l. of Launay, p.140

Ducluzeau.* List. CB 1932.
Madame Jean-Eugène Borie. 5ha.
R.2,000

Ducru-Beaucaillou, p.66

Duhart-Milon-Rothschild, p.71

Dupeyron. S.l. of Cannet, p.54

Duplessis-Fabre, p.61

Duplessis (Hauchecorne), p.62

Durfort-Vivens, p.55

Dutellier. S.l. of Ramage-la-
Bâtisse, p.87

Dutruch-Grand-Poujeaux, p.62

l'Eglise, p.131

de l'Eglise, p.131

l'Eglise-Clinet, p.131

l'Enclos, p.131

l'Escadre, p.138

de l'Espinglet. Prem. Côtes.
R.Raynaud. 30ha. R. & W

L'Estang. Côtes de Cast.
Robert Filliol. 23ha. R.10,000.
See p.142

l'Estruelle. Méd. GFA Ladra.
R.5,000

l'Evangile, p.131

La Fagnouse. St-E. Mme
Coutant. R.3,500

Falfas. Bg. Mme M. Jaubert.
17ha. R.8,750
de Fargues, p.106
Faubernet.* Bord. Sup. Adrien
& Guy Dufis. 8oha. R.33,000.
W.7,000.
Faurie-de-Souchard, p.118
Fayau, p.141
de Ferbos.* Cér. J. Perromat.
W.3,000
Ferrand.* Pom. SC. 15ha. W.
de Ferrand, p.118
Ferrande, p.97
Ferrière, p.55
Feytit-Clinet, p.132
les Fiefs-de-Lagrange. S.l. of
Lagrange
de Fieuzal, p.97
Figeac, p.119
Filhot, p.106
La Fleur, p.119
la Fleur-Milon, p.71
la Fleur-Pétrus, p.132
**Fleuron Blanc de Château
Loubens**. S.l. of Loubens
de Florimond. Bl. L.Marinier.
44.5ha. R.7,000. W.8,000
Fombrauge, p.119
Fonbadet, p.71
Fonchereau. E-D-M. Mme
Georges Vinot-Postry. 27ha.
R.5,000
Fonplégade, p.119
Fonrazade. St-Em. GC.
G.Balotte. 9ha. R.4,500
Fonréaud, p.64
Fonroque, p.119
Fonsèche. S.l. of Lamothe-Cissac
La Fontanelle. S.l. of Cantenac-
Brown
Fontenay, p.142
Fontesteau, p.85
Fort-de-Vauban. H-Méd.
A.Noleau. 7ha. R.2,500
Les Forts-de-Latour. S.l. of
Latour
Fourcas-Dupré, p.64
Fourcas-Hosten, p.64
Fourney. St-Em. GC. Vignobles
Rollet. 18ha. R.7,000
Fourtet, p.119
de France. Gr. B.Thomassin.
27ha. R.13,000
La France. E-D-M. SC. 6oha.
R.8,000. W.26,000
La France. Méd. CB 1932.
A.Feuvrier. 7ha. R.3,000
Franc-Grâce-Dieu, p.120
Franc-Mallet.* Pom. G.Arpin.
5ha. R.1,500
Franc-Mayne, p.120
Franquet-Grand-Poujeaux.*
Moul. CB. P.Lambert. 6ha.
R.2,500
de Fronsac. Fron. Seurin. 7ha.
R.2,200
La-Fuie-St-Bonnet. S.l. of La
Tour-St-Bonnet
"G" Château Guiraud. S.l. of

Guiraud, p.106
du Gaby, p.140
La Gaffelière, p.120
Gaillard. St-Em. GC. J.-J.
Nouvel. 2oha. R.10,000
de Gaillat.* Gr. Coste family.
8ha. R.4,000
Gallais-Bellevue. S.l. of
Potensac
Gallus, Cuvée, p.127
La Garde, p.98
Le Gardera, see Laurétan, p.141
Gardour. S.l. of Moncets
Le Gay, p.132
Le Gay. E-D-M. R.Maison.
4oha. R.12,000. W.4,000
Gazin. Gr. P.Michotte. 1oha.
R.4,000
Gazin, Pom, p.132
Gibeau. P-St-E. Bourlon-
Masseron family. 7oha. R.7,500
Gilette, p.106
Giscours, p.55
du Glana, p.66
Gloria, p.66
de Goélane. E-D-M. A.Castel.
5oha. R.20,000. W.5,000
Gombaude-Guillot.* Pom.
GFA. 7ha. R.2,400
Gontier. Bl. M.F.Levrand. 3oha.
R.12,500
Goumin. S.l. of Bonnet
La Grâce-Dieu.* St-Em. GC.
M.Pauty. 11ha. R.7,000
La Grâce-Dieu-Les-Menuts,
p.120
Grand-Abord.* Gr. M.Dugoua.
17ha. R.4,500. W.2,000
Grand-Barrail-Lamarzelle-
Figeac, p.120
Grand-Corbin, p.120
Grand-Corbin-Despagne, p.120
Grand-Duroc-Milon. Pau. CB
1932. Bernard Jugla. 6ha.
R.22,500
Le Grand-Enclos. Cér. Lataste.
3oha. W.13,000
Grand-Jour. Bg. Mme
Gaignerot. 25.5ha. R.12,500.
W.1,500
Grand-Listrac, p.64
Grand-Mayne, p.121
Grand-Monteil. Bord. Sup. Soc.
du Grand Monteil des Pontons et
de Lafite. 7oha. R.38,800.
W.1,200
du Grand-Moueys. Prem.
Côtes. N.Lacour & A.Icard.
42ha. R.9,200. W.3,800
Grand-Moulin. H-Méd. CB. SC.
35ha. R.7,000
Grand-Moulinet. Pom. J.-M.
Garde. 16ha. R.6,900
Grand-Pontet, p.121
de Grand-Puch. E-D-M. Société
Viticole. 175ha. R.40,000
W.5,500
Grand-Puy-Ducasse, p.71
Grand-Puy-Lacoste, p.72

de Suduiraut. 45ha. R.4,000.
W.8,000

du Juge.* Bord. Sup. (Cadillac).
P.Dupleich. 30ha. R.6,000
W.9,000

du Juge. Bord. Sup. (Haux).
J.Mèdeville. 24ha. R.9,000
W.5,500

Jumayne, p.140

Le Jurat. St-Em. GC.
E.Guinaudie. 8ha. R.3,500

Justa. Prem. Côtes.* Y.Mas.
20ha. R.8,000. W.5,000

Les Justices, p.107

Kirwan, p.56

de Labat.* H-Méd. Nony-Borie.
R.2,500

Labégorce, p.56

Labégorce-Zédé, p.56

Laborde. L-de-Pom. J.-M.
Trocard. 15ha. R.4,000

Labottière. Bord. Brand of
Cordier. R. & W.

Lachesnaye.* H-Méd. CBS.
H.Bouteiller. 20ha. R.5,000

Lacoste-Borie. S.l. of Grand-
Puy-Lacoste

Lafaurie. Prem. Côtes. A.
Croizet-Sauvestre. 25ha. R.5,000.
W.5,000

Lafaurie-Peyraguey, p.107

Lafayette. Bord. Brand of
Nathaniel Johnston. R.

Laffitte-Carcasset, p.78

Laffitte-Laujac. S.l. of Laujac

Lafite. Prem. Côtes. SCE.
R.11,500

Lafite-Canteloup. H-Méd. CB
1932. GFA. 10ha. R.5,000

Lafite-Rothschild, p.73

Lafleur, p.133

Lafleur-Gazin, p.133

Lafleur-du-Roy. Pom.
Y.Dubost. 3ha. R.1,750

Lafon, p.64

Lafon-Rochet, p.79

Lafüe. Ste-Cr. J.Sicres. R.2,000

Lagrange, Pom., p.133

Lagrange, St-Jul., p.67

Lagrave. Ste-Cr. J.-M.Tinon.
18ha. R.2,000. W.6,000

Lagüe.* Fron. Roux-Oulié. 10ha.
R.4,000

La Lagune, p.85

Lalande.* Listr. CB 1932. Mmes
Dubosc & Darriet. 10ha. R.5,000

Lalande. St. Jul. Société
d'Exploitation. 30ha. R.10,000

Lalande-Borie, p.67

Lalibarde. Bg. R.Dumas.
34.5ha. R.20,000. W.2,000

Lamarque. Ste-Cr. R.Bernard.
R.4,000. W.5,000

de Lamarque, p.86

Lamartine. S.l. of Cantenac-
Brown

Lamothe, p.107

Lamothe. Bg. P.Pessonier. 20ha.
R.7,000

Lamothe. Prem. Côtes.
J.Perriquet & F.Neel. 25ha.
R.3,000. W.6,000

Lamothe-Bergeron.* H-Méd.
CB. SC. Grand-Puy Ducasse.
50ha. R.25,000

Lamothe-Cissac. H-Méd. CGB.
G.Fabre. 35ha. R.16,000

Lamothe-Guignard, p.107

Landat. H-Méd. CB 1978. SC du
château Lamothe. 14ha. R.7,000

Lanessan, p.86

Langoa-Barton, p.67

Laniote, p.122

Lapelletrie. St-Em. GC. Jean
family. 12ha. R.6,000

Larcis-Ducasse, p.122

Lardit. Côtes de Cast. Jacques
Trepout. 11.5ha. R. See p.142

Larmande, p.122

Laroque, p.122

Larose-Trintaudon, p.86

Laroze, p.122

Larrivaux. H-Méd. CB 1932.
GFA. 20ha. R.6,000

Larrivaux-Hanteillan. S.l. of
Hanteillan

Larrivet-Haut-Brion, p.98

Lartigue.* St-Est. SC. 7ha.
R.3,000

Lartigue-de-Brochon. S.l. of
Sociando-Mallet

Lascombes, p.56

Lassalle. S.l. of Potensac, p.90

Lassègue. St-Em. GC.
J.P.Freylon. 22.5ha. R.13,000

Latour, p.73

Latour-à-Pomerol, p.133

Laujac.* Méd. CGB. Mme
H.Cruse. 30ha. R.12,500.

Launay, p.140

Laurensanne. Bg. J.-F.Levraud.
20ha. R.10,000. W.2,000

Laurétan, p.141

des Laurets, p.128

Laurette. Ste-Cr. F.Pons.
R.1,000. W.7,000

Lavalière. Méd. CB. Cailloux
family. 15ha. R.7,500.

Laville-Haut-Brion, p.98

Lavillotte, p.79

Lemoine-Nexon. S.l. of de
Malleret

Léon, & Dom. de Camélon.
Prem. Côtes. M.F.Mähler-Besse.
R.3,000. W.2,000

Léoville-Barton, p.68

Léoville-Las-Cases, p.68

Léoville-Poyferré, p.68

Lestage, p.64

Lestage-Darquier, p.62

Lestage-Simon, p.86

Letourt. S.l. of Hauterive

Ligondras. Marg. 1er Artisan.
P.Augeau. 7ha. R.3,000

Ligondras. Marg. Pierre
Augeau. 7ha. R.3,500

Liot.* Saut. CB. J.David. 20ha.
W.5,500.

Liouner.* Listr. CB 1932.
P.Bosq. 15ha. R.7,500
Liversan, p.86
Livran. Méd. CB. R.Godfrin.
50ha. R.20,000
Lognac. S.l. of Ferrande
Loubens, p.142
Loudenne, p.90
Louloumet. S.l. of Chicane
Loupiac-Gaudiet, p.142
La Louvière, p.99
de Loyac. S.l. of Malescot-St-
Exupéry
Lucas. S.l. of Dillon
Ludon-Pomiès-Agassac. S.l. of
Lagune
Lynch-Bages, p.73
Lynch-Moussas, p.74
du Lyonnat, p.128
MacCarthy, p.79
MacCarthy-Moula. St-Est. CB.
See Haut-Marbuzet, p.78
La Madeleine, p.122
Magdelaine, p.123
Magence, p.99
Magnol.* H-Méd. Barton &
Guestier. 17ha. R.5,000
Maillard. Prem. Côtes. F.
Germe, 20ha. R.4,000. W.4,000
Maison-Blanche, p.128
Maison Blanche. Pom.
G.Despagne. 4ha. R.1,500
Maison-Rose. S.l. of des Laurets
Maître d'Estournel. Bord.
Brand of Le Cercle d'Estournel.
R. & W.
Malagar. Prem. Côtes.
M.Dubourg. 13ha. R.2,000
W.4,500
Malarctic-Lagravière, p.99
Malescasse.* H-Méd. CB.
G.Tesseron. 40ha. R.13,000.
Malescot-St-Exupéry, p.57
de Malle, p.108
de Malleret, p.87
Malmaison. S.l. of Clarke
Maquin-St-Georges, p.128
de Marbuzet, p.79
de Marbuzet. S.l. of Cos-
d'Estournel
Margaux, p.57
Marquis-d'Alesme-Becker,
p.57
Marquis-de-Bressane. S.l. of
Hauterive
Marquis, Clos du. S.l. of
Léoville-Las-Cases
Marquis de St-Estèphe, p.79
Marquis-de-Terme, p.57
Marsac-Séguineau, p.57
Martinens, p.58
Martinon. E-D-M. Trollier.
35ha. R.5,000. W.15,000
de Martouret. E-D-M.
D.Lurton. 30ha. R.12,000
W.5,500
La Marzelle, p.120
Matras, p.123
Maucaillou, p.62

Maucamps.* H-Méd. CB.
I.Tessandier. 15ha. R.12,000
Mausse, p.140
Mauvesin.* Moul. CBS.
Vicomte & Vicomtesse de
Baritault du Carpia. 148ha.
R.21,000
Mauvezin, p.123
Du Mayne.* Saut. CB. SCI
Sanders. 8ha. W.2,000.
Mayne-d'Anice. S.l. of de
Chantegrive
Mayne-Binet. Cér. J.Perromat.
W.2,000
Mayne-Lévêque. S.l. of de
Chantegrive
Mayne-Vieil, p.139
Mazarin. Loup. Courbin-
Meyssan. 25ha. W.15,000
Mazeris-Bellevue, p.140
Mazeyres, p.133
Clos Mazeyres. Pom. Laymarie
& Fils, 9ha. R.3,500
Méaume.* Bord. Sup. (Guitres
& Coutras). A.Johnson-Hill.
24ha. R.7,500
Le Menotat. Bl. E.Cruse. 10ha.
R.6,000. W.1,000
Mendoce, p.137
Ménota.* Saut. CB. N.Labat.
16ha. W.4,500.
Meyney, p.80
Le Meynieu, p.87
Mille-Sescousses.* Bord. Sup.
J.Darricarrère. 75ha. R. &
W.45,000
Millet, p.99
La Mission-Haut-Brion, p.99
Les Moines. Méd. Claude
Pourreau. 21ha. R.12,000
des Moines. L-de-Pom.
H.Darnazou. 12ha. R.2,000
Monbousquet, p.123
Monbrison, p.58
Moncabon, Enclos de. S.l. of
Rauzan-Gassies
Moncets, p.136
Monconseil-Gazin. Bl.
M.Baudet. 15ha. R.5,000
Montalbert. St-Em. GC. SC.
12.5ha. R.6,000
Montalivet.* Gr. P.Coste,
P.Dubourdieu, R.Goffard. 15ha.
R.5,000. W.2,000.
Montbrun, p.58
Le Monteil-d'Arsac. S.l. of
d'Arsac
du Monthil.* Méd. CB 1932.
Jean Gabas. 20ha. R.9,500
Montlabert, p.123
Montrose, p.80
Mony. Prem. Côtes. Marquis de
Barbentane. 25ha. R.3,000.
W.10,000
Morange. Ste-Cr. F.Durr.
W.6,000
Morin, p.80
Moulin-d'Arvigny. S.l. of
Beaumont

Moulin-du-Cadet, p.123

Moulin-des-Carruades. S.l. of Lafite-Rothschild, p.73

Moulin-Duhart. S.l. of Duhart-Milon-Rothschild, p.71

Moulin-Haut-Laroque, p.139

Moulin-de-Laborde. List. Michel Hostens. 9.5ha. R.4,500

Moulin-de-Launay, p.141

Moulin-Pey-Labrie. C-Fr. Yvette Seurt. 8ha. R.3,500

Moulin-Riche.* S.l. of Léoville-Poyferré, p.68

Moulin-de-la-Roque. S.l. of La Tour-de-By, p.91

Moulin de la Rose. St. Jul. CB 1932. Guy Delon. 4ha. R.2,000.

Moulin Rouge. Côtes de Cast. J.-C. Bassilieaux. 23ha. R.14,000. See p.142

du Moulin Rouge.* H-Méd. CB. Veyries-Pelon family. 15ha. R.6,000

Moulin-de-St-Vincent. S.l. of Moulin-à-Vent

Moulin de Taffard.* Méd. Pierre Peyruse. 6ha. R.3,000

Moulin-à-Vent.* L-de-Pom. SC. 6ha. R.2,250

Moulin-à-Vent, Moulis, p.62

Moulinet, p.133

Moulinet-Lasserre. A.l. of René Moulis, p.63

Mourlet. S.l. of d'Archambeau, p.94

Mouton-Baronne-Philippe, p.74

Mouton-Cadet. Bord. Brand of La Baronnie. R. & W.

Mouton-Rothschild, p.74

Nairac, p.108

Nenin, p.133

Notton, S.l. of Brane-Cantenac

Olivier, p.100

L'Oratoire, p.123

les Ormes-de-Pez, p.80

Les Ormes-Sorbet, p.90

Palmer, p.58

Panigon.* Méd. CB. G.Lamolière. 25ha. R.12,500 W.300

Le Pape.* Gr. Société Fermière. 4.9ha. R.4,000

Pape-Clement, p.100

du Parc. H-Méd. René Gonzalvez. 10ha. R.6,000

Pardaillan. Bl. C.Carreau. 15ha. R.4,000. W.2,000

La Parde de Haut-Bailly. S.l. of Haut-Bailly

La Paroisse, p.87

La Patache. Pom. Mme Forton. 5ha. R.2,250

Patache-d'Aux, p.90

Patris, p.124

Paveil-de-Luze, p.58

Pavie, p.124

Pavie-Decesse, p.124

Pavie-Macquin, p.124

du Pavillon. Ste-Cr. d'Arfeuille. 11ha. W.5,000

Pavillon Blanc and Pavillon Rouge. S.ls. of Margaux, p.57

Pavillon-de-Boyrein. Gr. P.Bonnet & Fils. 20ha. R.

Pavillon-Cadet, p.124

du Pavillon & Grand-Renouil. C-Fron. Jean Ponty & Fils. 10ha. R.4,000

Pêcheur, Blanc du. Bord. Brand of Borie-Manoux. W.

Péconnet.* Prem. Côtes. Amiel family. 20ha. R.9,000

Pédesclaux, p.74

Perenne. Bl. M. & P.Oudinot. 48ha. R.20,000

Pernaud.* Saut. CB. P.Pascaud. 20ha. W.5,500

Perron. L-de-Pom. Massonié. 10ha. R.6,000

Petit-Faurie-de-Soutard, p.124

Petit-Village, p.134

Pétrus, p.134

Peychaud, p.137

Peymartin. S.l. of Gloria, p.66

Pey-Martin. Méd. CB. Jean Signoret. 10ha. R.6,500

Peyrabon.* H-Méd. CGB. J.Babeau. 53ha. R.17,500.

Peyrat. Prem. Côtes (Beguey). Mme David. 40ha. R.5,000. W.20,000

du Peyrat.* Prem. Côtes (Capian). SC. 63.5ha. R.6,000. W.15,000

Peyraud. S.l. of Bonnet, p.140

Peyreau.* St-Em. GC. M.Boutet. 13ha. R.6,200

Peyredon-Lagravette.* Listr. CB. P.Hostein. 6ha. R.3,000

Peyredoulle. Bl. J. & B. Germain. 16ha. R.6,200. W.1,500

De Peyrelongue, St-Em. GC. P.Cassat. 12ha. R.6,000

de Pez, p.81

Phélan-Ségur, p.81

Piada. Saut. CB. J.Lalande. 13ha. R.1,300. W.2,500

Pibran, p.75

Pichelèbre, p.140

Pichon. H-Méd. C.Fayat. 23ha. R.8,000

Pichon-Longueville-Baron, p.75

Pichon-Longueville-Comtesse-de-Lalande, p.75

Picourneau. S.l. of Le Bourdieu, p.83

Picque-Caillou, p.100

Pierredon.* Bord. Sup. (Gornac). P.Perromat. 45ha. R.10,000

Pipeau.* St-Em. P.Mestreguilhem & Fils. 25ha. R.11,500

Piron.* Gr. P.Boyreau. 20ha. R.2,000. W.7,500.

Pitray. Côtes de Cast. Vicomte

L. de Pitray. 26ha. R. See p.142

Plagnac.* Méd. CB. D.Cordier. 27ha. R.18,000

Plantey. Pau. G. Meffre. 30ha. R.13,000

Plantey-de-la-Croix.* S.l. of Verdignan

Plessis. S.l. of Moulin-de-Launay

Plince, p.134

La Pointe, p.134

Pomeys, p.63

Pomys. St-Est. CBS 1932. SARL Arnaud. 6ha. R.3,000

de Poncet. Prem. Côtes. J.L. David. 40ha. R.7,000. W.15,000

Pontac-Lynch, p.58

Pontac-Monplaisir.* Gr. J.Maufras. 14ha. R.3,500. W.1,500.

Pontet. Méd. CB 1978. Emile Courrian. 11ha. R.7,000

Pontet-Canet, p.75

Pontet-Chappaz. Marg. Vignobles Rocher-Cap de Rive SA. 6.5ha. R.3,500

Pontet-Clauzure.* St-Em. GC. SC. 10ha. R.4,000

Pontoise-Cabarrus.* H-Méd. CGB. F.Tereygeol. 22.5ha. R.13,000

De Portets.* Gr. J.-P. Théron. 14.5ha. R.6,000. W.2,000.

Potensac, p.90

Pouget, p.59

Poujeaux, p.63

les Pradines, p.81

Preuillac. Méd. CB 1932. Raymond Bouet. 30ha. R.19,000

Prieur du Château Meyney. S.l. of Meyney, p.80

Le Prieuré, p.124

Prieuré-Lichine, p.59

La Providence. Bord. Sup. Francis Cuvelier. 6ha. R.3,000

La Providence. Pom. J.Dupuy. 3ha. R.250

Puy-Blanquet.* St-Em. GC. R.Jacquet. 23ha. R.10,000

Puyblanquet-Carille. St-Em. GC. J.-F.Carille. 17ha. R.7,400

Puycarpin, p.142

Puy-Castéra.* H-Méd. CB. GFA du Castéra. 24ha. R.16,000.

Puyguilhem. Fron. Mlle J.Mothes. 10ha. R.5,000

Puymiran. E-D-M. Degueil. 45ha. R.23,000. W.13,000

Quentin. St-Em. GC. SC. 30ha. R.1,800

Les Queyrats.* Gr. Dulac family. 38.5ha. W.10,000. See also St-Pierre, p.101

de Quinsac. E-D-M. SC. R.5,000

"R". S.l. of Rieussec

Rabaud-Promis, p.108

Rahoul, p.100

Ramage-la-Bâtisse, p.87

La Rame. Ste-Cr. C.Armand. 36ha. R.5,000. W.15,000

de Ramondon. Prem. Côtes. M.Sangers & Mme van Pé. 8ha. R.7,000. W.6,000

Rausan-Ségla, p.59

du Raux. H-Méd. SCI du Raux. 10ha. R.5,000

Rauzan-Gassies, p.59

Raymond. E-D-M. Baron R. de Montesquieu. R.20,000. W.5,000.

Raymond-Lafon, p.108

Rayne Sec. Dry wine of de Rayne-Vigneau, p.108

de Rayne-Vigneau, p.108

René, p.134

Réserve de la Comtesse. S.l. of Pichon-Longueville-Comtesse

Réserve du Marquis d'Evry. S.l. of de Lamarque, p.86

de Respide. Gr. P.Bonnet & Fils. 40ha. R. & W.

Respide-Médeville.* Gr. C.Médeville. 7ha. R. & W.

du Retout. H-Méd. Gérard Kopp. 23ha. R.12,500

Le Reverdon. See Coutet, p.97

Reynier.* E-D-M. D.Lurton. 60ha. R.25,000. W.11,000

Reynon, p.141

Reysson.* H-Méd. CGB. SC. 46ha. R.13,000

de Ricaud, p.142

Richelieu. Fron. Y.Viaud. 20ha. R.6,000

Rieussec, p.109

Ripeau, 125

La Rivalerie. Bl. M.Bauchet. R.20,000

La Rivière, p.139

La Roche. Prem. Côtes. J.Palau. 20ha. R.4,000. W.4,000

de Rochemorin, p.101

Du Rocher. St-Em. GC. Baron S. de Montfort. 14ha. R.6,250

Rocher-Bellevue. Côtes de Cast. Vignobles Rocher-Cap de Rive SA. 15ha. R. See p.142

La Rochette. S.l. of des Laurets Côtes Rocheuses, p.127

De Rol. St-Em. GC. J.Sautereau. 7ha. R.3,000

de Rolland, p.109

Romer-du-Hayot, p.109

de la Ronceray. St-Est. CB. Jacques Pedro. 8ha. R.32,500

La Roque-de-By. S.l. of La Tour-de-By

Roquegrave. Méd. CB 1932. Joannon & Lleu. 25ha. R.13,000

de Roques. P-St-Em. M.Sublett. 15ha. R.8,000

Roquetaillade-Le-Bernet. S.l. of de Roquetaillade-la-Grange de Roquetaillade-La-Grange, p.101

Rosechatel. Bord. Brand of Schröder & Schÿler. R. & W.

La-Rose-Côte-de-Rol. St-Em.

GC. Y.Mirande. 8.5ha. R.3,500
La Rose-Maréchale. S.l. of
Coufran, p.85
La Rose-Peruchon. S.l. of du
Lyonnat
La Rose Pourret.* St-Em. GC.
B.Warion. 7ha. R.2,500
De Rouillac.* Gr. P.Sarthou &
J.Chambon. 5ha. R.1,500
Roumieu.* Bars. P.Goyaud.
14ha. W.3,500
Roumieu. Saut. CB. R.Bernadet.
20ha. W.2,000
Roumieu-Goyaud. Saut. CB.
Mme C.Craveia-Goyaud. 14ha.
W.
Roumieu-Lacoste.* Saut. CB.
Mme S.Dubourdier-Bouchet.
12ha. W.2,500
Rozier. St-Em. GC. J.-B. Saby.
16ha. R.7,000
Ruat. S.l. of Ruat-Petit-Poujeaux
**de la Sablière-Fongrave and
Domaine de Fongrave.*** E-D-
M. P.Perromat. 45ha. R. & W.
St-Amand.* Saut. L.Ricard.
20ha. W.5,000.
St-Christoly. Méd. CB 1932.
Hervé Héraud. 15ha. R.8,000
St-Estèphe. St-Est. CB 1932.
SARL Arnaud. 12ha. R.6,000
Ste-Hélène. S.l. of de Malle,
p.108
St-Paul. H-Méd. SC. 20ha. R.
de St-Pierre. St-Em. GC. L. &
J.P.Musset. 18ha. R.9,000
St-Roch. S.l. of Andron-Blanquet
de Sales. Pom. GFA. 47.5ha.
R.22,500
la Salle-de-Poujeaux. S.l. of
Poujeaux
Sarget du Gruaud-Larose. S.l.
of Gruaud-Larose
Le Sartre. Gr-Léo. GFA. 15ha.
R. & W.
Segonnes. S.l. of Lascombes
Ségur. H-Méd. CGB 1932. SC.
33ha. R.15,000
Ségur-d'Arsac. S.l. of d'Arsac

Séméillan Mazeau. List. CBS
1932. SC. 11ha. R.5,200
Senailhac.* E-D-M. Magnat.
6oha. R.15,000. W.8,000
Senilhac.* H-Méd. CB 1932. M.
& J.-L.Grassin. 12ha. R.6,000
Sergant. L-de-Pom. GFA des
Vignobles Jean Milhade. R.6,000
Sestignan. Méd. CB. B.de
Rozières. 12ha. R.5,000
Sigognac, p.91
Simon. Saut. CB. J.Dufour.
10ha. W.2,000
Soleil. P-St-Em. J.Soleil. 15ha.
R.7,000
Soudars.* H-Méd. CB.
E.Miailhe. 14.5ha. R.9,000.
le Souley-Ste Croix. H-Méd.
CB 1932. Jean Riffaud. 19ha.
R.10,000
Suau. Prem. Côtes. M.Raoux.
45ha. R.20,000
Taffard.* Méd. Paul Mottes.
16.5ha. R.7,500
du Tasta.* Prem. Côtes.
R.5,000. W.500
Tayac. Bg. P.Saturny. 23ha. R.
des Templiers. S.l. of
Larmande, p.122
Templiers, Clos des. L-de-
Pom. E. & J.-M.Meyer. 9.6ha.
R.3,800
Terfort. S.l. of Loubens
de Terrefort-Quancard. Bord.
Sup. Quancard family. 7oha.
R.38,000
Tertre-de-Launay. S.l. of
Moulin-de-Launay
Teysson.* L-de-Pom. Mme.
Servant. 13ha. R.6,000
de Thau. Bg. L.Schweitzer. 45ha.
15,000
Timberlay.* Bord. Sup.
R.Giraud. 75ha. R.50,000
W.6,000
Toinet-Fombrauge. St-Em.
B.Sierra. 8ha. R.2,900
La Tonnelle. St-Em. G.Arnaud

& Fils. 15ha. R.6,500

Toumalin, p.140

Toumilon, p.102

la Tour-d'Aspic. S.l. of Haut-Batailley, p.72

La Tour-de-Bessan, p.60

La Tour-Bicheau.* Gr. Y.Daubas & Fils. 20ha. R.7,000. W.1,300.

La Tour-Blanche, p.110

La Tour Blanche. Méd. CB 1932. SCA. 27ha. R.10,000

Tour-de-Bonnet. S.l. of Bonnet

La Tour-de-By, p.91

la Tour-Carnet, p.88

La Tour-Figeac, p.126

La Tour-Haut-Brion, p.102

La Tour-Haut-Caussan.* Méd. CB 1932. Philippe Courrian. 10.5ha. R.6,000

Tour-du-Haut-Moulin, p.88

La Tour-Léognan.* Gr. SC. R.5,000. W.3,000. Run jointly with Carbonnieux, p.95

Tour de Marbuzet.* St-Est. CB. 1932. Henri Duboscq. 7ha. R.3,000

La Tour-Martillac, p.102

Tour-du-Mirail, p.88

la Tour-de-Mons, p.60

Tour-du-Pas-St-Georges, p.129

La Tour-Pibran. Pau. CB 1932. J.-J.Gounel. 8ha. R.3,500

La Tour-du-Pin-Figeac (Giraud Belivier), p.126

La Tour-Prignac. Méd. CB 1932. SC. 120ha. R.50,000

La Tour-Puymirand. E-D-M. E.Fazilleau. 60ha. R.10,000 W.7,500

Tour-du-Roc. H-Méd. CB 1932. Philippe Robert. 12ha. R.4,500

La Tour-St-Bonnet, p.92

La Tour St-Joseph.* H-Méd. CB. M. & C.Quancard. 13ha. R.

Tour-St-Pierre. St-Em. GC. J.Goudineau. 10ha. 4,500

La Tour-Seran. Méd. CB. 1932. Patrick Peronno. 13ha. R.6,000

Tour-des-Termes, p.81

Tour-de-Tourteau, p.138

La Tour-Védrines. S.l. of Doisy-Védrines, p.105

Tournefeville. L-de-Pom. GFA Sautarel. R.6,000

des Tours, p.129

Tourteau-Choilet, p.103

Tourteran. A.l. of Ramage-la-Bâtisse, p.87

de Toutigeac, p.140

Trimoulet, p.126

des Troischardons. Marg. S de Fait Chardon Père & Fils. R.800

Tronquoy-Lalande, p.81

Troplong-Mondot, p.126

Trotanoy, p.135

Trottevieille, p.126

de Tuilerie. S.l. of Moulin-de-Launay, p.140

La Tuilerie.* Gr. F. & B.Dubrey. 20ha. R.4,500. W.4,000.

Les Tuileries. Bl. C.Alins. 25ha. R.10,000

Le Tuquet.* Gr. P.Ragon. 44ha. R.12,500. W.8,000.

de Tustal. E-D-M. Comte d'Armaillé. 45ha. R.6,000. W.14,000

La Vaillante. S.l. of Launay

La Valade, p.139

La Valière.* Méd. CB. Cailloux family. 15ha. R.7,500

Valrone. Bl. Bertolus & Poullet. 30ha. R.12,000. W.8,000

Verdignan, p.88

Vernous. Méd. CB 1932. SCI. 20ha. R.10,000

la Vicomtesse. S.l. of Laffitte-Carcasset

Videau. Prem. Côtes. 30ha. R.5,000. W.10,000

La Vieille France. Gr. M.Dugoua. 10ha. R.1,500

Vieux Château Certan, p.135

Vieux Château Landon. Méd. CB 1932. Philippe Gillet. 25ha. R.13,500

du Vieux-Clocher, p.92

Vieux-Colombiers. Méd. Soc. de Vinification de Prignac. 250ha. R.10,000

du Vieux-Moulin. Loup. Mme Jean Perromat. 18ha. W.5,000

Vieux-Robin. Méd. CB. François Dufau. 13ha. R.8,000

Vieux Sarpe.* St-Em. GC. J.-P.Janoueix. 6.5ha. R.4,000

La Vigerie. S.l. of Moulin-de-Launay, p.141

Villars, p.139

de Villegorge, p.88

Villemaurine, p.127

Vincent. Marg. CB 1932. Mme Jean Domec. R.2,000

Vin Sec de Doisy-Daëne. S.l. of Doisy-Daëne

La Violette. Pom. Vignobles S.Dumas. 3.3ha. R.2,000

Virou. Bl. Mme Monier. R.10,000. W.10,000

Vrai-Canon-Bouché. C-Fron. Roux-Oulié. 8ha. R.3,000

Vraye-Croix-de-Gay, p.136

"Y". S.l. of d'Yquem, p.110

Yon-Figeac, p.127

d'Yquem, p.110

CHATEAU PROFILES BY APPELLATION

This section focusses on properties that merit special consideration. It includes not only the great names of Bordeaux but also many less well-known producers whose wines deserve recognition. The entries are arranged by appellation, and each appellation is introduced with a description of its general character. In the case of the Médoc, which encompasses many important appellations, there is also a general introduction to the region.

Each entry begins, after the name of the property, with the following details, where obtainable and relevant: classification, owner, administrator, number of hectares planted with vines, number of cases produced annually, grape varieties and respective percentages used in production, and any secondary labels. See page 4 for a key to the abbreviations.

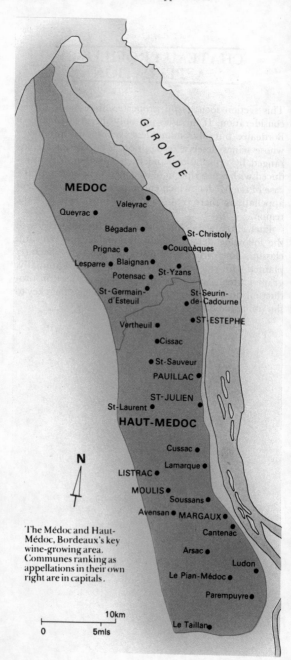

GIRONDE

MEDOC

Valeyrac
Queyrac ●
Bégadan ●
St-Christoly
Prignac ●
Couquèques ●
Lesparre ● Blaignan ●
Potensac ● St-Yzans
St-Germain-
d'Esteuil
St-Seurin-
de-Cadourne
Vertheuil ●
● ST-ESTEPHE
Cissac ●
● St-Sauveur
PAUILLAC
ST-JULIEN
St-Laurent ●
HAUT-MEDOC
Cussac ●
Lamarque ●
LISTRAC ●
MOULIS ●
Soussans ●
Avensan ● MARGAUX ●
Cantenac ●
Arsac ●
Ludon ●
Le Pian-Médoc ●
Parempuyre ●
Le Taillan ●

N

The Médoc and Haut-
Médoc, Bordeaux's key
wine-growing area.
Communes ranking as
appellations in their own
right are in capitals.

10km

0   5mls

THE MEDOC APPELLATIONS

Médoc has been the great ambassador for the red wines of Bordeaux the world over. From the early 18th century, when wealthy and discerning Englishmen first paid a premium to obtain better wines, until the second half of the 20th century, the fame of the region has been spearheaded by the treasure trove of the Médoc.

With its proximity to the city of Bordeaux, commercial and political centre of the Gironde, it was natural that the Médoc should be devploped earlier and more thoroughly than any other piece of land in the region. In the 17th and 18th centuries, the great wine estates were put together in much the same form as we know today. Because of the poor, gravelly soil, mixed subsistence farming easily gave way to specialized viticulture. A glance at the map shows the Médoc to be a very narrow but lengthy strip of land running along the estuary of the Gironde from just outside the modern suburbs of northern Bordeaux, at Blanquefort and Le Taillan, to St Vivien, 70km (44 miles) to the north. In few places do the vineyards extend more than 10km (6 miles) inland from the river, and mostly lie to the east of the main Bordeaux-Lesparre-Soulac road. This is where the ridges of gravel are at their deepest and purest. As you go north, the soils get heavier and the gravel more interspersed with clay or sand, while, to the west, the land becomes sandy and the pine forests of Les Landes begin.

Viticulturally, the Médoc is divided into two distinct areas: the Haut-Médoc in the south and the Bas-Médoc (called simply Médoc for appellation purposes) in the north. Within the Haut-Médoc, six communal appellations have been carved out. In addition, the name Haut-Médoc itself constitutes a seventh appellation, encompassing wines not covered by the communal appellations. The latter correspond to the area where the great majority of the finest vineyards lie. This is vividly illustrated by the following figures which show the proportion of the area under vine in the five appellations occupied by the Crus Classés (the remaining two contain no Crus Classés). Haut-Médoc 5.5%, Margaux 68%, St Julien 75%, Pauillac 72.5%, St Estèphe 19.5%.

Although more and more of the Crus Bourgeois now château-bottle at least a proportion of their wines, many smaller vineyards find it makes economic sense for them to join cooperatives where the methods of vinification have been modernized, rather than face the large capital cost of modernizing their own *cuviers*. Members of cooperatives account for the following proportions of the areas under vine in these appellations: Médoc 42.5%, Haut-Médoc 17.5%, Pauillac 18%, St Estèphe 26%, Listrac 24%, Moulis 6.5%.

Standards in cooperatives have improved considerably in the past few years and they are now undoubtedly a positive influence on quality.

The predominance of the Cabernet Sauvignon grape in all the vineyards of the Médoc ensures a certain family resemblance, a crispness of definition on nose and palate and a tendency for the tannin to be dominant in the first year or so in bottle. The development of bouquet, combined with delicacy and character of flavour, comes with bottle-ageing. Médoc wines need this ageing, and even quite modest *crus* keep and improve very well.

MARGAUX

Alone of the six commune appellations, this is not restricted to the one that bears its name. Also included are most of Arsac and all of Cantenac, Labarde and Soussans. The area under vine increased by 30% between 1972 and 1983.

The outstanding characteristics of the appellation are finesse and breed, the result of deep, poor, gravelly ridges and a high proportion of Cabernet Sauvignon. But the variations of emphasis are considerable. Labarde wines tend to have more body and richness, the Cantenacs are more elegant and often softer, as is du Tertre, the sole Cru Classé of Arsac. Many Margaux wines have more tannin and are slower to evolve.

Château d'Angludet

Cru Bourgeois Supérieur Exceptionnel 1932. Owner: M & Mme Peter A. Sichel. 30ha. 12,000 cases. CS 45%, Mer 35%, CF 15%, PV 5%.

Angludet was unfortunate not to be classified in 1855. At that time it was divided up and had much declined in importance since the 18th century, when it had been ranked with the leading growths. Now, under Peter Sichel's devoted care, the wines are becoming steadily better as the vineyard matures.

This excellent vineyard, situated on the plateau of Cantenac, produces wines that are finely perfumed and combine great finesse with elegance and vigour. I have been especially impressed with the 1978 vintage.

Château Bel-Air-Marquis-d'Aligre

Cru Bourgeois Supérieur Exceptionnel 1932. Owner: Pierre Boyer. 17ha. 4,500 cases. CS 30%, CF 20%, Mer 35%, PV 15%. Second label: Château Bel-Air-Marquis-de-Pomereu.

Confusingly, this is one of three Margaux properties sporting the name Marquis in its title, and the only one not classified. It lies at the back of Margaux, with a part of the vineyard in the adjoining commune of Soissans.

Pierre Boyer is a perfectionist who makes his wines with great care and low yields. Only organic fertilizers are used in the vineyards. The wine has real finesse and a certain unctuousness combined with delicacy and freshness.

Château Boyd-Cantenac

3e Cru Classé. Owner: Pierre Guillemet. 18ha. 7,500 cases. CS 67%, Mer 20%, CF 7%, PV 6%.

This is a property with a chequered history. It lost much of its vineyards to Cantenac-Brown in 1860, disappeared as a name for 45 years before reappearing again in 1920, then lost its buildings to Château Margaux. Now the wine is made at Château Pouget, Pierre Guillemet's other property.

Although no longer as important as it was in 1855, nor of the standard expected of a Troisième Cru, it produces well-made wines, rich and supple in style and certainly worthy of a *Cru Classé* once more; 79, 78, 75, 71 and 70 were all very successful years here.

Château Brane-Cantenac

2e Cru Classé. Owner: Lucien Lurton. 85ha. 29,000 cases. CS 70%, CF 13%, Mer 15%, PV 2%. Second label: Château Notton.

Brane-Cantenac owed its name and pre-eminence in 1855 to Baron de Brane, famed as a viticulturist and responsible for the rise of Mouton. Now it belongs to another famed viticulturist, Lucien Lurton, the largest vineyard owner in the Médoc today.

With vineyards enjoying a prime position on the plateau of Cantenac, this property produces a wine noted for its delicacy, finesse and breed, quintessential Margaux qualities, and this in spite of its high proportion of Cabernet Sauvignon – a sure indication of the influence of soil on grape varieties. Like many Margaux wines it can often be drunk young with enjoyment, but lasts well, as demonstrated by its lovely 1966. Among recent vintages, the 82 is outstanding, and very good wines were made in 81, 79 and 78.

Château Cantenac-Brown

3e Cru Classé. Owner: Societé Civile du Château Cantenac-Brown. Administrator: Aymar du Vivier. 32ha. 15,000 cases. CS 75%, Mer 15%, CF 8%, PV 2%. Secondary labels: Château la-Fontanelle (Margaux), Château Lamartine (Bordeaux Supérieur).

The English name Brown derives from John Lewis Brown, a Bordeaux merchant of English origin and an artist famous for his animal pictures. He was also responsible for the unusual château, described as being in the "Renaissance anglaise" style. It now belongs to the du Vivier family, formerly owners of de Luze, who still distribute the wine.

Cantenac-Brown today does not enjoy the reputation (or sell for the price) it once did. The wine is more tannic with less finesse than the best Cantenacs and there is a certain coarseness. Efforts are being made by the du Viviers to improve matters.

Château Canuet

Cru Bourgeois. Owner: Jean and Sabine Rooryck. 11ha. 5,000 cases. Mer 50%, CS 45%, PV 5%. Second label: Château Dupeyron.

The Rooryck family – Flemish in origin – owned Château Labégorce until the death of Jean Rooryck's mother in 1965 caused the family to sell. Then Jean and his wife bought a modest house in the centre of Margaux and some vines to go with it.

In recent years their wines have won several gold and silver medals at the Paris Concours Agricole as the production of their young vineyard steadily improves.

Château Dauzac
5ᵉ Cru Classé Owner: F. Chatellier et Fils. 50ha. 15,000 cases.
CS 60%, Mer 30%, CF 5%, PV 5%.
Until recently this property in Labarde had suffered a long period of neglect and obscurity. The restoration began when W.A.B. Miailhe from neighbouring Siran bought the vineyard in 1964. Its present owners, the Chatellier family from Champagne, took over in 1978, since when considerable effort has gone into improving both vineyard and buildings.

The wines at present have a certain coarseness but show signs of improvement. A property to watch.

Château Desmirail
3ᵉ Cru Classé. Owner: Lucien Lurton. 18ha. 4,000 cases. CS 80%, Mer 10%, CF 9%, PV 1%.
This famous old growth has been resurrected by Lucien Lurton, vineyard owner extraordinary of Margaux (see Brane-Cantenac, Durfort-Vivens etc). The wines are perfumed, soft and elegant in spite of the high proportion of Cabernet Sauvignon.

Château Deyrem-Valentin
Cru Bourgeois 1932. Owner: Jean Sorge. 10ha. 5,000 cases. CS 45%, Mer 45%, CF 5%, PV 5%.
This small property is situated in the best part of Soussans, and neighbours include Lascombes, Malescot and the two Labégorces. It has belonged to the present family since 1928, and Jean Sorge is very much a working resident proprietor.

The wines have the bouquet and finesse associated with the appellation, but are rather light in body.

Château Durfort-Vivens
2ᵉ Cru Classé. Owner: Lucien Lurton. 20ha. 5,500 cases. CS 80%, CF 12%, Mer 8%. Second label: Domaine de Cure-Bourse.
The names come from the comtes Durfort de Duras, who were the proprietors from the 15th century until the Revolution of 1789, and Vivens was added in 1824, but the Vivens were typically related to the Durforts. From 1937 until 1961 it was under the same ownership as Château Margaux, when it was sold to its present owner. The actual château is still inhabited by Bernard Ginestet, son of the former owner of Château Margaux.

The contrast between Durfort and Brane-Cantenac is always an interesting one. Durfort is always firmer and more tannic but usually has less finesse and charm. In recent vintages, however, the wines have more richness and fruit to match their tannin. Especially successful years are 83, 82, 81, 78 and 75.

Château Ferrière
3ᵉ Cru Classé. Owners: Mme André Durand-Feuillerat (héritiers). 5ha. 4,500 cases. CS 47%, Mer 33%, PV 12%, CF 8%.
This small growth has been farmed by Château Lascombes on behalf of its owners since 1960. A small quantity of wine is thus declared under this name at each vintage, but effectively the wine has lost its separate identity.

The wines are pleasantly light and soft, but hardly deserving of Troisième Cru Classé status any more. The wine is largely sold in France.

Château Giscours
3ᵉ Cru Classé. Owner: GFA du Château Giscours. Administrator: Pierre Tari. 81ha. 29,500 cases. CS 75%, Mer 20%, CF 3%, PV 2%.
Since its aquisition by the Tari family in 1952, much time and money has been invested in this property to restore it to its former glory. Now it is one of the largest and most important properties in the Margaux appellation, as well as one of the most consistent.

The wines of Giscours are deep-coloured with a pronounced bouquet combining richness and fruit, while the wine itself is very fruity, vigorous and full-bodied. If not as stylish as the wines of Cantenac and Margaux, the wine clearly has breed. Because of their power, these wines require eight to ten years' ageing in the best vintages before being anywhere near their best. But the delicious 1980 was excellent at four years old. The wines of Château Giscours are marketed world-wide by Gilbey-Loudenne, an IDV subsidiary.

Château La Gurgue
Cru Bourgeois Supérieur 1932. Owner: Société Civile du Château la Gurgue. Administrator: Mme Bernadette Villars. 12ha. 5,000 cases. CS 70%, Mer 25%, PV 5%.
A very well placed vineyard, together with Desmirail it is the closest

neighbour to Château Margaux on its western boundary. There was a change of ownership in 1978 which should provide the capital to maintain and improve the quality of this good bourgeois *cru*.

This is the delicate, perfumed type of Margaux, with style and breed, nice fruit, not a lot of body but plenty of flavour and refinement. Certainly a wine to watch and follow.

Château d'Issan
3e Cru Classé. Owner: Mme Emmanuel Cruse. 32ha. 12,000 cases. CS 75%, Mer 25%.

Regum mensis arisque deorum ("for the tables of kings and the high altar of the gods") says the inscription over the gateway at d'Issan. This is one of the oldest properties and the most splendid château in the whole Médoc, with its beautiful early-17th-century château sitting within the moat of its medieval predecessor.

After a long period of neglect, d'Issan was bought by the Cruse family in 1945 and both château and vineyard have been patiently restored to their former glory. Formerly this was a Cruse (négociant) exclusivity; now it is sold on the market, and there have been marked improvements in the wine in recent years. This is a wine of great individuality, combining a power and richness rare in Cantenac with great breed and a lovely perfume. Outstanding wines were made in 83, 82, 81, 79 and 70. The 73 must be one of the most delightful wines of the vintage. This is very much a château on the up – and at present offers remarkable value for money.

Château Kirwan
3e Cru Classé. Owner: Schröder and Schÿler. 31ha. 11,300 cases. CS 40%, Mer 30%, CF 20%, PV 10%.

Château Kirwan is named after an Irishman from Galway who lost his head in the French Revolution. It now belongs to the Bordeaux firm of Schröder and Schÿler, who bottled the wines in their Bordeaux cellars until 1966; 1967 was the first vintage to be château-bottled.

A lot of work and investment has gone into improving the quality of Kirwan. New wood was used in the barrel-ageing for the first time in 1978. The recent vintages are deep-coloured, powerful, concentrated wines which are beginning to attract more favourable comments again. Personally I find them still a little short on Margaux charm with a tendency to dryness.

Château Labégorce
Cru Bourgeois Supérieur 1932. Owner: Jean-Robert Condom. 29ha. 11,000 cases. CS 55%, Mer 40%, CF 5%.

This is certainly one of the best unclassified wines of Margaux, together with its close neighbour Labégorce Zédé. The vineyards are well placed in Margaux and Soussans, and the château has nothing bourgeois about it. The wines have Margaux finesse and delicacy. The distribution is in the hands of Dourthe frères.

Château Labégorce-Zédé
Cru Bourgeois Supérieur 1932. GFA Labégorce Zédé. Administrator: Luc Thienpont. 26ha. 9,500 cases. CS 50%, Mer 35%, CF 10%, PV 5%. Second label: **Château de l'Amiral.**

For some years the wines of Labégorce Zédé took second place to those of its neighbour Labégorce. Now, since Luc Thienpont took over in 1979, standards have improved and fine wines are being made; the emphasis is on finesse and breed with a superbly perfumed bouquet, and this is certainly a wine to watch. Although the appellation is Margaux the greater proportion of the vineyard area lies in Soussans.

Château Lascombes
2e Cru Classé. Owner: S A Lichine (subsidiary of Bass-Charrington). Administrator: Alain Maurel. 94ha. 35,000 cases. CS 65%, Mer 30%, CF 3%, PV 2%. Second label: **Château Segonnes.**

Historically Lascombes was a small property until its purchase in 1951 by Alexis Lichine and an American syndicate, who subsequently sold to the giant UK brewery group Bass-Charrington in 1971. In the past 20 years its vineyards and production have been greatly increased until this is now one of the largest properties in the Médoc.

In recent years there have been some disappointing wines made here, lacking the style and breed of which this growth is capable, and its results in blind tastings tend to confirm this. However, there are some signs of improvement. Certainly a stricter selection is necessary if wines comparable to other Deuxièmes Crus are to be made again regularly, and the recent launching of a new second label is a positive sign of this.

Just under half the output of this château consists of rosé.

Château Malescot-St-Exupéry
3e Cru Classé. Owner: Roger Zuger. 34ha. 15,000 cases. CS 50%, Mer 35%, CF 10%, PV 5%. Secondary labels: Château de Loyac, Domaine du Balardin.

Since acquiring the property in 1955 from the English firm of W.H. Chaplin, the Zuger family have done much to rebuild a *cru* which had greatly declined in size and standing. The charming château, now restored and lived in again, stands in the centre of the village of Margaux, while the vineyards are in Margaux (adjoining Château Margaux) and in Soussans.

The reputation of Malescot is once again good. The wines have a fine bouquet and finesse, but I find a harshness and sometimes a certain edginess which detracts from the final impression.

Château Margaux
1er Cru Classé. Owner: Société Civile du Château Margaux (Mentzelopoulos family). Administrator: Paul Pontallier. 85ha. Red: 17,500 cases; CS 75%, Mer 20%, and CF 5%. White: 3,500 cases; SB 100%. Secondary labels: Pavillon Blanc and Pavillon Rouge du Château Margaux.

This great château has had its ups and downs, but new heights of quality and consistency have been achieved since the Mentzelopoulos family acquired the property in 1977. A new underground cellar has been built, the château and gardens restored to their former glory, and much work has been done to improve the vineyard.

At its best Margaux is one of the most sumptuous and sensual wines of the Médoc, with all the perfume and finesse of fine Margaux as found in its neighbours but allied to more body and remarkable character and individuality. After producing some great vintages in 45, 47, 49, 50 and 53, its wines became less outstanding and less consistent, although the 66 stands out in this lean period. Now, from 78 to 83 it has consistently produced wines which are each among the outstanding examples of their respective vintages.

A second wine, Pavillon Rouge du Château Margaux, is now made as a result of the stricter selection now practised. The first vintage was 1979. The wines are lighter and clearer than the Grand Vin, but have breed and charm and are ready to drink much earlier.

An excellent white wine, Pavillon Blanc du Château Margaux, made only from Sauvignon grapes from a vineyard in Soussans, is now a wine of real distinction. Its bouquet and breed are remarkable, but so, unfortunately, is the price!

Château Marquis-d'Alesme-Becker
3e Cru Classé. Owner: Jean-Claude Zuger. 9ha. 4,150 cases. CS 40%, Mer 30%, CF 20%, PV 10%.

This small and little known Cru Classé was owned by the English firm of W.H. Chaplin and run partly with Malescot. The present proprietor is the brother of Roger Zuger at Malescot and the château is the original building of Château Desmirail. The vineyards are in Soussans and Margaux.

With its small production and long obscurity it remains a wine hard to find. But I have found it possessed of elegant, stylish fruit with a firm backbone. It needs time to develop.

Château Marquis-de-Terme
4e Cru Classé. Owner: Famille Sénéclauze. 35ha. 12,000 cases. CS 45%, Mer 35%, CF 15%, PV 5%.

A good proportion of this wine is sold direct on the French market, with the result that it is not so widely known on export markets as its size would lead one to suppose. Much work has recently been done to make good deficiencies in the *chais*, which is now modern and well equipped. The vineyard is very well kept. The yields, however, are high.

Whenever I have come across this wine I have found it to have charm and a certain easy appeal, without being among the best of Margaux in terms of finesse or originality.

Château Marsac-Séguineau
Cru Bourgeois 1932. Owner: Société Civile du Château Marsac-Seguineau. Administrator: Jean-Pierre Angliviel de la Beaudelle. 10ha. 5,000 cases. CS 65%, Mer 35%. Second label: Château Gravières-de-Marsac.

This is a full-flavoured, supple wine which nevertheless lasts well. The vineyard is in Soussans. The wines are exclusively distributed by the négociants Mestrezat, who are also in effect the owners and have done much to reorganize the vineyards since taking over.

Château Martinens

Cru Bourgeois Supérieur 1932. Owners: **Simone Dulos and Jean-Pierre Seynat-Dulos. 30ha. 7,000 cases. Mer 40%, CS 30%, PV 20%, CF 10%.**

The pleasing château at Martinens was built in 1767 by three maiden ladies from London, Ann, Jane and Mary White. But they sold after only nine years. The present owners have run the property since 1945. It lies in Cantenac and enjoys an excellent reputation for stylish, attractive wines.

Château Monbrison

Cru Bourgeois. Owners: **Elizabeth Davis & Sons. 14ha. 5,500 cases. Mer 35%, CS 30%, CF 30%, PV 5%.** Second label: **Clos Cordat.**

Davis sounds English but is in fact American. The property was bought in 1921 by Robert Meacham-Davis, an American commissioner in the Red Cross, and the present proprietor is his daughter. She is now assisted by her three sons Bruno, Jean-Luc and Laurent Vonderheyden.

I have found the wine to be most attractive, well structured with plenty of fruit and balancing tannin.

Château Montbrun

Cru Bourgeois 1932. Owner: **J. Lebègue & Co.** Administrators: **Jacques and Alain de Coninck. 8ha. 3,500 cases. Mer 75%, CS and CF 25%.**

This small but well-placed vineyard in Cantenac was once part of Château Palmer. With its high proportion of Merlot, it produces rich full-bodied wines, appropriate for a property run by men from the Libournais. It is distributed by the négociants J. Lebègue & Co. – now unconnected with the English firm of the same name.

Château Palmer

3e Cru Classé. Owner: **Société Civile du Château Palmer.** Administrator: **B. Bouteiller. 45ha. 12,500 cases. CS 55%, Mer 40%, CF 3%, PV 2%.**

Named after a British general who fought under Wellington, Palmer is now owned by Dutch and British proprietors (Mähler-Besse and Peter Sichel). The château lies in the hamlet of Issan, and most of its vineyards were once part of Château d'Issan's domain. The charming château itself was built in the years 1857–60 when the property was owned by the Péreire family.

The reputation of Palmer has soared in the past 20 years. This was one of the first of the "Super-Seconds", a reputation which effectively dates from the superlative 61. The Chardon family (father Pierre and sons Claude and Yves) have had much to do with the quality and consistency of this splendid wine. The wine is characterized by its opulence and richness which are almost burgundian in the best years, yet this is combined with real finesse and breed. In recent years 70, 71, 75, 76, 78, 79 and 81 were all great successes. The 82 lacks the richness and concentration of the best 82s and cannot be compared with the 61, but is nevertheless a fine and attractive wine.

Château Paveil-de-Luze

Cru Bourgeois. Owner: **GFA du Château Paveil.** Administrator: **Baron Geoffroy de Luze. 24ha. 7,000 cases. CS and CF 70%, Mer 30%.** Second label: **Château de-la-Coste.**

A fine vineyard on deep, well-drained gravel in Soussans with a charming château in the chartreuse style, Paveil has now belonged to the de Luze family for over a century. The wines were always sound but often rather anonymous, and bottled in de Luze's cellars in Bordeaux. Now the de Luze family have parted company with the firm that bears their name and the wine is château-bottled and seems to be improving. At its best this is a wine of some style and distinction, with lots of charm and breed rather than body. A wine to watch.

Château Pontac-Lynch

Cru Bourgeois Supérieur 1932. Owner: **GFA du Château Pontac-Lynch.** Administrator: **Serge Bondon. 9ha. 3,000 cases. CS and CF 45%, Mer 47%, PV 8%.**

A little known *cru* today, bearing two the famous names, Pontac-Lynch apparently sold for higher prices in the middle 18th century than its famous neighbours which are today classified. The wines have been winning medals recently and should be worth looking out for.

Château Pouget
4e Cru Classé. Owner: **GFA des Châteaux Boyd-Cantenac et Pouget.** Administrator: **Pierre Guillemet. 10ha. 3,500 cases. CS 66%, Mer 30%, CF 4%.**
Under the same ownership as Château Boyd-Cantenac, Château Pouget is the château for both wines, and this is where both wines are made. An attempt is said to be made to differentiate between the two *crus* although tastings suggest the best *cuves* go into Boyd. Pouget is exclusively distributed by Maison Dubos Frères of Bordeaux.

The wines are well made, rich and supple in style, and certainly worthy of Cru Classé status; 70, 71, 75, 78 and 79 were all very successful years.

Château Prieuré-Lichine
4e Cru Classé. Owner: **Alexis Lichine. 60ha. 25,000 cases. CS 55%, Mer 33%, PV 6%, CF 6%.** Second label: **Château de Clairefort.**
This property has been restored and the vineyard enlarged and reconstructed since it was bought by Alexis Lichine in 1952. The charming château in Cantenac was formerly the Priory and is now very much Alexis Lichine's European home (there is now no connection with the négociant company of the same name).

The quality and reputation of this *cru* have deservedly grown in recent years. The wines are full-bodied and rich, and a very consistent standard is maintained. Here they think that 83 is better than their 82, fine as that is. Time alone will tell. Other vintages that have particularly impressed me are 81, 79, 78, 76 and 70.

Château Rausan-Ségla
2e Cru Classé. Owner: **Holt Frères et Fils (Lonrho group). 42ha. 10,000 cases. CS 66%, Mer 28%, CF 4%, PV 2%.**
This is one of the oldest and most famous *crus* in Margaux, but unfortunately its wines have for some years failed to match their high classification. Having belonged to the Cruse family for several generations, it was bought by the Liverpool firm of John Holt (now part of Lonrho) in 1960, since when it has been managed and marketed by the famous négociant Louis Eschenauer.

In theory this is a long-lasting wine which develops great finesse; in practice too many vintages have been austere and charmless. Efforts are now being made to put this right, and a delightful 80 was made, which has structure and power as well. Let us hope we shall soon be seeing some more wines that are truly worthy of this famous name.

Château Rauzan-Gassies
2e Cru Classé. Owner: **Mme Paul Quié et J.-M. Quié. 30ha. 8,300 cases. CS 40%, Mer 39%, CF 20%, PV 1%.** Second label: **Enclos de Moncabon.**
Until the French Revolution of 1789, this was part of the same property as Rausan-Ségla. There is no château. Since 1943 it has belonged to the Quié family. In the past some great wines were made. In recent years the wines have been consistent but not top flight.

The style of the wine is more powerful and richer than many Margaux, more in the character of Cantenac, with delicacy and charm developing in bottle. Recently efforts have been made to modernize and improve matters here, so the wines should be worth watching.

Château Siran
Cru Bourgeois Supérieur 1932. Owner: **William-Alain B. Miailhe. 35ha. 12,500 cases. CS 50%, Mer 25%, PV 15%, CF 10%.** Secondary labels: **Châteaux Bellegarde, St-Jacques.**
This is something of a show-place for a Cru Bourgeois, but then the proprietor Alain Miailhe is convinced that it should be a Cru Classé, and is eloquent on the topic. There is a heliport, an anti-nuclear shelter well stocked with the best vintages, and a park famous for its cyclamens.

The wines have a charming bouquet and have become noticeably richer and fuller in flavour since around 1970. There is some point of comparison with nearby Giscours, and the wines have more charm and breed than their other classified neighbour Dauzac.

Château Tayac
Cru Bourgeois Owner: **André Favin. 34ha. 15,000 cases. CS 65%, Mer 25%, CF 5%, PV 5%.**
This is the largest of the Crus Bourgeois of Margaux, lying in Soussans. Its present good reputation is the work of the present proprietor, who inherited the property in 1960. The wines are perfumed and robust with something agreeably rustic in their make-up.

Château du Tertre

5ᵉ Cru Classé. Owner: **Philippe Capbern Gasqueton. 48ha. 14,000 cases. CS 80%, CF 10%, Mer 10%.**

The word *tertre* means a knoll, a piece of high ground, and Château du Tertre is a splendidly situated vineyard on the highest ground in the Margaux appellation, in Arsac. The soil is classically pebbly. Since taking over the property in 1961, Phillipe Gasqueton (of Château Calon-Segur) has steadily restored the vineyard, buildings, and now the château itself.

I believe that this is one of the most underrated of the Cru Classés at the present time. The wines have a beautifully vivid fruit and considerable finesse, breed and charm. The record for consistency is also impressive. The 1980, for instance, is really fine and has more concentration than many wines of this vintage. The 83 and 82 were outstanding successes.

Château la Tour-de-Bessan

Owner: **Lucien Lurton. 21ha. 8,000 cases. CS 90%, Mer 10%.**

The *tour* is a ruined watch-tower of the 15th century dating from the last years of English rule. The vineyard in Soussans is the humblest part of Lucien Lurton's Margaux empire, and produces light, supple wines with breed and charm. A chance to buy a Lurton Margaux at a more modest price.

Château la Tour-de-Mons

Cru Bourgeois Supérieur 1932. Owner: **Clauzel-Binaud-Cruchet.** Administrator: **Bertrand Clauzel. 30ha. 10,000 cases. CS 45%, Mer 40%, CF 10%, PV 5%.**

A very old property in Soussans with a long-standing reputation. Until recently the families that own it also owned Château Cantemerle. For many years la Tour-de-Mons has been spoken of as a candidate for classification.

Unfortunately the distribution of this wine was for many years a monopoly of the old house of H.O. Beyermann and, as their fortunes declined, so this excellent wine was not as widely sold as it deserved to be. Their under-investment, as at Cantemerle, affected consistency and quality. At its best this is a long-lived wine of breed and real finesse.

MOULIS

This is the smallest of the six communal ACs, but there are more outstanding Crus Bourgeois than in Listrac. The area under vine has increased by as much as 47% in the last decade but is still only a modest 405 hectares. The vineyards here lie north-west of Margaux and directly west of Arcins. The wines are powerful and rich, with the best having fruit and finesse as well. These are long-keeping wines of marked attraction.

Château Anthonic

Cru Bourgeois Supérieur. Owner: **Pierre Cordonnier. 18ha. 5,000 cases. Principally CS and Mer.**

This *cru* has carried its present name only since 1922. It appeared in the first edition of Cocks and Féret in 1850 under another name, and changed names once more between then and 1922. The château is on the outskirts of the village of Moulis, and the vineyards are some of the oldest in the commune.

Recently the vineyards have been in the throes of reconstruction. When I tasted the 1981 vintage in 1984, I found it deep-coloured with well-projected fruit on the nose, but tasting slightly stalky like a wine with too much *vin de presse*, although the structure was good and it obviously needed time to develop. Certainly a good solid wine, but not in the front rank of Moulis.

Château Bel-Air-Lagrave

Cru Bourgeois 1932. Owner: **Mme Jeanne Bacquey. 15ha. 5,500 cases. CS 60%, Mer 35%, PV 5%.**

This vineyard is on the gravelly ridges of Grand Poujeaux, certainly the best sector of the Moulis vineyards. It has been in the same family for 150 years. The owners believe in hard pruning and low yields to produce the best quality.

The wines are clearly carefully made. Their charm and fruit is emphasized, and they are softer and more refined than many from this appellation, with individuality and a definite finesse and balance which firmly removes them from any suggestion of the rustic. Very attractive wines were made here in 1979 and 1981. Certainly a wine to watch.

Château Biston-Brillette

Cru Bourgeois 1932. Owner: Michel Barbarin. 18ha. 7,000 cases. Mer 50%, CS and CF 50%.

An old-fashioned and rather rustic label hardly does justice to the excellent wines now being made here. Typically Moulis with its dense texture, there is also a hint of complexity about its spicy concentrated fruit which lifts it from the general run of wines from this appellation. The emphasis on fruit and balance makes this a wine which can be enjoyed young, without sacrificing its keeping qualities.

Château Branas-Grand-Poujeaux

Owner: Jacques de Pourquéry. 6ha. 4,000 cases. CS 60%, Mer 35%, PV 5%.

A small property with a well-placed vineyard and a most enthusiastic owner determined to make fine wines. In a blind tasting of 1981 Moulis wines held in 1984 I placed this wine on the same level as some Cru Bourgeois Exceptionnels. The wine had both charm at this early stage and a fine middle flavour and richness with real style and breed. All the wine is aged in casks, of which one-third are new each year. A wine to watch, if you can find it!

Château Brillette

Cru Grand Bourgeois. Owner: Société Civile. Administrator: Mme Berthault. 30ha. 11,000 cases. CS 55%, Mer 40%, PV 5%.

When Raymond Berthault bought this property in 1976 it had greatly declined and there was much to be done. The new proprietor was the owner of Viniprix and Euromarche, and Brillette was to be a hobby. Bertrand Bouteiller (Château Pichon-Longueville-Baron) acts as *régisseur* and Professor Peynaud has advised. One-third new wood is used each year.

Unfortunately Raymond Berthault died in 1981, but his widow and son-in-law continue along the lines already laid down. This was always a good solid Moulis; now it looks like moving into the leading category.

Château Chasse-Spleen

Cru Grand Bourgeois Exceptionnel. Owner: Société Civile. Administrator: Mme Bernadette Villars. 62ha. 25,000 cases. CS 50%, Mer 45%, CF 2%, PV 3%.

Chasse-Spleen has for long been recognized as not only the leading *cru* of Moulis, but as deserving Cru Classé status. From the First World War until 1976 it belonged to the Lahary family and was very well run. Then it was sold to its present owners who include a bank, but the most important partner is the Société Bernard Taillan whose director is the dynamic Jacques Merlaut, whose daughter, a qualified oenologist, manages the property. The curious name Chasse-Spleen is attributed to a quip of Lord Byron's to the effect that the wine chased away spleen (ill-humour or melancholy).

The wines often have an initial toughness, even coarseness, but this is quickly dispelled and the true character of the wine emerges. In mature vintages the wines quickly develop an almost opulent fullness of fruit on the nose, a lovely flavour with concentration, structure and real breed. It is extremely consistent and makes delicious bottles in lesser years such as 80. The 81 is rather slow developing for the year, but the 79 is already most attractive, and the 78 very fine. The 75 is a long-term *vin de garde*. This is a wine which does not take as long to mature as you might think, and which keeps well and seldom disappoints.

Château la Closerie-Grand-Poujeaux

Cru Bourgeois 1932. Owner: M. Donat family. 3,500 cases.

This small vineyard was the creation of a former *régisseur* of Chasse-Spleen. Since 1941 it has belonged to the Donat family. For many years now the redoubtable Mlle Donat has run the property and is one of the great characters of Moulis. Everything is done in a very traditional way, and long-lived, solid wines are the result, with the emphasis on body and richness, rather in the same style as Dutruch.

Château Duplessis-Fabre

Cru Bourgeois. Owner: Société Civile du Château Fourcas-Dupré. Administrator: Patrice Pagès. 14ha. 5,500 cases. Mer 45%, CS 42%, CF 8%, PV 4%, Mal 1%.

This property belongs to the Pagès family, who have also made such an excellent job of running Château Fourcas-Dupré in recent years. Powerful assertive wines with just enough suppleness are made here – good honest middle-of-the-road wines.

Château Duplessis (Hauchecorne)

Cru Grand Bourgeois. Owner: Société Civile des Grands Crus Réunis. Administrator: Lucien Lurton. 17.5ha. 8,000 cases. CS 65%, Mer 20%, Mal 10%, PV 5%.

The wine of this château has for some time been labelled simply as Duplessis. It is now proposed that the word "Hauchecorne" should be added to the label in smaller letters to avoid confusion with the nearby Duplessis-Fabre.

The wines here are rich and supple and are made for reasonably early drinking.

Château Dutruch-Grand-Poujeaux

Cru Grand Bourgeois Exceptionnel. Owner: François Cordonnier. 25ha. 10,000 cases. CS and CF 60%, Mer 35%, PV 5%.

The wines of Dutruch have long enjoyed a deserved reputation for quality and consistency. The present owner took over from M. Lambert in 1967, but in fact they were related.

In the 1960s I noted that the wines here were characterized by their body and richness, and this is still the case. Recently both 81 and 79 were most successful, and an attractive 80 was also made. These are wines which repay keeping.

Château Gressier-Grand-Poujeaux

Cru Bourgeois Supérieur 1932. Owner: Héritiers de Saint-Affrique. Administrator: Bertrand de Marcellus. 18ha. 9,000 cases. CS 50%, Mer 40%, CF 10%.

This fine old property has been in the hands of the same family since 1724, and the family arms of the Saint-Affriques, with its three Negro heads, gives the label a very distinctive look. Improvements and modernizations have been made in recent years, and new oak is now used in the maturation process.

The wines have always had more fruit and finesse than those of many neighbouring properties, and have maintained a consistent standard over many years. Recently the 81 and 79 were both excellent and among the best wines in the commune.

Château Lestage-Darquier

Cru Bourgeois Supérieur 1932. Owner: François Bernard. 4ha. 1,800 cases. CS 50%, Mer 40%, CF 10%.

With such a small production it is hardly surprising that this wine is little known. The vineyard is well placed on the gravelly ridges of Grand Poujeaux and has belonged to the Bernard family for several generations. I have found the wines very deep-coloured with a bouquet dense with rich fruit and with a very distinctive assertive flavour, tannic and with the promise of something quite fine when mature.

Château Maucaillou

Cru Bourgeois. Owner: Famille Dourthe. 55ha. 19,000 cases. CS 45%, Mer 35%, CF 15%, PV 5%.

Maucaillou is the pride of the Dourthe family. They no longer control the négociant firm which bears their name, but they have kept this château, where the business started. Three-quarters of the vintage is aged in new oak, unusually for a non-classified growth, and there is a very modern stainless-steel installation for the fermentation.

In a blind tasting of 79 Moulis wines held in 1984 I placed Maucaillou first. The wines combine the power of Moulis with a really beautiful flavour, real breed and charm. This is a *cru* which often competes well in blind tastings with the Crus Classés.

Château Moulin-à-Vent

Cru Grand Bourgeois. Owner: Dominique Hessel. 24ha. 10,000 cases. CS 65%, Mer 30%, PV 5%. Second label: **Moulin-de-St-Vincent** (3,000 cases).

Moulin-à-Vent may seem an odd name for a Bordeaux château, but in the Middle Ages mixed agriculture was the norm in the Médoc, and many ruined mills can still be found. Since buying the property in 1977, Dominique Hessel has made many improvements, enlarging the vineyard and maturing the wine in casks instead of vats.

The wines have a fine flavour and are rich and vigorous, developing a complex bouquet with bottle age. This now deserves to be numbered with the leading *crus* of Moulis.

Moulin-de-St-Vincent, the second label, used to be an exclusivity of Ginestet. Under the present management a deliciously fruity, early-maturing wine is being produced.

Château Moulis
Cru Bourgeois Supérieur. Owner: Jacques Darricarrère. 12ha.
4,500 cases. CS 60%, Mer 40%.
In the last century this was a vast estate with around 100 hectares. Now it
is a modest one with vineyards grouped around the château just outside
the village of Moulis. There is a modern stainless-steel installation for
vinification, and the wines are matured in wood. All the wine is château-
bottled.

Château Pomeys
Cru Bourgeois Supérieur 1932. Owner: Xavier Barennes. 8ha.
2,500 cases. CS 67%, Mer 33%.
This small property has now been in the same family for seven generations.
It is very traditionally run and its wines have a good reputation.

Château Poujeaux
Cru Grand Bourgeois Exceptionnel. Owner: François & Philippe
Theil. 50ha. 25,000 cases. CS 35%, Mer 35%, CF 15%, PV 15%.
Second label: **Château la Salle-de-Poujeaux.**
If Moulis is the name of the appellation, Poujeaux is where most of the best
crus are, and there are none better than the Poujeaux of the Theil family. A
third of the wine is put in new oak, and everything here is meticulously
done.

The wines are deep-coloured with an arresting bouquet – sometimes
there are overtones of tobacco and a flavour which is stylish and fine
although tannic and powerful. This is a long-lived wine which deserves
long maturing in the best vintages, and is certainly always one of the best
wines in the appellation. Unusually for a wine of this class it is sold entirely
direct and not through the Bordeaux trade.

Château Ruat-Petit-Poujeaux
Cru Bourgeois 1932. Owner: Pierre Goffre-Viaud. 15ha. 5,000
cases. CS and CF 65%, Mer 35%. Second label: **Château Ruat.**
Petit Poujeaux is a hamlet just outside Moulis and well away from Grand
Poujeaux. Ruat was the name of a pre-Revolution property, dispersed at
the time of the Revolution, but patiently pieced together again after the
present proprietor's great-grandfather had bought the domain in 1871.
The wines have charm, fruit and typical Moulis richness and solidity, with
a tendency to evolve more quickly than many wines of this appellation.
This is good middle-of-the-road Moulis.

LISTRAC

Listrac and its neighbour Moulis differ in important respects from the
other four commune appellations. They contain no Crus Classés, and they
are not bordering on the river, where the best crus are, but are on a plateau
inland. But both produce excellent wines whose distinctive characteristics
are increasingly appreciated.

The area under vine here has increased by over 33% in the last decade.
The wines were often considered in the past to be tough and astringent,
but are today markedly less rustic, quite powerful but with finesse and
fruit.

Château la Bécade
Cru Bourgeois. Owner: Jean-Pierre Théron. 23ha. 13,000 cases.
CS 75%, Mer 25%.
This is a well-placed vineyard lying to the northeast of Listrac on the road
between St-Julien and Margaux. Its well-made, typical wines have won a
number of medals in recent years. No wood is used in the maturing, and
this makes the wines ready to drink young.

Château Cap-Leon-Veyrin
Cru Bourgeois 1932. Owner: Alain Meyre. 12ha. 7,000 cases.
Mer 50%, CS 45%, PV 3%, CF 2%.
This is an amalgamation of two vineyards dating from 1908. The wines
are matured in cask, including a proportion of new oak. These are
powerful, long-lived wines which repay keeping.

Château Clarke
Cru Bourgeois. Owner: Baron Edmond de Rothschild. 121ha.
30,000 cases. CS 49%, Mer 37%, CF 10%, PV 4%. Second label:
Château Malmaison.
This must be one of the most remarkable new developments in Médoc.
Baron Edmond de Rothschild has undertaken a long-term scheme of
expansion in terms of the most modern installation and vineyard plantings

that will take some years to realize. What has been done is worthy of a Cru Classé.

Prior to the 82 vintage I find the wines rather lean, austere, and marked by new wood. The 82, however, gives a fair idea of the potential of this *cru* as the vineyard matures. There is a strong assertive flavour typical of Listrac, but there is also plenty of fruit and richness, and the new oak has been completely absorbed. There are good facilities for receiving visitors between June and September. An attractive rosé is also made.

Château Fonréaud

Cru Bourgeois. Owners: **Héritiers Chanfreau**. Administrators: **Mme Leo Chanfreau and M. Jean Chanfreau**. 20,500 cases. CS 66%, Mer 31%, PV 3%.

The château here is something of a landmark on the main Lesparre road south of Listrac. Part of the crop is aged in vat, and part in cask. The wines tend to be elegant, attractive, fruity and easy to drink when young.

Château Fourcas-Dupré

Cru Grand Bourgeois Exceptionnel. Owner: **Société Civile**. Administrator: **Patrice Pagès**. 42ha. 22,000 cases. CS 50%, Mer 38%, CF 10%, PV 2%.

Guy Pagès lived at and managed this château from 1967 until his untimely death in 1985. During this time he established high standards and made many improvements. He is succeeded by his son Patrice, already well versed in the affairs of the property. There are both stainless-steel and concrete vats for fermentation, and casks from leading Crus Classés are used for ageing.

The wines of Fourcas-Dupré are very perfumed, quite tannic and powerful in the best years but supple and attractive in lesser ones. The comparison with the neighbouring Fourcas-Hosten is interesting, especially as Patrice Pagès has assisted in the running of the latter for several years. There is a tendency for the Hosten wines to have more depth and richness, especially noticeable in years like 80 and even 79. I found them closest together in the excellent 78.

Château Fourcas-Hosten

Cru Grand Bourgeois Exceptionnel. Owner: **Société Civile**. Administrator: **Bertrand de Rivoyre and Patrice Pagès**. 40ha. 18,000 cases. CS 55%, Mer 40%, CF 5%.

Until 1972 this château belonged to the Saint-Affriques of Gressier, and the wines were made and kept there. It now belongs to a syndicate of French, Danes and Americans, with Bertrand de Rivoyre, head of the négociants Louis Dubroca, acting as administrator. The *chais* and *cuvier* have been reconstructed. Some new wood is now used for ageing, and the vineyard has been gradually enlarged.

The wines of Fourcas-Hosten have exceptional colour and are notable for their power and richness, with a very assertive character but more fruit combined with tannin than the other *crus* of Listrac. This is a very consistent wine now, with 76 and 80 now at their best and 79 still needing some time. The 78 is outstanding.

Cave Coopérative Grand Listrac

Owner: **Coopérative**. 160ha. 66,650 cases. Mer 60%, CS and CF 30%, PV 10%.

This cooperative has long enjoyed an excellent reputation, especially in France, where Grand Listrac was for many years the best buy on the French Railways. Today there are 70 members. Three Listrac properties are sold under their château names: Capdet, Clos du Fourcas and Vieux Moulis, as are two Moulis wines: Guitignan and Bouqueyran.

Château Lafon

Cru Grand Bourgeois. Owner: **Jean-Pierre Théron**. 11.5ha. 6,500 cases. CS 75%, Mer 25%.

The property is run jointly with the proprietors of another Listrac *cru*, la Bécade. When he bought it in the late 1960s Jean-Pierre Théron found no more than a dilapidated ruin. Everything had to be restored and the vineyard reconstructed and enlarged.

The wines are kept only in vat, not wood, and this makes them ready to drink early. These are pleasant, commercial wines.

Château Lestage

Cru Bourgeois Supérieur. Owner: **Héritiers Chanfreau**. Administrators: **Mme Leo Chanfreau and M. Jean Chanfreau**. 52ha. 25,500 cases. Mer 55%, CS and CF 41%, PV 4%.

Under the same ownership and management as Château Fonréaud. The château is a large, ornate 19th-century mansion. Most of the wines are aged in vat rather than cask, which tends to produce supple, early-maturing wines. But I have usually found this wine quite tannic and sometimes a little dry. It certainly needs bottle age in the better years.

Château Saransot-Dupré
Cru Bourgeois Supérieur 1932. Owner: **Yves Raymond. 10ha. 4,000 cases. Red: CS 50%, Mer 50%. White: Sem 50%, Sauv 25%, Musc 25%.**
Yves Raymond is the third generation of his family to own this *cru*, although the family have lived in Listrac for 300 years. The property totals 225 hectares, including woods and pasture. A flock of sheep is kept to provide all the manure necessary for the vineyard.

The wines have a reputation for being rich and supple. A small quantity of white wine. AC Bordeaux, is also made.

ST-JULIEN

This is the commune with the highest proportion of Crus Classés. The increase in the area under vine has been only 20% here in the last decade. The soils here have more clay than Margaux, and there is quite a difference between the vineyards near the Gironde and those further inland, where more fleshy wines are made. These are wines of great character and originality, with more body and vivid fruit than those of Margaux. They match the best Pauillacs for longevity.

Château Beychevelle
4ᵉ Cru Classé. Owner: **Société Civile.** Administrator: **Maurice Ruelle. 72ha. 25,000 cases. CS 60%, Mer 28%, CF 8%, PV 4%.**
This is one of the most beautiful châteaux in the Médoc, and in the summer months it is set off by a superb bank of flowers at its roadside entrance. When it belonged to the Duc d'Epernon, who was an admiral of France at the end of the 16th century, ships passing by in the Gironde were required to lower their sails as a salute. So Beychevelle is a corruption of *baisse-voile*, meaning "lower-sail". Recently (1984) the Achile Fould family have sold an important holding to a pension fund, and this has enabled much-needed extensions to the *chais* to be undertaken.

At its best Beychevelle is a glorious example of everything that makes the wines of St-Julien so attractive: a bouquet of great elegance and immediate impact, together with a ripe, fresh flavour that asks to be drunk from an early age, although the harmony of the wine also ensures good keeping.

In recent years the 83, 82, 81, 79, 78 and 75 are all most successful. There has in the past been some inconsistency, so that lesser years in particular were unreliable, but recent improvements should lead to more consistency in future.

Château Branaire-Ducru
4ᵉ Cru Classé. Owner: **Société Anonyme du Château Branaire-Ducru.** Administrator: **Jean-Michel Tapie. 48ha. 20,000 cases. CS 60%, Mer 20%, CF 15%, PV 5%.**
The extremely simple, classical façade of the château here faces Beychevelle but can easily be missed as it stands well back from the road. It would be a pity to miss the wine though. Most of the vineyards lie further inland than those of Beychevelle and Ducru-Beaucaillou, and the wines have less finesse but more body and are not without breed. Jean-Michel Tapie has continued the work begun with his father when they bought the château in 1952, and the reputation of Branaire has risen steadily over the years.

The wines have a very marked character which often comes through in blind tastings. The bouquet is noticeably powerful with an almost Pauillac assertiveness and a certain chocolate character in the fat years which is most distinct. The wine has a lot of body and fruit and is extremely supple, so that it is often possible to enjoy a Branaire when other wines are still not ready. This is a very consistent wine, and excellent examples were made in 83, 82, 81, 79, 78, 76 and 75.

Certainly this is a wine to follow in terms of value for money. It is not yet an "investment" wine, but is one of exceptional attractiveness.

Château la Bridane
Cru Bourgeois. Owner: **Pierre Saintout. 15ha. 8,000 cases. CS 55%, Mer 45%.**
This is one of the relatively few Crus Bourgeois in St-Julien, and it has long

enjoyed a good reputation. Much of the wine is exported. Recently the Cabernet Franc has been eliminated, and the Merlot increased. This is good, attractive St-Julien at an accessible price.

Château Ducru-Beaucaillou

2e Cru Classé. Owner: Jean-Eugène Borie. 49ha. 17,000 cases. CS 65%, CF 5%, Mer 25%, PV 5%. Second label: **Château la Croix.**
This château acquired its name and reputation in the first part of the 19th century when it belonged to the Ducru family. The Beau-Caillou was the name of the vineyard itself. The distinctive château, with its massive Victorian towers and simple, classical façade between them, has been made familiar from the distinctive yellow-brown label. Unusually for Bordeaux, the *chais* are situated beneath the building. The reputation of the *cru* today is the work of Jean-Eugène Borie, a resident proprietor who is one of the most widely respected wine-makers in the Médoc. Ducru-Beaucaillou was recently the first of the Médoc Crus Classés on the open market to break away from the pack and establish a higher price for itself than the other Second Growths, to create the "Super-Seconds" (Palmer had achieved a higher price earlier but was available only through the two négotiant owners, Mälher-Besse and Sichel).

The wines here have long had elegance, lightness and breed (Jean-Eugène Borie's first great vintage was 1953). In recent years they have acquired a little more firmness and richness, especially in the best vintages, although the beauty of flavour and finesse are still the hallmark, rather than the power one finds in Léoville-Las-Cases. In recent years, 83, 82, 81, 79 and 78 all produced classic examples, with 80 and 77 providing attractive, early-drinking wines.

Château du Glana

Cru Grand Bourgeois Exceptionnel. Owner: **Gabriel Meffre.** 45ha. 17,000 cases. CS 68%, Mer 30%, PV 2%.
Château du Glana is not one of the more romantic wines of the Médoc. Strictly speaking, it has no château today, and the ugly little red-brick villa that appears on the label is not now part of the property. More obvious is the massive and very functional *chais* sitting amidst the vineyards nearby, close to Gloria and Ducru-Beaucaillou. This and Gloria are the two largest Cru Bourgeois of St-Julien.

The reputation of du Glana has in the past been rather mixed. I can only speak about recent vintages, and have found the wine well made, easy, fruity and delicious. Du Glana is commercial in the good sense; it provides just the sort of wine, with the character of the appellation, that the wine-lover today looks for and can enjoy without long keeping.

Château Gloria

Cru Bourgeois. Owner: **Henri Martin.** 45ha. 16,000 cases. CS 65%, Mer 25%, CF 5%, PV 5%. Secondary labels: **Châteaux Haut-Beychevelle-Gloria, Peymartin.**
Gloria is the life work of Henri Martin, one of the great figures of the Médoc. As Grand Maître of the Commanderie du Bontemps he has also done much to promote the Médoc in general over many years. He is now ably assisted by his son-in-law Jean-Louis Triaud. The vineyard has been put together in a generation from bits and pieces of Cru Classé vineyards only. For this reason it has not joined the Syndicat des Crus Bourgeois, and Gloria sells for the same price as some Fifth Growths.

The wines are generous and supple, with breed and fullness and richness of flavour. It is a wine noted for its consistency. The problem is that it is almost certainly not as good as the classified growths of St-Julien, although superior to some lesser Margaux and Pauillac classifieds, and of course it is more expensive than most Crus Bourgeois.

Château Gruaud-Larose

2e Cru Classé. Owner: **Cordier family.** 82ha. 35,000 cases. CS 62%, Mer 25%, CF 9%, PV 4%. Second label: **Sarget du Gruaud-Larose.**
If Léoville-Las-Cases and Ducru-Beaucaillou are the archetypal St-Julien's of the riverside vineyards, Gruaud-Larose is the classic example of a St-Julien from the plateau that lies between the riverside properties and St-Laurent. This very large estate was created in the 18th century, divided in the 19th and then reunited by the Cordiers in 1934. Today this property, together with nearby Talbot, is their showplace and indeed the flagship of this leading négociant house.

As with some other Crus Classés sold as *négoce* exclusivities, Gruaud sells at a more modest price than it would on the open market. It would be a mistake to allow this to influence our assessment of the intrinsic merits of this outstanding *cru*, for Gruaud is certainly worthy to be placed beside Las-Cases and Beaucaillou as a "Super-Second", in quality if not in price.

The wines here have great concentration and richness and are decidedly tannic in the past few years, but with maturity they acquire a soft, velvety texture with great breed and charm. Very fine wines were made in 83, 82, 81, 79, 78, 76 and 75. The 80 is slower in developing than most of the wines of this vintage.

The new second wine is well worth looking out for. It is packed with fruit and can of course be drunk earlier than the Grand Vin, but still has plenty of structure.

Château Hortevie
Cru Bourgeois. Owner: Henri Pradère. 3.5ha. 1,500 cases. Cabernets 70%, Mer 25%, PV 5%.
This very small vineyard is a good example of the remarkable quality of the *terroir* of St-Julien. In competent hands it cannot avoid producing a wine of charm and breed. The vineyard lies behind the village of Beychevelle, and its proprietor, who is also the co-owner of Terrey-Gros-Caillou, runs the property jointly. This is a wine of real quality.

Château Lagrange
3ᵉ Cru Classé. Owner: Château Lagrange SARL. Administrator: Marcel Ducasse. 49ha. 19,000 cases. CS 65%, Mer 35%. Second label: les Fiefs-de-Lagrange.
In 1983 Lagrange was sold to the giant Japanese firm of distillers and wine merchants, Suntory, and so became the first Bordeaux Cru Classé to be bought by a Japanese company. The vineyard here is very well placed on the plateau of St-Julien behind Gruaud-Larose. One of its attractions for the new owners was that, although there are 49ha in production, there is considerable potential for greatly increasing this. Already another 32ha have been, or are about to be, planted. A complete overhaul of all the buildings, including the château, is in hand, and a new *chais* is being constructed to cope with the greatly increased production envisaged. The new owners have brought in Marcel Ducasse to manage the property while Michel Delon of Leoville-Las-Cases acts as consultant.

There was a time when the wines at Lagrange were tough and coarse in style, but matters have been improving even in the 1960s, and the 1978 had real St-Julien fruit and charm. So all the evidence was there to suggest that something well above the rather modest reputation of recent years was possible. The 82, made by the old owners but sold by the new ones, is an excellent example of the vintages, with a scent of prunes and great depth of flavour and fruit, tannin and complexity; while the 83 has a lot of character and finesse with real depth of flavour. Certainly this is a wine to watch.

A new second wine, les Fiefs-de-Lagrange, has been introduced to improve the selection for the Grand Vin. The first vintage is 1983.

Château Laland-Borie
Cru Bourgeois Supérieur. Owner: Jean-Eugène Borie. 18ha. 8,000 cases. CS 65%, Mer 25%, CF 10%.
This *cru* has been created by Jean-Eugène Borie, owner of Ducru-Beaucaillou, from a vineyard that was formerly part of Lagrange. The new vineyard was planted only in 1970 but is now making very stylish and elegant wines, with charming fruit and medium weight. The first important vintage was the 79, and since then the wines have steadily improved.

The wine offers an excellent opportunity for sampling Jean-Eugène Borie's deft hand with St-Julien, at a modest price.

Château Langoa-Barton
3ᵉ Cru Classé. Owner: Société Fermière. 20ha. 8,000 cases. CS 70%, Mer 15%, PV 8%, CF 7%.
This château has the distinction of having belonged to the same family since 1821, longer than any other Cru Classé. At the time when Hugh Barton acquired the property it was known as Pontet-Langlois. It will come as no surprise to anyone familiar with the vagaries of French spelling of proper names to know that Langlois has become Langoa. The 18th-century château is one of the finest in the Médoc, not as well placed as Beychevelle but not far behind it in pure architectural terms. The wines of Langoa and the Barton portion of Léoville were never château-bottled until 1969, being removed to Barton & Guestier's Bordeaux cellars for bottling.

The wines of Langoa accurately reflect their classification. Usually ready to drink earlier than those of Léoville-Barton, they have a classic St-Julien character but are generally lighter in texture, less tannic but with lots of elegance, fruit and charm – and real breed. The vintages here follow those of Léoville-Barton very closely, with marvellous wines in 83, 82 and 81, a good 80, an elegant if light-weight 79 and a superb 78. Every now and then it does something surprising, as with an unusually good 74 or a 71 which seems even better than the Léoville. A relationship not dissimilar to that between Gruaud-Larose and Talbot.

Château Léoville-Barton

2e Cru Classé. Owner: Société Fermière. 39ha. 16,000 cases. CS 70%, Mer 15%, PV 8%, CF 7%.

Like its neighbour Poyferré, Léoville-Barton was until the 1820s a part of the enormous estate of the Marquis de Las Cases. In 1826 Hugh Barton, who had already bought Langoa only five years before, acquired what was then a quarter share of the original Las-Cases estate and used the cellars of Langoa for making and housing the produce of his new acquisition. A hundred and sixty years later the Barton family still own the property, with Anthony Barton having recently taken on the burden of management from his uncle Ronald, who still lives in the château.

Léoville-Barton, under Ronald Barton's long stewardship, remained a very traditionally-made wine. The wines are finely perfumed, very powerful and rich in tannin at first, then developing that beautiful fruit and richness of flavour which are hallmarks of the best St-Juliens. The style tends towards more richness than Las-Cases, but with a shade less elegance. There were some inconsistencies in the 1970s, with neither 73 nor 79 being as good as the general level of those vintages. But since then, with stricter selection now evident, very good results were obtained in 80, and outstanding wines were made in 81, 82 and 83. Earlier, 78, 76 and 75 are the years to look for. With the marked improvement at Leoville-Poyferré from 1980 onwards, it is going to be especially interesting in the future to compare the three Léovilles side by side again.

Château Léoville-Las-Cases

2e Cru Classé. Owner: Société Civile. Administrator: Michel Delon. 85ha. 30,000 cases. CS 65%, Mer 18%, CF 14%, PV 3%. Second label: Clos du Marquis.

The label of this wine states "Grand Vin de Léoville du Marquis de Las Cases" – no mention of château – and serves to remind us that this is the residue of what was in the 18th century the most important estate, not only in St-Julien but also in the Médoc. With its magnificent *clos* adjoining Latour on a gravel ridge within sight of the Gironde, Las-Cases represents half the original estate and runs from the village of St-Julien to Latour. The original château, standing at the southern entrance to the village, is actually divided between Las-Cases and Poyferré, with the Las-Cases portion on the left-hand side.

The Société Civile is still composed of descendants of the Las Cases family. In 1900 they appointed the famous viticulturalist Théophile Skawinski as manager. On his retirement in 1930 he was succeeded by his son-in-law André Delon, grandfather of the present administrator Michel Delon. In the 1960s the reputation of Las-Cases recovered from a poor patch, the result of extensive replanting after the Second World War. During the 70s its reputation has soared to fresh heights, so that today Las-Cases is once more regarded as the leading wine in St-Julien.

In style it is firmer and slower to mature than other St-Juliens. Recently the wines seem to have filled out and are now not only elegant but also very concentrated and powerful. The bouquet is especially characteristic, reserved at first but slowly evolving to become elegant and firm. Great wines were made in 83, 82, 81, 79 and 78, all true *vins de garde*. The 80 is slower in developing than most, but the 76 is now drinking well. Las-Cases is certainly now one of the stars of the "Super-Seconds".

The Clos-du-Marquis is one of the best and most consistent of the secondary wines.

Château Léoville-Poyferré

2e Cru Classé. Owner: Cuvelier family. Administrator: Didier Cuvelier. 63ha. 18,500 cases. CS 65%, Mer 35%. Second label: Château Moulin-Riche.

Like Léoville-Barton, Léoville-Poyferré originally represented a quarter portion of the Las-Cases estate, which was acquired by the Baron de Poyferré. Unlike the other two Léovilles, Poyferré has not had the same continuity of ownership since that time, and its fortunes have been more varied. At its best, in the past it has produced wines as fine as Las-Cases, as in 28 and 29. But at that time, although under different ownerships, both were managed by Théophile Skawinski. Now, after a period of inconsistency, a member of the younger generation of the Cuvelier family has assumed responsibility, and the results are beginning to show. First of all the *cuvier* was completely modernized in 1980, then more new wood was introduced and a capable new *maître de chais*, with the reassuringly *médocain* name of Dourthe, took over.

The 1980 vintage is the watershed here: not obviously a great vintage but elegant and fine – good by the general standard of the year. The 81 has a fine flavour, with structure, fruit, elegance and breed. The 82 is a glorious example of this exceptional year, a great bottle in the making, while the 83 has length, concentration and harmony. Although good wines were made before this (a particular favourite of mine being the delicious 73) the *cru* was not reaching the heights of which it is capable. Now the future looks exciting.

Château St-Pierre

4e Cru Classé. Owner: Henri Martin. 20ha. 5,000 cases. CS 70%, Mer 20%, CF 10%.

This property has certainly had a very chequered history. The name derives from a Monsieur St-Pierre who acquired the property in 1767. Then in 1832 it was divided between different branches of the family, and the suffixes Bontemps-Dubarry and Sevaistre appeared. Although reunited by its Belgian owners after the Second World War, parts of the vineyard had been sold off, notably to Gloria and du Glana. Then in 1982 Henri Martin of Gloria bought the château – now being restored – and most of the vineyard. The original Sevaistre *chais* was bought by Jean-Eugène Borie for his Lalande-Borie, while St-Pierre is now housed in the same *chais* as Gloria, itself originally the St-Pierre-Bontemps *chais*, which Henri Martin had originally bought without the name.

St-Pierre had made elegant, perfumed, stylish and typically St-Julien wines for some years, but Henri Martin's skills now look like lifting it to higher plains; quite apart from his flair for publicizing his wines, the 82 and 83 are certainly lovely wines of great breed, and very clearly superior to Gloria.

Château Talbot

4e Cru Classé. Owner: Jean Cordier. 101ha. Red: 40,000 cases. CS 71%, Mer 20%, CF 5%, PV 4%. White: 2,500 cases. Secondary labels: Connetable Talbot, Caillou Blanc du Château Talbot (Bordeaux Blanc AC).

It is Talbot's misfortune that it is always obliged to stand in the shadow of Gruaud-Larose. The name commemorates the Earl of Shrewsbury who was killed commanding the English forces at Castillon la Bataille in 1453, although it seems doubtful that he ever actually owned the estate. As with all Cordier properties, Talbot is beautifully kept and very well equipped.

Talbot has long been noted for its consistency. The wines generally have less tannin and concentration than those of Gruaud-Larose, and are ready to be drunk sooner, but they also keep very well. The charm of Talbot is its harmony. The wines are beautifully perfumed and have great St-Julien refinement in their fruit. Not surprisingly 83 and 82 promise to be superb. The 81 is developing well and has great finesse. The 80 is delicious (I prefer it at present to the Gruaud), while the 79 is already drinkable. The 78 is a more long-term wine, with 76 another attractive wine for drinking now. There is a fine 75 of real attraction, which still needs time. Because of Cordier's pricing policy Talbot is always marvellous value for money, especially if bought early.

The new second wine, Connetable Talbot, is really delightful, ideal for early drinking, with lots of vivid St-Julien fruit. The white wine is pleasant, fresh and clean, but nothing more.

Château Terrey-Gros-Caillou

Cru Bourgeois. Owners: André Fort & Henri Pradère. 15ha. 8,000 cases. Cabernets 65%, Mer 30%, PV 5%.

Ever since I came across this *cru* for the first time – it was the 66 vintage – I have been greatly impressed by the real breed and finesse of this wine. Certainly it is one of the very best of the very best of the Cru Bourgeois in St-Julien. The vineyard is in several parcels, the most important of which is behind the village of Beychevelle where the *chais* is – and adjoining Talbot and Léoville-Barton. Another is next to Gruaud-Larose, and yet another adjoins Beychevelle and Ducru-Beaucaillou.

A very fine 83 here epitomized the virtues of this wine, with its very vivid

St-Julien fruit on the nose and its lovely flavour, combining richness and exceptional breed. This is due not only to good vineyards but also to fine winemaking. Certainly this is a wine to look for if you enjoy St-Julien but do not want to pay Cru Classé prices all the time.

PAUILLAC

The fame of Pauillac is assured from the reflected glory of its three First Growths: Lafite-Rothschild, Mouton-Rothschild and Latour. The area covered by the Crus Classés here is greater than in any other appellation, even though it has only 18 as against 21 in Margaux. The area under vine has increased by 27% in the decade 1972–83.

It is here that the Cabernet Sauvignon achieves its most characteristic results, producing that marked blackcurrant style for which it is justly famous. The wines are the most powerful in terms of both bouquet, body and flavour of all Médocs. The best *crus* combine this with a finesse that develops with ageing, but some lesser *crus* have a certain coarseness.

Château Batailley

5ᵉ Cru Classé. Owner: Emile Castéja. 50ha. 22,000 cases. CS 73%, Mer 20%, CF 5%, PV 2%.

The early reputation and classification of Batailley date from the period of Guestier's ownership. Now another négociant, Emile Castéja of Borie-Manoux, is in charge. There is sometimes a tendency to undervalue châteaux that are not sold through the Bordeaux market, especially if, in their pricing policy, they are more concerned with offering continuity to their customers than looking over their shoulders at what their neighbours are doing. The real worth of Batailley should not be underrated on account of its relatively modest price.

Interestingly, all of the present vineyard is on land classified in 1855. It lies at the back of Pauillac on the road to St-Laurent. The wines here are very consistent, solid and dependable. In the past Batailley occasionally produced something memorable (53, 61 and 64 are examples). Otherwise it was sound but unexciting. Now the wines consistently have more fruit and concentration as well as being more stylish. Years to look out for are 82, 81, 79, 78, 76 and 75.

Château Clerc-Milon

5ᵉ Cru Classé. Owner: Baron Philippe de Rothschild. 30ha. 8,700 cases. CS 70%, Mer 20%, CF 10%.

This rather neglected property was bought by Baron Philippe de Rothschild in 1970. The vineyard is well placed between the road and the river, north of Pauillac and close to both Mouton and Lafite. Milon is the name of the small village where the property lies, and Clerc was the name of the proprietor at the time of the 1855 classification.

Naturally much work has been done to improve the vineyard and the *cuvier* and *chais*; and the Rothschild team are confident of doing good things here given time. I have to confess that so far I have been disappointed, even in recent vintages such as 78 and 79. The wines used to be light but supple. Now they are still small wines but seem rather charmless and mean, as if new wood was too much for the structure. But one must wait and see.

Château Colombier-Monpelou

Cru Grand Bourgeois. Owner: Bernard Jugla. 15ha. 7,000 cases. CS 68%, Mer 18%, CF 6%, PV 5%, Mal 3%. Second label: Grand Canyon.

For many years this was the best wine to come out of the Pauillac cooperative. Then in 1970 it was bought by Bernard Jugla, proprietor of the adjoining Château Pédesclaux. Because Colombier parted company with its château and *chais* in 1939 (these now serve as the headquarters of La Baronnie, négociant company of Baron Philippe de Rothschild) a completely new installation had to be built. The wines are fermented in metal vats and aged in casks of which a third are new each year. This is good, honest Pauillac which enjoys a growing reputation. The wines have a certain elegance and suppleness, with pleasing fruit.

Château la Couronne

Cru Bourgeois Supérieur Exceptionnel 1932. Owner: Mme des Brest-Borie. 4ha. 1,750 cases. CS 70%, Mer 30%.

This very small vineyard was created in 1879 by Armand Lalande, who was then owner of Léoville-Poyferré and Brane-Cantenac. It lies in the south of Pauillac, inland from the Pichons and Batailley. Since 1952 it has been managed by Jean-Eugène Borie of Ducru-Beaucaillou on behalf of his sister.

The wines are true Pauillacs, but their aggressiveness is quickly shed as they develop excellent fruit. They are very harmonious and supple wines, which maintain a consistent standard comparable to many Cinquièmes Crus Classés.

Château Croizet-Bages
5e Cru Classé. Owner: Mme L. Quié. Administrator: Jean-Michel Quié. 22ha. 8,500 cases. CS 37%, CF 30%, Mer 30%, PV and Mal 3%.

This *cru* was created by the brothers Croizet in the 18th century. Its *chais* and *cuvier* are in the little hamlet of Bages, close to its more famous neighbour Lynch-Bages, on high ground in the south of Pauillac. It has belonged to the Quié family since 1930 and is now administered by Jean-Michel Quié, son of Mme Quié. There is no château.

The wines are attractively robust, full-flavoured Pauillacs, which mellow fairly quickly, yet in my experience still keep very well. If they seldom reach the heights, they also rarely disappoint. This is a *cru* which deserves its classification.

Château Duhart-Milon-Rothschild
4e Cru Classé. Owner: Domaines Barons de Rothschild. 45ha. 12,500 cases. CS 70%, Mer 20%, CF 10%, PV 4%. Second label: Moulin-Duhart.

When the Rothschilds of Lafite bought the neighbouring vineyard of Duhart-Milon in 1962 it was in a very sorry state, with only 16ha of vineyards in production and a high proportion of Petit Verdot. The wines were often very undistinguished. It takes a long time to see the results when a vineyard has to be almost entirely reconstituted, but now this is happening and Duhart is again taking its place as a leading Pauillac.

The vineyard lies mostly on the plateau of the Carmandes, and the *chais* and *cuvier* are in Pauillac. There is no château.

By the early 70s a wine of elegance and charm was being produced - not a heavy-weight, but rather in the mould of Haut-Batailley. For me the vineyard really came of age with its 78, a wine of immense breed, elegance and outstanding length. The 79 is more powerful and richer, the 80 a light-weight charmer, the 81 and 82 both very elegant middle-weight wines, with the 82 a true wine of the year, with massive fruit but complex and fine.

This is a wine that certainly deserves to be placed among the leading Pauillacs today and has truly realized its potential again.

Château la Fleur-Milon
Cru Grand Bourgeois. Owner: André Gimenez. 13ha. 5,000 cases. CS 45%, Mer 35%, CF 20%.

The vineyards of this *cru* are indeed well placed. Its *chais* is in the village of Le Pougalet (there is no château), and the various small plots of vineyard adjoin Mouton-Rothschild, Lafite-Rothschild, Duhart-Milon and Pontet-Canet. But this promising position is not reflected in the wine. The present owner has been in charge since 1955, a real working proprietor whose wines are still bottled from cask to cask. I find the wine very *artisanal*, rather coarse and tough, with the sort of stalkiness that suggests too much *vin de presse*.

Château Fonbadet
Cru Bourgeois Supérieur 1932. Owner: Pierre Peyronie. 15ha. 6,500 cases. CS 60%, Mer 19%, CF 15%, Mal 4%, PV 2%. Secondary labels: Châteaux Haut-Pauillac, Padarnac, Tour-du-Roc-Milon, Montgrand-Milon.

This charming 18th-century château lies to the south of the village of St-Lambert, just past the two Pichons as you drive from Bordeaux. The trees in its park stand out like an oasis in the sea of vines. The present owner is very much the working, resident proprietor.

The proportion of new casks used is 25%. This is a sound, classic Pauillac, which often does very well in blind tastings and fully deserves its excellent reputation. One factor is the very old vines, apart from meticulous care in the wine-making.

Château Grand-Puy-Ducasse
5e Cru Classé. Owner: Société Civile. Administrator: Jean-Pierre Angliviel de la Beaumelle. 36ha. 17,500 cases. CS 70%, Mer 25%, PV 5%. Second label: Artiges-Arnaud.

Until the present proprietors bought it in 1971, Grand-Puy-Ducasse was a very small vineyard of only 10ha, adjoining Mouton and Pontet-Canet. The new owners bought two additional vineyards, one adjoining Batailley and Grand-Puy-Lacoste on the plateau behind Pauillac, the other adjoining the two Pichons, so that it now has vineyards in all three main sectors of Pauillac. The château is a pleasing neo-classical building on the quayside near the centre of the village of Pauillac. For many years it also served as the Maison du Vin.

The new regime here seems to be producing fine results. The wines are classic Cabernet Sauvignon blackcurrant Pauillacs, but the structure is supple, rich and harmonious. The 75, for instance, was splendid. The wines are now very consistent. This is another example of a *cru* which, because it is marketed exclusively by a négociant (Mestrezat) at very reasonable prices, can be underrated. It is an excellent buy for the consumer.

Château Grand-Puy-Lacoste

5e Cru Classé. Owner: Borie family. Administrators: Jean-Eugène Borie & Xavier Borie. 45ha. 12,000 cases. CS 70%, Mer 25%, CF 5%. Second label: Lacoste-Borie.

This *cru* has for long had an excellent reputation for constantly producing typically robust and fine Pauillacs. Raymond Dupin was owner here from 1932 until extreme old age caused him to sell to the Borie family in 1978. If some things had begun to slip in his last few years this should not detract from the achievement of the Dupin years. The Bories decided to replace the old *cuvier* after the 1980 vintage with stainless steel, and the dilapidated château is being renovated.

Most of the vineyard is in one piece in front of the château on the plateau of Bages and is of the highest quality. The consistency and excellence of the wines reflect this. These wines are really powerful and often rather tannic and tough at first. The Bories are still making very concentrated wines, but are trying to emphasize the fruit a little more. The vintages of 83, 82, 81, 79 and 78 are all excellent examples of these years. Under the new regime this *cru* is becoming more fashionable – and expensive – but it does produce classic *vin de garde*.

Château Haut-Bages-Libéral

5e Cru Classé. Owner: Société Civile. 26ha. 10,000 cases. CS 70%, Mer 25%, PV 5%.

This *cru* has had a chequered history. When it was bought by the Cruses in 1960 it lost part of its vineyard to Pontet-Canet and its wines were Bordeaux-bottled in Cruses' cellars. With the introduction of compulsory château-bottling for the Crus Classés in 1972 and the sale of Pontet-Canet, the Cruses were obliged to build a new installation for handling the wines. In 1980 they sold to a company, which also runs Chasse-Spleen and La Gurgue, who have made important investments to bring the property and vineyards up to standard. So the future looks much brighter than the past.

The vineyard, as the name suggests, is on the plateau of Bages, and adjoins Latour, Lynch-Bages, and Pichon-Longueville-Baron. The other part of the name has no political connotations but was the name of its 19th-century owner at the time of the classification.

In the last years of the Cruse management there were improvements in the wine, which was rich with good fruit, sometimes delicious as in 76, sometimes rather one-dimensional and hollow, as in 79. But the future certainly promises better things – a *cru* to watch.

Château Haut-Bages-Monpelou

Cru Bourgeois. Owner: Emile Castéja. 10ha. 3,000 cases. Cabernets 70%, Mer 30%.

One of the lesser lights of the Borie-Manoux stable. The vineyard was once part of Duhart-Milon. The wines are full-bodied but elegant and drinkable relatively young. This is pleasant, dependable, easy-to-drink wine at a modest price.

Château Haut-Batailley

5e Cru Classé. Owner: Mme des Brest-Borie. Administrator: Jean-Eugène Borie. 20ha,. 7,500 cases. CS 65%, Mer 25%, CF 10%. Second label: Château la Tour-d'Aspic.

When the Borie family bought Batailley in 1942 they divided it between the two brothers: Marcel, who was the négociant, and François, who bought Ducru-Beaucaillou. Haut-Batailley is much the smaller part. Its vineyard had to be replanted and took time to mature. There is no château, as the house stayed with the main part of the property, and the wine is vinified at La Couronne.

There is a marked contrast in styles between Haut-Batailley and Batailley, with the former producing wines of less weight but real elegance. If one compares Haut-Batailley with Grand-Puy-Lacoste one sees the same sort of contrast. Grand-Puy and Batailley are more assertively, even aggressively Pauillac. Haut-Batailley is extremely consistent, the beautifully balanced fruit and mature tannins making it drinkable relatively young but still able to age attractively.

Château Lafite-Rothschild

1er Cru Classé. Owner: **Groupe Rothschild. 90ha. 25,000 cases.** CS 70%, Mer 15%, CF 13%, PV 2%. Second label: **Moulin des Carruades.**

Lafite has experienced something of a renaissance in recent years. In the 1960s and early 70s there had been far too many disappointments for a wine of Lafite's standing. So in 1975 Professor Peynaud was called in to advise. Then Jean Crété was appointed *régisseur*, with his invaluable experience under Michel Delon at Léoville-Las-Cases behind him, and young Baron Eric de Rothschild took over as the family member in charge. The combination of these changes has been most beneficial for Lafite and shows up vividly in the glass. Jean Crété retired in 1984 and was followed by Gilbert Rokvam. The old practice of keeping the wine in cask for three years, irrespective of the character of the vintage, has been abandoned, and this has certainly had a very good effect.

The features that one notices about recent Lafite vintages, compared with those of previous years, are their depth of colour, richness and concentration of flavour. The wines of 75, 78, 79, 81, 82 and 83 are all great classic *vins de garde*, while 76 and 80 are good examples of their vintages which can be drunk and enjoyed earlier.

To drink a bottle of Lafite should be one of the ultimate experiences for any wine-lover, and it is good to know that in future there should be no disappointments.

Château Latour

1er Cru Classé. Owner: **Pearson group.** Administrator: **Jean-Louis Mandrau. 60ha. 16,000 cases.** CS 80%, CF 10%, Mer 10%. Second label: **les Forts de Latour (8,000 cases).**

Since 1963 Latour has been controlled by the Pearson group of London. Their director with responsibility for Latour has, since 1984, been Alan Hare, while the management on the spot has now been assumed by Jean-Louis Mandrau. The legendary Jean-Paul Gardère remains as consultant, having guided Latour's fortunes since Pearson's took over.

Latour has produced monumental wines for generations. The modernization of the *cuvier* and improvements in the vineyard have simply tended to make the wines more accessible. But retrospective tastings show that Latour has lost none of its legendary characteristics: its great depth of colour, classic Cabernet nose and remarkable concentration of fruit and tannin. Admirers of Latour often used to bemoan the fact that they doubted they would live long enough to enjoy the most recent vintages. The 66 is a great wine only just approaching its best, while the 70 is still not ready. But 64, 67, 71 and 76 provide classic wines which are delicious now. Vintages that promise greatness for the future are 75, 78, 79, 81 and an 82 which takes it place beside the wonderful 61.

Les Forts de Latour is produced partly from vineyards that never go into the Grand Vin and partly from younger vines of Latour. There is a shorter fermentation, and the wine has the characteristics of Latour but with less concentration, so it develops more quickly. The wine is not placed on the market until it is ready to drink.

Château Lynch-Bages

5e Cru Classé. Owner: **Cazes family.** Administrator: **Jean-Michel Cazes. 80ha. 28,000 cases.** CS 70%, Mer 18%, CF 10%, PV 2%. Second label: **Château Haut-Bages-Averous (7,000 cases).**

Lynch-Bages is a wine that arouses markedly varying opinions among claret-lovers. Some admire it unreservedly; others call it the poor man's Mouton or claim that it lacks finesse and breed. Objectively this is a marvellously attractive, almost plummy, Pauillac with a really concentrated blackcurrent bouquet and flavour. At the same time it is less tannic and aggressive than many Pauillacs, with an emphasis on fruit and suppleness. It also has a fine record of making good wines in lesser vintages.

The château, which is the home of Jean-Michel Cazes who now runs Lynch-Bages, stands on the edge of the plateau of Bages, commanding views across the Gironde, with the vineyards behind it. In recent years there has been an impressive programme of enlarging and modernizing both *cuvier* and *chais*. Certainly standards have never been higher than they are today. Recent outstanding years have been 83, 82, 81, 78 and 75.

Haut-Bages-Averous is something of a cross-breed. There are 5 hectares of good Cru Bourgeois, the produce of which is assembled with those vats of Lynch-Bages that have been eliminated from the Grand Vin. The result is a light, deliciously fruity and easy-to-drink wine.

Château Lynch-Moussas

5e Cru Classé. Owner: Emile Castéja. 25ha. 12,500 cases. CS 70%, Mer 30%.

Although this *cru* has belongd to the Castéja family for many years, there were many members of the family involved until Emile Castéja was able to buy out the others in 1969. At that time the production had fallen to less than 2,000 cases, and the property was in a very rundown condition. Emile Castéja, who is also responsible for all Borie-Manoux's properties (see Batailley etc) has had to rebuild and re-equip *cuvées* and *chais*, and replant the vineyard.

The vineyard adjoins Batailley and is the most westerly of all Pauillac *crus*, where part of the vineyard lies near the hamlet of Moussas, there is also some near Duhart-Milon and Lafite to the north, and near Pichon and Latour to the south.

Before the restoration this was a pleasant but rather light wine, without much distinction. An indication of the progress now being made came at a recent blind tasting of 80 Crus Classés, where it did better than several better-known Pauillacs. I was struck by the aromatic, rather minty bouquet, and by the attractively fruity flavour and interesting individuality, an achievement in a small year such as 80. This is certainly a wine to watch.

Château Mouton-Baronne-Philippe

5e Cru Classé. Owner: Baron Philippe de Rothschild. 50ha. 15,000 cases. CS 65%, Mer 20%, CF 15%.

Just a few hundred yards from the front gate of Mouton-Rothschild stands a curious unfinished building, a classical portico sliced down the middle as if it were a piece of cake. This is Mouton-Baronne-Philippe, so named to commemorate the late wife of the proprietor. Originally known as Mouton d'Armailhac, it was acquired by the Baron in 1933 and renamed Mouton-Baron-Philippe in 1956, the "Baron" being changed to "Baronne" in 1975.

This property, although only a stone's throw away from the great Mouton, is run entirely separately but with equal care. The wines are true Pauillacs but less rich and opulent than those of their big brother. In the most successful years the wines do have a very good concentration, but in some lesser ones they can be slightly mean and dull. As one would expect, they are nearer in style to their other neighbour than to the great Premiers Crus.

Château Mouton-Rothschild

1er Cru Classé 1973. Owner: Baron Philippe de Rothschild. 72ha. 20,000 cases. CS 85%, CF 7%, Mer 8%.

The Mouton-Rothschild we know today is the life's work of one man – Baron Philippe, who, from the day he took charge in 1923, set about making something special of it. He was the first to introduce compulsory château-bottling, along with the other First Growths – only then Mouton was not a First. He hit upon the idea of having an artist design a special motif for each year's label, something which has happened every year since 1945. Finally he cut through the petty jealousies of Bordeaux to see Mouton proclaimed an official Premier Cru Classé in 1973.

The wines of Mouton are quintessential Pauillacs, curiously closer in style to Latour, on the other side of the commune, than to its near neighbour and long-time rival, Lafite. There is a similar concentrated blackcurrant bouquet and flavour, combined with a richness and opulence that disguise the tannin more than at Latour. There have been some ups and downs in recent vintages, but both 81 and 82 are outstanding, as was the 78.

Château Pédesclaux

5e Cru Classé. Owner: Jugla family. Administrator: Bernard Jugla. 18ha. 8,300 cases. CS 70%, Mer 20%, CF 5%, PV 5%.

This is one of the more obscure of the Crus Classés. Its vineyards and *chais* are just to the north of the village of Pauillac, near to Pontet-Canet. The name comes from a *courtier* (wine-broker) who was proprietor at the time of the 1855 classification. It was bought by the Jugla family in 1950, and the facilities have been improved and the production increased under their management. Belgium is the principal export market.

The reputation of Pédesclaux is for making solid, honourable Pauillacs rather than exciting ones – but then prices too are suitably modest.

Château Pibran
Cru Bourgeois. Owner: **Billa family. 9ha. 4,000 cases. Cabernets 70%, Mer 24%, PV 6%.**
This *cru* lies just outside Pauillac to the north-west and adjoins Pontet-Canet. It has belonged to the Billa family since 1941, and it is they who have built up the property since then. In good years all the wine is château-bottled. These are attractively fruity wines, with a good reputation.

Château Pichon-Longueville-Baron
2e Cru Classé. Owner: Société Civile de Pichon-Longueville. Administrator and co-proprietor: **B. Bouteiller. 30ha. 14,000 cases. CS 80%, Mer 20%.**
The château here is a notable landmark on the *route des châteaux*, with its slender turrets and high-pitched roof giving it a fairy-tale look. Unfortunately it is today little more than a shell, and the present owners live at Château Lanessan. In 1855 the property was undivided and, apart from Mouton (now elevated to Premier Cru status), was the only Pauillac in the Deuxième Cru category. The vineyard is superbly situated, adjoining Latour.

There was a time when Pichon-Baron (as it is usually called to distinguish it from the neighbouring Comtesse) was normally the better of the two wines. Not so today. The wines are classic Pauillacs, bold and powerful with a marked blackcurrant flavour and considerable breed. Unfortunately there has been a lack of consistency in recent years. While the Comtesse has moved ahead the Baron has not, and one feels that the full potential here is not at present being fulfilled. My favourite among recent vintages is the 79.

Château Pichon-Longueville-Comtesse-de-Lalande
2e Cru Classé. Owner: **Mme H. de Lencquesaing. 60ha. 25,000 cases. CS 46%, Mer 34%, CF 12%, PV 8%.** Second label: **Réserve de la Comtesse.**
Unlike its neighbour, the Baron, Pichon-Comtesse has a charming château which is now lived in for much of the time by the present owner and administrator, Mme de Lencquesaing, and her husband. It was her father, Edouard Miailhe, who originally acquired the property in 1926. He made various improvements, notably a partly submerged *chais* with a terrace above giving a splendid view of Château Latour and the Gironde. But it is really since his daughter took over in 1978 that the reputation of Pichon-Comtesse has soared into the top category of Second Growths. A new *cuvier* was ready for the reception of the 1980 vintage, further extensions have been made to the *chais*, and the facilities for receiving guests and providing tastings have been much improved. Also important has been the role of Monsieur Godin, who became *chef de culture* in 1970 and then *régisseur* in 1975. He is one of the new breed of Bordeaux managers who combine a modern technical training with an inbred feel for the *métier*.

The wines here have always had great finesse and breed. The fact that part of the vineyard lies in St-Julien helps to give the wine a special character, more opulent and feminine than a Pauillac, yet richer than a St-Julien. The introduction of the Réserve de la Comtesse has led to a more rigorous selection and a corresponding rise in quality. Outstanding wines have been made in 78, 79, 81, 82 and 83, while 80 and 84 have produced wines above the general level of these years.

Château Pontet-Canet
5e Cru Classé. Owner: **Guy Tesseron. 75ha. 30,000 cases. CS 68%, Mer 20%, CF 12%.** Second label: **les Hauts de Pontet.**
This large property lies north of Pauillac and adjoins Mouton-Rothschild. For many years it was the pride of the Cruse family, who sold it in 1975 to Guy Tesseron, member of a well-known Cognac family whose wife is a Cruse. The château and the fine *chais* and underground cellar, found in few properties in the Médoc, are most impressive. Unfortunately, during the latter years of the Cruse regime the reputation of Pontet-Canet declined. The wine was bottled in their Bordeaux cellars and not at the

château. Now all the wine is château-bottled.

One had hoped that under the new ownership the fortunes of Pontet-Canet would rapidly be restored, but it is taking rather longer than one had hoped. Often these powerful tannic wines seem to lack breed, and sometimes they seem dry and austere. The introduction of the new second label in 1982 should result in a stricter selection. The best recent vintages have been 75, 81 and 82.

Cave Coopérative La Rose Pauillac.
Owner: **Groupement des Propriétaires-Viticulteurs de Pauillac.** 110ha. 52,000 cases. CS and CF 45%, Mer 40%, PV 15%.

This cooperative, founded during the years of crisis in 1933, marked the beginning of the cooperative movement in the Médoc. At its inception there were just 52 members. Today there are 125 of them, cultivating 110ha of vineyards. Most of the wine is sold under the label of La Rose Pauillac, but Château Haut-Milon and Château Haut-St-Lambert make their own declaration, while Château le Fournas-Bernadotte is vinified at the cooperative, but the *élevage* is then done by the proprietor.

This cooperative enjoys a reputation for producing good, solid Pauillacs which are fruity and not too tannic or austere.

ST-ESTEPHE

In many ways a transitional area between the two parts of Médoc. There is a wide range of qualities from the breed and power of its leading *cru*, Cos-d'Estournel, to some rather lean, austere wines with a distinct *goût de terroir*. But improved methods of vinification have rendered many wines less rustic than they were. There has been little change in the area under vine, which has increased by only 5% in the past decade.

Château Andron-Blanquet
Cru Grand Bourgeois Exceptionnel. Owner: **Mme Cécile Audoy.** 15ha. 6,000 cases. Mer 35%, CS 30%, CF 30%, PV 5%. Secondary labels: **Château St-Roch, Blanquet.**

Since 1971 Andron-Blanquet has been under the same ownership and direction as Cos-Labory, whose vineyards its adjoins at some points. This is a wine which in my experience has that strong *goût de terroir* found in some St-Estèphes, especially when young, but this is matched by sufficient fruit and richness to ensure that with some ageing the fruit produces a pleasing wine, but with quite a strong flavour. A wine of character – if you like the character!

Château Beau-Site
Cru Grand Bourgeois Exceptionnel. Owner: **Emile Castéja.** 27ha. 15,000 cases. CS and CF 60%, Mer 40%.

The name means "beautiful spot", and when one looks at the view from the little courtyard in front of the château and *chais* one can see why it was chosen. The village of St-Corbian, where it is situated, is on high ground, and there is a splendid prospect across the vineyards of Calon-Ségur and towards the Gironde. The property is owned by the Castéja family and distributed exclusively by the firm of Borie-Manoux, the Bordeaux négociant.

The wines, like many St-Estèphes, have quite a strong flavour at first, but soon develop the richness to produce harmonious and pleasing wines. Sometimes there can be a touch of austerity about the finish, but this usually rounds off with ageing. I have found the most impressive of recent vintages to be 82, and 78, but the 79 promises well and the 76 is robust and harmonious. This is a good Cru Bourgeois.

Château Beau-Site-Haut-Vignoble
Cru Bourgeois 1932. Owner: **Jean-Louis Braquessac.** 20ha. 8,000 cases. CS 60%, Mer 30%, PV 10%.

In the same village of St-Corbian as Beau-Site is Beau-Site-Haut-Vignoble. This wine is distinctly more *artisanal*. Although carefully made, it is not in the same class as its neighbour. There is a lack of richness combined with toughness, giving a certain leanness – features characteristic of many lesser St-Estèphes. Nevertheless, this is an honourable and typical St-Estèphe.

Château Calon-Ségur
3e Cru Classé. Owner: **Familles Capbern-Gasqueton et Peyrelongue.** Administrator: **Philippe Gasqueton.** 48ha. 15,000 cases. CS 60%, CF 20%, Mer 20%. Second label: **Marquis de Ségur.**

This is the oldest of the leading St-Estèphe *crus*. In the 12th century it was given to a bishop of Portiers, Monseigneur de Calon, while in the 18th century it belonged to the famous Marquis de Ségur, who was proprietor of Lafite and Latour. He is supposed to have said that, although he made his wine at Lafite, his heart was at Calon – hence the heart-shaped device seen on the label and in many places at the property. Since the death of his father in 1962, Philippe Gasqueton has run the property and continued the wine's reputation for consistency. In 1984 a large new underground cellar was completed. It is L-shaped and runs along two sides of the *chais*, 60 metres long on one side and 50 metres on the other. The beautiful old wooden *cuvier* is still preserved but has not been used since 1973. The new stainless-steel *cuvées* are of 100 hectolitres each, which represents half a day's picking. This makes for better control and selection.

This is a wine which seldom comes top in comparative tastings of cask samples of Cru Classé St-Estèphes, but then often does better in bottle. The wines are noticeably softer and fruitier, and more generous than Cos or Montrose, but less fine perhaps. In a blind tasting in Paris in 1976 for *La Nouvelle Guide de Gault-Millau*, Calon received the highest average mark of a group of leading Cru Classés. The vintages tasted were 66, 70, 71 and 73. In recent vintages the 83 is very attractive and the 82 among the leading wines of the vintage. 81, 79 and 78 are all good and there is a delicious early-drinking 80. Calon was always a great favourite in England, but in recent years its reputation has been rather eclipsed. Perhaps it has just not made the headlines, but all the evidence points to this being just the sort of wine one wants – easy to drink yet lasting well, with plenty of character, and not over-expensive.

Château Capbern-Gasqueton

Cru Grand Bourgeois Exceptionnel. Owner: Famille Capbern-Gasqueton. Administrator: Philippe Gasqueton. 30ha. 10,000 cases. CS 60%, Mer 25%, CF 15%. Second label: **Le Grand Village Capbern** (exclusively distributed by Dourthe).

The château is a solid mansion in the centre of St-Estèphe. The vineyard is in two parts, one adjoining Calon-Ségur, the other near Meyney. The château is the home of Philippe Gasqueton and his family, and has been in the family for many generations. All the wine is matured in casks, but no new wood is used.

As at Calon-Ségur, Philippe Gasqueton succeeds in emphasizing the fruit and avoiding the harshness often associated with St-Estèphe. A very attractive 83 was made here, with lots of fruit and ripeness but also plenty of character, while the 79 is rather light-structured but with well-balanced fruit and a pleasing flavour.

Château Chambert-Marbuzet

Cru Bourgeois 1932. Owner: Société Civile (H. Duboscq & Fils). 8ha. 3,800 cases. CS 70%, Mer 30%.

Another outpost of the Duboscq empire around Marbuzet (see Haut-Marbuzet). Again, the wine is very well made and most attractive, even when young, yet clearly has the ability to age well. I have found the wine scented and packed with fruit, well supported by ripe tannin, all with an attractive flavour.

Château la Commanderie

Cru Bourgeois 1932. Owner: Gabriel Meffre. 16ha. 6,000 cases. CS 60%, Mer 40%.

This is a northerly outpost of Gabriel Meffre's empire. At one time all the wines were made at du Glana; now they have their own *chais*. The name goes back to the Middle Ages, when this was a *commanderie* of the Knights Templar. It is situated in the southern part of the commune, between Marbuzet and Leyssac. The wine is exclusively distributed by Dourthe and Kressmann, depending on the market.

Château Cos-d'Estournel

2ᵉ Cru Classé. Owner: Domaines Prats. Administrator: Bruno Prats. 54ha. 18,000 cases. CS 60%, Mer 40%. Second label: **Château de Marbuzet.**

Cos is a landmark familiar to all who travel the *route des châteaux* on account of its pagoda-like façade, strikingly placed on a hill overlooking Lafite. This building is in fact the *chais*, for there is no château. The present ownership dates back to 1919 when it was bought by Fernand Ginestet, the grandfather of Bruno Prats. He has been in charge here since 1971. Cos has usually been considered as the leading *cru* of St-Estèphe, and certainly develops more finesse and breed in bottle than any other, as well as being very long-lived. There was a period in the 1960s when it was less convincing, but since Bruno Prats assumed the direction, Cos has become established as one of the leading Deuxièmes Crus Classés once more.

When this wine is in cask it is always most impressive, concentrated and tannic but finely balanced with great breed. There is often a dull patch in the early years in bottle, but then the fruit, balance and breed come into their own. This is a most rewarding wine to keep. Fine and often exceptional wines were made in 83, 82, 81, 79 and 78. The 80 is less evolved than most wines of the year.

Château Cos-Labory

5e Cru Classé. Owner: Mme Cecile Audoy. 12ha. 6,700 cases. CS 40%, Mer 35%, CF 20%, PV 5%.

The style of the wines here is light and elegant, and they mature rather quickly. There is certainly more refinement here than is usual in St-Estèphe, but not the weight and character of the leading growths. Among recent vintages I have liked the 80 as much as any – comparatively speaking – for its charm and drinkability.

Château Coutelin-Merville

Cru Grand Bourgeois. Owner: Guy Estager. 16ha. 6,000 cases. CS and CF 65%, Mer 30%, PV and Mal 5%.

Until 1972 this property was run jointly with Château Hanteillan in Cissac, whose vineyards it adjoins. But then inheritance problems forced the sale of the Cissac property, so this *cru* now stands on its own. The wines are matured in cask, but there is no new oak. The wine has power and good structure which require bottle-ageing to round off and give of their best.

Château Le Crock

Cru Grand Bourgeois Exceptionnel. Owner: Cuvelier family. Administrator: Didier Cuvelier. 31ha. 15,500 cases. CS 65%, Mer 35%.

Since 1903 Le Crock has belonged to the Cuvelier family, who also now own Léoville-Poyferré. This property is now managed by the enthusiast Didier Cuvelier who is assisted by Francis Dourthe, the Poyferré *maître de chais*.

I do not know what the wines were like in the past, but recently they have been most impressive. They are scented, powerful and complex on the nose, with a marked and agreeable personality, rich, with structure and depth on the palate. In a blind tasting of 79 Crus Bourgeois in 1984 Le Crock was on the same level as Meyney. On this form it must be one of the leading Crus Bourgeois of St-Estèphe, a wine to look out for, especially since its revitalized management took charge.

Château Haut-Marbuzet

Cru Grand Bourgeois Exceptionnel. Owner: Henri Duboscq. 38ha. 18,500 cases. Mer 50%, CS 40%, CF 10%.

In the last 20 years or so, Henri Duboscq has built up a formidable reputation for his wines. Situated around the village of Marbuzet, just to the south of Montrose, this was his starting point. Now he has added MacCarthy-Moula, Chambert-Marbuzet and then Tour-de-Marbuzet to his empire.

One remarkable feature for a Cru Bourgeois is that all the wine is matured in new oak, something which even most Cru Classés do not attempt. One might expect this to result in austere, tannic wines, especially in St-Estèphe, yet in my experience the wines are outstandingly attractive. The colours are deep and dense, the nose rich and concentrated with fruit and well-married oak, the wine very well balanced and stylish with an outstanding flavour, possible to drink when relatively young and yet a good keeper. The consistency is also unusual; the 72 for example was one of the few wines from this vintage that one could drink with real pleasure.

Château Houissant

Cru Bourgeois Supérieur 1932. Owner: Jean Ardouin. 20ha. 10,000 cases. CS 70%, Mer 30%.

This *cru* is well situated on high ground inland from Montrose, in the southern sector of the appellation. The wines have long enjoyed a solid and consistent reputation. Not currently rated because it is not a member of the Syndicat, this is nevertheless a commendable Cru Bourgeois.

Château Laffitte-Carcasset

Cru Bourgeois 1932. Owner: Vicomte Philippe de Padirac. 20ha. 8,000 cases. CS 65%, Mer 35%. Second label: Château la Vicomtesse.

The name is not an attempt to ape the Premier Cru Classé but the name of an 18th-century owner. It is well placed, lying just past the Cave Coopérative going north. The wine is carefully made, and the emphasis is on finesse, although the wines also have plenty of body. It is not a member of the Syndicat des Crus Bourgeois.

Château Lafon-Rochet

4e Cru Classé. Owner: Guy Tesseron. 45ha. 12,000 cases. CS 80%, Mer 20%.

Since Guy Tesseron (a Cognac négociant married to a Cruse) bought this *cru* in 1960, he has made great efforts to rebuild its reputation. There was much to be done, in the vineyard as well as the *chais*, and an entirely new château was built, designed in a suitably traditional mould. It is clearly visible from the road just past Cos d'Estournel on the *route des châteaux*.

I had felt by the mid 1970s that the wines were beginning to come of age and show clear improvements. However, looking back over regular tasting notes and seeing the results of some blind tastings in bottle, I find descriptions like "austere", "mean", "dry finish" coming up with monotonous regularity. So what has gone wrong? One of the first things Guy Tesseron did here was to reduce drastically the Merlot content of the vineyard and increase the Cabernet Sauvignon to 80%. This compares to only 60% at Cos d'Estournel and Calon-Ségur, and 65% at Montrose. The reason why the proportions of Cabernet Sauvignon in St-Estèphe are significantly lower, even for Cru Classés, than in Pauillac, St-Julien or Margaux lies in the heavier soil with its clay content. The Cabernet simply does not ripen as well in these soils and Merlot is essential to obtain balanced wines. It seems to me that at Lafon-Rochet they have treated the vineyard as if it were in Margaux and paid the penalty. The most attractive vintage at present is the 79.

Château Lavillotte

Cru Bourgeois. Owner: Jacques Pedro. 12ha. 5,500 cases. CS 75%, Mer 25%.

This offers a good example of the vagaries of French spelling. When this *cru* hit the headlines by coming out above some Crus Classés in a Gault-Millau blind tasting, I rushed off to my Cocks and Féret to look it up, but there was no entry under this name. Later it transpired that it was entered as La Villotte! The château label spells the name as one word. Jacques Pedro is a perfectionist, and this comes through in his wines. They are matured in cask and not filtered, so decanting is essential, even for a vintage such as 78.

It is not hard to see why this wine did so well in a blind tasting. It tends to be heavily perfumed and rich with distinctly minty overtones and real intensity. The flavour is fine and speaks of breed and complexity. I particularly like its attack and fruit up-front. Yet there is also finesse, with slightly less body than one had expected.

Château MacCarthy

Cru Grand Bourgeois. Owner: Jean Raymond. 6ha. 3,000 cases. CS 65%, Mer 35%.

As we know from the history of Lynch, Dillon and Kirwan, exiled Irishmen did well in Bordeaux in the 18th century, not to mention ones like Barton who came of their own volition. The MacCarthys are not so famous, but they were people of consequence two centuries ago, and have left behind this small property and a street in Bordeaux to keep their name alive.

Once this *cru* embraced most of the vineyards and land around the village of Marbuzet; now only 6 hectares are left, and most of the land now belongs to the Duboscqs. The reputation today is for decent wines that do not see much wood and are drinkable after four or five years.

Château de Marbuzet

Cru Grand Bourgeois Exceptionnel. Owner: Domaines Prats. 7ha. 10,000 cases. Mer 56%, CS 44%.

The handsome château here is the home of the Prats family of Cos-d'Estournel, which has no château of its own. The wine is vinified at Cos and is in fact treated as the second wine there, because the production here is blended with vats not suitable for inclusion in the Grand Vin of Cos. So as at Haut-Bages Averous and Lynch-Bages, this is not quite a straight second wine. The result is a pleasing harmonious wine which ages more quickly than the Cos, and so fulfils a useful commercial purpose.

Cave Coopérative Marquis de St-Estèphe

Owner: Société de Vinification de St-Estèphe.

The cave here was founded in 1934 by just 42 viticulteurs. Now there are over 200 "adherents", and this is one of the most up-to-date and best-run cooperatives in Médoc, or anywhere else in Gironde. Only grapes from the St-Estèphe appellation are received here. Apart from the wine sold under its own marque of Marquis de St-Estèphe, a number of the more important properties are kept separate and bottled *à la propriété* to be sold under their own names. These are the following: de Mignot, Lille-Coutelin, Gireaud, Moutinot, L'Hôpital, Le Roc, Haut-Coteau, La Croix des Trois Soeurs, Palmier, Faget, Les Pradines, La Croix de Pez, Balangé, Ségur de Cabanac, Graves de Blanquet, Tour de Pez, Haut-Verdon, Ladouys, Les Combes, Violet, Lartigue. Of course the quality of these wines varies according to the soil and the *cépages* planted, but all are carefully made. No wood is employed, and the wines normally show well after four to six years.

Château Meyney
Cru Grand Bourgeois Exceptionnel. Owner: **Domaines Cordier.** 50ha. 27,000 cases. CS 70%, Mer 24%, CF 4%, PV 2%. Secondary label: **Prieur du Château Meyney.**

St-Emilion abounds with old ecclesiastical buildings, or their remains, but they are rare in Médoc, and Meyney certainly has the best-preserved example. The present buildings, finely situated on a ridge with views across the Gironde, date from 1662–66. The large courtyard, even today, has a rather monastic atmosphere. The old name Prieuré des Couleys used, until recently, to appear on the label.

The wines balance fruit and tannin very judiciously; they are quite dense in texture and strong but always juicy in flavour. I find that they are normally at their best when on the young side, and that although they seem to have the structure for ageing, if kept too long they dry up and acquire a bitter finish. Of recent vintages 80 and 79 in their different ways represent Meyney at its most delicious for drinking now. 78 is not so ready while 75 and 70 are probably at their peak. 81 and 82 promise well but need time. This is clearly one of the leading non-classified wines of St-Estèphe, in my judgement just behind de Pez and Phélan-Ségur, because lacking a little in breed.

Château Montrose
2e Cru Classé. Owner: **Jean-Louis Charmolüe. 67ha. 23,000 cases.** CS 65%, Mer 25%, CF 10%.

Disappointingly for the Scots, the name conceals no Scottish affiliations but refers to the old name for this vineyard, the rose-coloured hill. This is the most recently planted of all the great Crus Classés, developed from completely uncultivated land, formerly part of Calon-Ségur, at the beginning of the 19th century. Like the neighbouring Meyney, it commands fine views of the Gironde from its ridge nearby. Montrose has belonged to the Charmolüe family since 1896 and is meticulously run by them. The present owner, Jean-Louis Charmolüe, is a resident working proprietor, like his much respected mother before him. The *cuvier* is still completely traditional, with beautifully kept wooden vats, and this is a very traditional wine. The only modern note is struck by a new *chais*.

I have always admired Montrose in cask. Although less marked by Cabernet Sauvignon than it used to be, it has a lovely clean, crisp, tannic flavour with new oak, tannin and fruit well matched. But this is not a wine to hurry over, and plenty of patience is required. Thus the 80 and 79 are still not ready to drink, or even very approachable, especially surprising perhaps for the 80. I have noted 82 as having great promise, and 79 and 78, 76 and 75 as fine wines for the future.

Château Morin
Cru Grand Bourgeois. Owners: **Marguerite & Maxime Sidaine.** 10ha. 4,750 cases. CS 65%, Mer 35%.

This *cru* is situated just outside St-Corbian, in the northern sector of the appellation, and has been in the same family for several generations. It still uses a delightful old label, distinctly 19th-century in appearance, and the property is run on very traditional lines. The strongly flavoured wines are, however, reasonably supple and are of good repute.

Château les Ormes-de-Pez
Cru Grand Bourgeois. Owner: **Cazes family.** Administrator: **Jean-Michel Cazes. 30ha. 12,500 cases.** CS 50%, Mer 35%, CF 10%, PV 5%.

The great gift for wine-making which the Cazes family have brought to Lynch-Bages is also evident here. I have frequently been agreeably surprised over the years by the consistently attractive wines made at les

Ormes-de-Pez. Even in difficult years the wines are usually supple and fruity, quite without the leanness or austerity of many St-Estèphes. In 1981 new stainless-steel fermentation vats were installed here and a new ageing *chais* constructed. Previously the wines had been kept at Lynch-Bages.

The wines have plenty of concentration, but are very well balanced with suppleness, fruit and plenty of character. Very good wines were made in 83, 82 (especially promising and rich), 81, 79 and 78. While les Ormes-de-Pez sometimes lacks the breed of its neighbour de Pez, it also seldom disappoints, and this makes it one of the best and most reliable of the Crus Bourgeois of St-Estèphe.

Château de Pez

Cru Bourgeois Supérieur 1932. Owner: Société Civile (Robert Dousson). 23.2ha. 14,500 cases. CS 70%, CF 15%, Mer 15%.
This is a very old property, and its grand twin-turreted château is clearly visible from the *route des châteaux* as it winds through the hamlet of the same name. It is situated just to the west of St-Estèphe. Ever since Robert Dousson took over the management here for his aunt in 1955, the reputation of this *cru* has grown, and for some years now it has been regarded as a candidate for classification, and the best non-classified *cru* in the commune.

The quality which de Pez has, and which is missing in other Crus Bourgeois of the commune, is breed. This comes out very clearly in blind tastings. There is an attractive spiciness on the nose, together with elegance, charm, and a lot of fruit, while the flavour has good concentration and richness, with breed and balance. Some years can be a little lean, but the balance is preserved. Very fine examples were made in 82, 79, 78, 76 and 75 of the years I have seen. Distribution world-wide is in the hands of Gilbey-Loudenne.

Château Phélan-Ségur

Cru Grand Bourgeois Exceptionnel. Owner: Société Anonyme (President, Xavier Gardinier). 52ha. 22,000 cases. CS 60%, Mer 30%, CF 10%.
As with neighbours Meyney and Montrose, this is a château you will not see from the *route des chateaux*. The very handsome château is on the southern edge of St-Estèphe village on high ground with a fine view across the river. There is a massive *chais*, but there still seems to be a lack of space. In 1985 the Delon family, who have owned the property since 1924 agreed to sell to Xavier Gardinier, the President Director-General of Champagne Pommery.

At its best this *cru* can make very fine long-lasting wines which are rich and supple, with complexity and breed. On the other hand one comes across poor bottles which seem rustic and coarse and savour of old casks. There is an inconsistency which puts the *cru* at a disadvantage compared to de Pez or Meyney. Yet with its finely placed vineyards, the main part adjoining Montrose and the rest north of the village next to Calon-Ségur, this should be an exceptional wine. One will watch the new regime with interest and hope for a brilliant future.

Château les Pradines

Owner: Jean Gradit. 8ha. 3,500 cases. CS 60%, Mer 35%, CF 5%.
Here is a good example of what vinification at a cooperative can achieve – the wines here are all bottled *à la propriété* and sold exclusively by Louis Dubroca. They have that positive, assertive character of St-Estèphe, but with very clean fruit and a complete absence of leanness. The wines see no wood, but need two to four years in bottle to give of their best. This is a very pleasing wine with plenty of agreeable character.

Château Tour-des-Termes

Cru Bourgeois 1932. Owner: Jean Anney. 26.5ha. 13,500 cases. CS 55%, Mer 35%, PV 10%.
A good-sized property situated near the village of St-Corbian in the north of the appellation. The wines I have come across are well made, robust with plenty of character, but also supple and quite fine. They are aged in cask. This is a wine of a good standard, not a member of the Syndicat des Crus Bourgeois.

Château Tronquoy-Lalande

Cru Grand Bourgeois. Owner: Arlette Castéja. 16.5ha. 7,000 cases. Mer 50%, CS and CF 50%.
I have always been attracted by the charming château here with its two distinctive towers at each end of a chartreuse-style building. Lalande is the

name of the place, Tronquoy that of an early-19th-century owner. In the early part of that century this *cru* was included in several unofficial classifications, but did not make the all-important one in 1855.

This is now a carefully managed property, for which Dourthe have the exclusivity and provide technical assistance. The wines are matured partly in *cuve* and partly in wood.

HAUT-MEDOC

The decline which this area suffered in the years of depression has now been triumphantly reversed. The area under vine increased by over 66% to 2,899 hectares between 1972 and 1983. The importance to the region as a whole of this increase in plantings may be gauged by the fact that if this increase is added to that in the Médoc AC, it amounts to 2,300 hectares – the equivalent to the whole area planted in Médoc AC in 1976.

This is *par excellence* the area of the Crus Bourgeois, which here account for 62% of the area in production and cover a greater area than in any other part of Médoc. Wines are produced in 15 very diverse communes but only in ten of these are more than 100 hectares planted and the most important are St-Seurin, St-Laurent, Cussac, St-Sauveur, Cissac and Vertheuil.

The styles of wine vary considerably, with the largest-producing northern communes making robust, full-flavoured wines, and softer, lighter ones being made in the south.

Château d'Agassac

Cru Grand Bourgeois Exceptionnel. Owner: **Société Civile.** Administrator: **Philippe Capbern Gasqueton.** 30ha. 9,000 cases. CS 60%, Mer 40%.

This is one of the few remaining examples of a genuine medieval fortress to survive in the Médoc. It is also the most important *cru* in Ludon, after La Lagune, and the only member there of the Syndicat des Crus Bourgeois. Since Philippe Gasqueton (see Calon Ségur, Capbern and du Tertre) took over 20 years ago, marked improvements have been made, and the reputation of the wine is much enhanced. The wine is matured in oak casks but no new wood is used. The yields are low, usually only around 30hl/ha.

This is a wine of marked and attractive individuality, vividly perfumed, with a very special fruitiness and pronounced flavour. Much of the crop is traditionally exported to Holland. It is a pity this wine is not better known in the Anglo-Saxon world.

Château d'Arsac

Cru Bourgeois Supérieur 1932. Owner: **SARL SOFAGA.** Administrator: **R. de Rijcke.** 11.5ha. 5,500 cases. CS 80%, Mer 15%, CF 5%. Secondary labels: **Château Ségur-d'Arsac, Château Le Monteil-d'Arsac.**

This *cru* is something of a curiosity, since it is the only one in Arsac not to benefit from the Margaux AC (it carries the Haut-Médoc AC). This is because at the time when the AC was being settled there were no vines planted and the proprietor did not bother to apply for it. The present owner took over in 1959 and has since reconstructed the vineyard. There are also 150ha of pasture supporting 500 sheep, and extensive woods. The wine is aged in casks, of which 20% are new.

Big, deep-coloured, traditional wines are made here, high in extract with tannin and fruit well matured and quite an assertive character. There is not the breed of du Tertre, but the wines become aromatic and supple with bottle age. The proprietor hopes to be granted the Margaux AC when the appellation is next reviewed.

Château Beaumont

Cru Grand Bourgeois. Owner: **Bernard Soulas.** 85ha. 30,000 cases. CS 56%, Mer 36%, CF 7%, PV 1%. Second label: **Château Moulin-d'Arvigny.**

In marked contrast to their neighbour, Tour-du-Haut-Moulin, the wines of Beaumont tend to be light, fruity and ready to drink early. They are very perfumed, with well-integrated new oak, tannin and fruit making for a very harmonious whole, most attractively flavoured. The 83 is very good, 82 will be for earlier drinking than most Médocs, but is very attractive, and there is a pleasant 79. I have also tasted a fruity, light 76.

The second wine, Château Moulin-d'Arvigny, is a selection of about 25% of the production, mostly from young vines, and is designed for early drinking. The 82 is delicious and already drinkable.

Château Belgrave
5ᵉ Cru Classé. Owner: GF A. Administrator: **Patrick Atteret. 55ha. 18,000 cases.** CS 60%, Mer 35%, PV 5%.
Until the CVBG group (Dourthe-Kressman) bought this property in 1979, it had suffered from under-investment and downright neglect for decades. So it is hardly surprising that the wine is little known or its reputation negligible. And yet the vineyard is well situated on gravelly ridges behind Lagrande, so the potential should be there. Now the new owners have carried out extensive improvements to the *chais*, and new casks are being used for maturation. Patrick Atteret, the CVBG's chief oenologist, is responsible for the direction of this project.

It is really too early to say just how good this wine can become, it will probably need at least another five years to judge the achievements of the new regime. The 80 when tasted blind in 85 did modestly, but was quite attractive in a light, soft, fruity way.

Château Bel-Orme-Tronquoy-de-Lalande
Cru Grand Bourgeois. Owners: **Mme L. Quié & Jean-Michel Quié. 24ha. 10,000 cases.** CS 30%, CF 30%, Mer 30%, CF and Mal 10%.
Not to be confused with Tronquoy-Lalande in nearby St-Estèphe, this property once belonged to the Tronquoy family. The words *bel-orme* mean "beautiful elm".

The wines here are powerful, solid and traditional, and they last marvellously, as is proved by some bottles of the 1920s that I have sampled. They tend to lack the bouquet of wines further south in the Médoc, but develop a warmth and richness of texture with age.

Château le Bourdieu
Cru Bourgeois. Owner: **Monique Barbe. 30ha. 25,000 cases.** CS 50%, Mer 30%, CF 20%. Secondary labels: **Châteaux Victoria, Picourneau.**
Probably the most reputed *cru* in Vertheuil today, the vineyards run from the village of that name to the boundary with St-Estèphe. The wine is matured in cask, and perhaps a woman's hand can be found in this carefully made wine, which combines robustness with finesse. The style is that of a good, lush St-Estèphe.

Château Cambon-la-Pelouse
Cru Bourgeois Supérieur 1932. Owner: **Indivision Carrère Fils, Frère and Gendre. 60ha. 35,000 cases.** Mer 50%, Cs 30%, CF 20%.
The *cru* has recently been resurrected by an energetic family of growers from St-Emilion, where they own Château Grand Barrail-Lamarzelle-Figeac.

The wines here have real breed, with the emphasis on elegant fruitiness. They are soft and develop quickly for early drinking – no casks are used in the maturation, but this is a good example of how clean, fresh and attractive such wines can be. It clearly makes very good commercial sense. Very good wines were made in 83 and 81, with the 82 producing something extra. I noted a lovely scent of cherries and liquorice, a delicious flavour, rich but also complex. This looks like a *cru* with a future.

Château de Camensac
5ᵉ Cru Classé. Owner: **Forner family. 60ha. 20,000 cases.** CS 60%, CF 20%, Mer 20%.
Like the other Crus Classés of St-Laurent, Camensac had sunk into a state of complete obscurity and neglect when it was rescued by the Forner brothers in 1965. Of Spanish origins (they produce a fine Rioja) and new to Bordeaux, they sought the help of Professor Emile Peynaud in rebuilding this *cru*. Much of the vineyard had to be replanted, and the *chais* and *cuvier* completely modernized and re-equipped.

In the early 1970s I noted that light-textured, fruity, harmonious wines were being made, which were eminently drinkable. But more recently the wines seem to have a stronger, coarser flavour, even when, as with the 82, there is a lot of richness and ripeness. In 1985 the 78 was still very tannic and coarse, solid, but without any highlights. Perhaps as the vines age the residual character of the soil is re-asserting itself, for there is no reason to believe the wine is any less carefully made. Still a wine to watch.

Château Cantemerle
5ᵉ Cru Classé. Owner: **Société Assurances Mutuelles du Batiment et Travaux Publics.** Administrator: **Jean Cordier. 53ha. 20,000 cases.** Mer 40%, CS 40%, CF 18%, PV 2%.
This famous old property, after a period of decline, has now been rapidly restored to its former glory. It achieved a great and deserved reputation

when Pierre Dubos was proprietor, a regime which lasted over 50 years and corresponded roughly with the first half of this century. Then came the division among a number of heirs, a constant problem in France, and the result was a lack of money and direction, so decline and decay set in. The turning point came in 1980 with the sale to a syndicate of which Domaines Cordier are part. Cordier are responsible for the management and marketing, their partners have provided the finance. The *cuvier* and *chais* have been modernized, with stainless-steel fermentation vats taking the place of the old wooden ones.

The style of Cantemerle leans towards lightness and elegance combined with good richness in the middle flavour. With the *cuvier* being rebuilt at the time, I found the first vintage of the new regime disappointing and dull. The 81 was better but not special, but then in 82 and 83 superb wines were made, with an opulence and richness only encountered in exceptional years. So the future looks bright indeed.

Château Caronne-Ste.-Gemme
Cru Grand Bourgeois Exceptionnel. Owners: **Jean & François Nony-Borie.** 45ha. 23,000 cases. CS 65%, Mer 35%.
This very good *cru* is deservedly becoming much better known since François Nony-Borie became involved in the management in the early 1980s. The family has owned it since 1900. The vineyards are separated from Camensac and the rest of St-Laurent by the Jalle du Nord, which divides St-Julien from Cussac, and the nearest vineyard is Lanessan in Camensac. So the situation of the vineyards is rather special.

My overall impression of the wines here is that they are very well made, have more style and breed than most St-Laurent wines with nothing rustic about them. But there is a strong assertive character which clearly comes through, nicely balanced with fruit, and resulting in some complexity. The 83 is tannic but has plenty of fat, bigger than the 81 and finer perhaps than 79. The 82 is excellent, with the concentration typical of the year. 81, 80, 79 and 78 are all good examples of these years. This is really a top Cru Bourgeois, with excellent keeping qualities.

Château Cissac
Cru Grand Bourgeois Exceptionnel. Owners: **M & Mme Louis Vialard** and **Mlle Danielle Vialard.** 30ha. 13,500 cases. CS 75%, Mer 20%, PV 5%.
Cissac has been inseparably linked for over a generation with Louis Vialard, who comes from an old *médocain* family. They have owned it since 1885, and Louis Vialard has lived here since 1940. Everything is traditional: old vines, wooden fermenting vats, and of course ageing in cask, of which 50% are normally new, an unusually high proportion for a Cru Bourgeois.

In 1971 Louis Vialard made some important changes in his methods. He stopped adding *vin de presse*, using only free-run juice; he began vintaging later, and he increased the proportion of Cabernet Franc, at the expense of the Cabernet Sauvignon. In 1983 he gave a tasting of the vintages of the 60s and 70s to assess the results. For me the most noticeable difference was caused by the *vin de presse*; it gave the older vintages a background of flavour and complexity lacking in most of the younger wines, except for the 75, itself a year exceptionally rich in tannin and extract. In otherwise excellent years such as 76, 78 and 79, a certain leanness was perceptible. The Cabernet Franc at Cissac tended to lack body and colour, somewhat diluting the final blend, and this grape has now been eliminated. This is a fine *cru*, whose wines have real breed and elegance, and reward keeping.

Château Citran
Cru Grand Bourgeois Exceptionnel. Owner: **Jean Cesselin.** 84ha. 32,000 cases. Mer 65%, CS 35%.
This is the most important *cru* in Avensan. Part of the vineyard lies close to the village, but the oldest part is between the château and Paveil-de-Luze. When the Miailhe family bought the property in 1945 there was hardly any vineyard left. For many years, until 1980, Jean Miailhe of Château Coufran ran the property and expanded the vineyards to their present size and established a fine reputation for the wine. He then handed over to his sister and brother-in-law, the present proprietors.

The wines have a good reputation. I have found them to have an excellent bouquet with pronounced fruit. They have a good flavour and balance with a certain earthiness, but can be dry in lesser years or in years of high yield such as 79.

Château Coufran

Cru Grand Bourgeois. Owner: **Société Civile**. Administrator: **Jean Miailhe. 64ha. 33,600 cases. Mer 85%, CS 10%, PV 5%**. Second label: **Château La Rose-Maréchale.**

The very high proportion of Merlot here is unusual for the Médoc, even on these heavier soils. The result is an easy, supple, fruity wine for early drinking without much style or personality and distinctly on the light side. But this is good commercial claret and fulfils its declared purpose of producing easy-to-enjoy Médoc at a very reasonable price.

Château Dillon

Cru Bourgeois 1932. Owner: **Lycée Agricole de Bordeaux-Blanquefort. 35ha, 18,500 cases. Red: Mer 50%, CS 44%, CF 6%. White: Sauv 100%**. Second label: **Château Lucas (Bordeaux Blanc).**

This *cru* takes it name from an emigré Irishman who was a general in the French army and acquired the property in 1754. It has belonged to the Lycée Agricole since 1956, and they have made improvements in the *cuvier* in order to carry out temperature-controlled fermentation. At their best, the wines produced here are light and elegantly flavoured, but there have been lapses in consistency. Some good wines were made in the 1970s especially the 70, 75 and 79. But then a new parcel of young vines was added and little or no selection was employed, and the wines have taken a step backwards again. So one must wait and see.

Château Fontesteau

Cru Grand Bourgeois. Owner: **Jean Renaud. 11ha. 5,000 cases. Mer 40%, CS 30%, CF 30%.**

From 1939 until 1984 the owner of Fontesteau was René Eglise. Since 1984 it has been owned by Jean Renaud. The name comes from *fontaines d'eau*, because there are a number of old wells on the property. The wines are made quite traditionally, with fermentation in concrete vats and ageing in casks. I found the 79 vintage had a note of *goût de terroir*. It was already attractive and desirable at five years old, but rather lacked personality, which is unusual for the St-Sauveur commune. It will be interesting to see what the new owner achieves.

Château Hanteillan

Cru Grand Bourgeois. Owner: **SARL du Château Hanteillan. 83ha. 35,000 cases. CS 48%, Mer 42%, CF 6%, PV and Mal 4%**. Second label: **Château Larrivaux-Hanteillan.**

In 1972 this property was bought by a group of partners connected to France's largest construction company. A high proportion of Merlot reflects the clay present in parts of the vineyard. The property used to share the same owners as Château Coutelin-Merville in St-Estèphe, and the vineyards adjoin one another. Despite Coutelin-Merville's superior appellation, I have found that Hanteillan today makes a more impressive wine.

The rich, well structured 79 showed how well the rather young vineyard is maturing, as well as the careful selection which had been exercised in a year of high yield. This is a serious wine with some real breed, which should be followed with interest as the vineyard matures.

Château Lagune

3ᵉ Cru Classé. Owner: **Société Civile Agricole**. Administrator: **Jean-Michel Ducellier. 55ha. 25,000 cases. CS 55%, CF 20%, Mer 20%, PV 5%**. Second label: **Château Ludon-Pomiès-Agassac.**

The restoration of La Lagune began when it was bought by Georges Burnet in 1957. This dynamic man replanted the vineyard and reconstructed the *chais*, where he installed a marvellous system of stainless steel pipes to bring the new wine straight from the vats to the barrels and also to carry out racking entirely mechanically and without contact with the air. It was a revolutionary system when installed over 25 years ago, but no one else has yet copied it, which seems surprising. Unfortunately Burnet did too much too quickly and ran short of money so had to sell in 1961, having made the mistake of selling that great year *sur souche* (on the vine, before the harvest). It was bought by the Champagne house of Ayala for whom Jean-Michel Ducellier is today the administrator. The *régisseuse* is a woman, the redoubtable Madame Boyrie, and her meticulous hand is visible everywhere.

Now the vineyard has come of age a series of splendid wines have given La Lagune an enviable reputation. This is a wine of great elegance, very perfumed, usually rather marked by new wood at the start (100% new wood is usual here) but this is soon absorbed to give a very rich, supple flavour with great finesse. The years 83, 82, 81, 79, 78, 76 and 75 are all great successes. I think the 80 has suffered slightly from the new wood policy and could have been better with less. A wine clearly of 2ᵉ Cru Classé standing today.

Château de Lamarque

Cru Grand Bourgeois. Owner: Société Civile Gromand d'Evry. Administrator: Roger Gromand. 47ha. 25,000 cases. CS 50%, Mer 25%, CF 20%, PV 5%. Second label: Réserve du Marquis d'Evry.

The château here is the best preserved and most impressive fortress in the Médoc to have survived from the English period in Aquitaine. Although parts of it date from the 11th and 12th centuries the main structure is 14th century with some 17th-century alterations. It lies between the *route des châteaux* and the ferry to Blaye, but is well concealed amid the trees of its park. Until recently the wine of Lamarque was unknown, but a reconstruction of vineyards and *chais* was undertaken in the 1960s which is now bearing fruit. The château has been handed on by inheritance since 1841 when it was acquired by the Comte de Fumel, passing via a daughter to the present owner Marie-Louise Burnet d'Evry, who married Roger Gromand. He is the driving force behind the renaissance of Lamarque, and with Professor Emile Peynaud's constant advice and supervision he has again established a reputation for the wines. The wine is matured in casks, a quarter of which are new each year.

In the 1970s I found the wines light and agreeable in the good vintages, but without much personality. On tasting the 83, however, I noted sappy, scented fruit on the nose, a fine flavour with lots of richness and extract, and great harmony. Clearly the vineyard has come of age, and this is now a wine to watch.

Château Lanessan

Cru Bourgeois Supérieur 1932. Owner: Bouteiller family. Administrator: Hubert Bouteiller. 40ha. 12,000 cases. CS 75%, Mer 20%, CF and PV 5%.

Since 1790 this property has effectively been in the same family, the Delbos, whose name still appears on the label alongside that of Bouteiller, handed from father to son till 1909, when the daughter of the last male Delbos inherited. She was married to Etienne Bouteiller. Hubert Bouteiller, the present member of the family in charge, has his house here. A feature of Lanessan unrelated to wine is the carriage museum, where the original stables and harness room are displayed together with a fine assortment of carriages.

The wines of Lanessan have a strong and marked personality. There is a tendency to firmness at first, but in good years the wines have great fruit and richness and considerable breed. They are also very consistent. There is a great capacity for ageing. I have tasted a number of old vintages going back to 1916, all of them well preserved and many outstanding. Recently 83, 82 and 81 were all very fine examples of these years. A useful and elegant 80 was made, and even the 77 was good. This is a wine for those who love fine Médocs for their own sake and are not slaves to labels.

Château Larose-Trintaudon

Cru Grand Bourgeois. Owner: Société Civile. 172ha. 80,000 cases. CS 60%, CF 20%, Mer 20%.

Bought and developed by the Forner family in the 1960s this is now the largest vineyard in the Médoc. Mechanical harvesting is used, but all the wines are matured in casks of which 30% are new each year.

The aim is to produce fruity, light-textured wines which can be drunk young, and the 76 is a good example of this. I was surprised to find the 79 still rather aggressive at five years old, but pleasantly scented and spicy.

Château Lestage-Simon

Cru Bourgeois. Owner: Charles Simon. 32ha. 16,600 cases. Mer 68%, CS 22%, CF 10%.

The wines here are typical of St-Seurin: fine, robust and solid, with the Merlot giving fruit and suppleness. I was once given a bottle of the 29 by a former proprietor, and it had kept splendidly. Today's wines are made for earlier drinking but are none the worse for that.

Château Liversan

Cru Grand Bourgeois. Owner: Prince Guy de Polignac. 48ha. 20,000 cases. CS 49%, Mer 38%, CF 10%, PV 3%.

Since 1983 Liversan has been owned by the Polignacs, formerly the principal share-holders of Champagne Pommery. They immediately installed a new *cuvier* with stainless steel fermentation vats. The wines are now to be aged in oak with a good proportion of new wood. The 83 was rich, strong and assertive in cask, typical of this area behind Pauillac – good four-square Médoc and very attractive. With the dedication of the new owners to quality and plenty of mature vines in the vineyard, this is one worth following again, and should produce one of the best Crus Bourgeois among the inland communes north of St-Laurent.

Château de Malleret
Cru Grand Bourgeois. Owner: Société Civile (Marquis du Vivier). 59ha. 25,000 cases. CS 70%, Mer 15%, CF 10%, PV 5%. Second label: Château Lemoine-Nexon.

These wines are extremely scented and elegant, very fruity with real length of flavour and a quite seductive charm. Despite the high proportion of Cabernet Sauvignon and the small amount of Merlot, the character of the delightful 80 seems to suggest Merlot rather than Cabernet first, which emphasizes again the important role of the soil. Very good wines were also made in 79 and 81.

Château Le Meynieu
Cru Grand Bourgeois. Owner: Jacques Pédro. 14ha. 5,000 cases. CS 70%, Mer 30%.

The energetic and meticulous Jacques Pédro is mayor of Vertheuil as well as proprietor of this *cru* along with Lavillotte and Domaine de la Ronceray. His aim is to make very typical Médocs with plenty of tannin but developing bouquet and finesse in bottle.

Cave Coopérative La Paroisse
Owner: Union de Producteurs. 120ha. 61,000 cases.

The Coopérative founded in 1935 now has 60 adherents and is considered the best coop in the Haut-Médoc appellation. Most of the wine is sold in bulk to négociants or under the La Paroisse brand, but a few property wines are kept separate. These are: Château Quimper, Domaine du Haut et de Brion, Château Le Tralle, Domaine de Villa and Château Maurac.
   These are solid, well balanced wines which resemble the lesser St-Estèphes but usually have more flesh.

Château Ramage-la-Bâtisse
Cru Bourgeois. Owner: Société Civile. 52ha. 25,000 cases. CS 60%, Mer 40%. Alternative label: Château Tourteran. Second label: Château Dutellier.

This is a combination of several properties which have been put together since 1961. The wines are very scented (I detected a smell of violets) and extremely fruity and easy to drink. It is easy to see why they have created quite a reputation for themselves in a short while.

Château Sénéjac
Cru Bourgeois Supérieur 1932. Owner: Charles de Guigné. 18ha. 7,500 cases. CS 40%, CF 24%, Mer 30%, PV 6%.

There is an international air about Sénéjac. The proprietor is an American citizen of French origin, and he is now assisted by a woman oenologist from New Zealand. The wines are good and have made progress recently. They are completely different from those of de Malleret, the other important *cru* of Pian. They are deep-coloured and perfumed, but classically austere and tannic. These wines are made to last and do last, as the older vintages show. They have a good following among many traditional English wine merchants, and one can see why.

Château Sociando-Mallet
Cru Grand Bourgeois. Owner: Jean Gautreau. 30ha. 18,500 cases. CS 60%, Mer 30%, CF 10%. Second label: Château Lartigue-de-Brochon.

The aim here is to produce very traditional Médocs. There is long vatting, for maximum extraction of colour and tannins, and maturing in casks, of which between a third and half are new – a very high proportion for a Cru Bourgeois. When young the wines are very taut and marked by new wood at a stage when other wines are beginning to be drinkable. The 79, for instance, was like this in 84. But with patience the wines develop a fine flavour and character.

Château du Taillan
Cru Grand Bourgeois. Owner: Henri-François Cruse. 20ha. 8,000 cases. CS 55%, Mer 40%, CF 5%. White wine: Château La Dame-Blanche.

This has belonged to the Cruses since 1896. The château and the even older cellars are classified as historic monuments. The wine is kept mostly in large wooden *foudres* of 80 to 170hl, but 20% passes through new casks of the conventional size.

The aim here is to produce supple, easy-to-drink wines without much tannin. The white wine, La Dame-Blanche, is made from 67% Sauvignon and 33% Colombard, which gives the wine a character rather different from the usual Bordeaux Blanc, with much more obvious flowery fruit.

Château la Tour-Carnet
4e Cru Classé. Owner: Mme Marie-Claire Pelegrin. 31ha. 14,000 cases. CS 33%, Mer 33%, CF 33%, PV 1%.

Like so much else in St-Laurent, la Tour-Carnet was on its last legs when Louis Lipschitz bought it in 1962. In the early days the Ginestets gave technical assistance and sold the wine on an exclusive basis. After Louis Lipschitz died his daughter and her husband continued the work.

The wines are conscientiously made, and one-third new wood is used in making them. At their best the wines are vivid in colour, very fruity and intense in flavour, but light. The 76 was very attractive but hardly of Quatrième Cru standing, but I found the 80 irony, austere and dry – a disappointment for the year. Certainly a number of unclassified wines are better than this.

Château Tour-du-Haut-Moulin
Cru Grand Bourgeois. Owner: Laurent Poitou. 32ha. 12,000 cases. CS and CF 50%, Mer 45%, PV 5%.

The vineyards of this *cru* lie beside those of Beaumont around the village of Cussac, but the wines are very different. Laurent Poitou is the fourth generation of his family to own this *cru*, and he makes fine traditional wines. They are aged in wood, of which 25% is new. The result is a wine of exceptional colour and rich in extract. Tannic and powerful but well balanced, these wines have great character, and with ageing their very real breed emerges.

Château Tour-du-Mirail
Cru Bourgeois 1932. Owners: Helène & Danielle Vialard. 18ha. 9,000 cases. CS 70%, Mer 25%, PV 5%.

This property has belonged to the daughters of Louis Vialard of neighbouring Château Cissac since 1970. Louis Vialard himself supervises the winemaking, but everything is quite separate from Cissac. Vinification is in stainless steel vats, and the wines are matured in cask. They have a lot of flavour and a well projected and quite perfumed bouquet. At the same time they are fairly light in body and have a certain Cabernet Sauvignon "edge". Despite their firmness, I find these wines are at present more enjoyable when fairly young (five to seven years), before the fruit begins to fade. This is an honourable Cru Bourgeois, but at present lacks the style and charm of Cissac.

Château Verdignan
Cru Grand Bourgeois. Owner: Société Civile. Administrator: Jean Miailhe. 47ha. 30,000 cases. CS 55%, Mer 40%, CF 5%. Second label: Château Plantey-de-la-Croix.

Coufran is the last château in the Haut-Médoc and this is the last but one – and both are administered or owned by Jean Miailhe. Verdignan has an attractive château with a tall turret, easily visible from the road. When Jean Miailhe bought it in 1972 the reputation of Verdignan was not very good. I remember wines of rather tough character during the 1960s. Now Jean's son Eric is in charge of the winemaking, as he is at Coufran. The wine is fermented in stainless steel and matured in cask. As one would expect of a wine from St-Seurin, this is solid and well-structured with a strong flavour, but it also has lots of fruit, something that was constantly lacking in the past.

Château de Villegorge
Cru Bourgeois Supérieur Exceptionnel 1932. Owner: Lucien Lurton. 12ha. 2,700 cases. Mer 60%, CS 30%, CF 10%.

Villegorge has long enjoyed a good reputation. It was one of only six Crus Bourgeois classified as Exceptionnel in 1932, and was again classified as an Exceptionnel in 1966. However, Lucien Lurton took it out of the Syndicat after he bought it in 1973, so it did not feature in the 78 classification made by the Syndicat. The soil here is extremely gravelly, resembling that of Margaux. Largely abandoned by vignerons, it has in recent years become prey to gravel merchants, so the countryside is now scarred with pits filled with water. Lucien Lurton is now engaged in a battle to prevent further dispoiling of his countryside. The fermentation is in stainless steel, and the wine is matured in cask with 25% new wood. The vineyard here is particularly prone to frost damage, and the result is low and irregular yields. The high proportion of Merlot is most unusual in the Médoc.

The wines of Villegorge have always been deep-coloured, with a very strong character, and they remain so under Lucien Lurton with the difference that they are now rather more polished and less rustic than they sometimes were. Excellent wines were made in 83, 82 and 81.

MÉDOC AC

The fortunes of this area have revived considerably in recent years. Between 1972 and 1983 the area under vine has increased by 62%, from 1,836 hectares to 2,977. Wine is now produced in 16 communes, of which the most important are Bégadan (by far the largest), St Yzans, Pregnac, Ordonnac, St-Christoly, Blaignan and St-Germain-d'Esteuil.

Because of the heavier soils, even where there are good outcrops of gravel, more Merlot is found here than in the Haut-Médoc and therefore a lower proportion of Cabernet Sauvignon. The wines are pleasantly perfumed, especially when young, and develop quite a lot of finesse in bottle. They are mostly light in body but well flavoured. There are plenty of good Crus Bourgeois – nine were designated as Grands Bourgeois in 1978.

Cave Coopérative Bellevue

Owner: Société Coopérative de Vinification d'Ordonnac. 226ha. 100,000 cases. Mer 50%, CS 45%, CF 5%.

The cooperative at Ordonnac was founded in 1936 and has 75 members drawn from this commune and the neighbouring one of St-Germain-d'Esteuil. The following individual *crus* are vinified here: Château de Brie, Château Belfort, Château Lagorce, Château Moulin-de-Buscateau, Château Moulin-de-la-Rivière, Château l'Oume-de-Pey, Château La Rose-Picot, Domain du Grand-Bois and Château Les Graves. The coop is also a member of Uni-Médoc, the association of *caves coopératives* of Médoc, and supplies much wine in bulk for négociants' own brands as well as under its own marque of Pavillon de Bellevue. This is good, dependable Médoc.

Château La Cardonne

Cru Grand Bourgeois. Owner: Domaines Rothschild. 85ha. 35,000 cases. CS 72%, Mer 23%, CF and PV 5%.

This large property, the most important in Blaignan, has been part of Domaines Rothschild since 1973, since when the vineyard has been considerably expanded, and the existing buildings restored and the equipment replaced. The vineyard is very well placed on the highest plateau of the region. The wines do not see wood at all, being entirely matured in vat prior to bottling.

I have found the wines deep-coloured, very perfumed, very fruity, frank and fresh. This is archetypal Médoc, straightforward and easy to enjoy young.

Château Castéra

Cru Bourgeois. Owner: Alexis Lichine & Co. 45ha. 15,000 cases. CS and CF 60%, Mer 40%.

This is one of the principal *crus* of St-Germain-d'Esteuil. It is an old property which has links with the Black Prince, who beseiged the original château. Since 1973 it has belonged to Alexis Lichine & Co., the important Bordeaux négociants, who have enlarged the vineyard and modernized the *chais*. This is a good solid enjoyable Médoc, developing a mellow, fruity character, full and soft when quite young. Can be enjoyed from three years onwards.

Cuvée de la Commanderie du Bontemps

The word *cuvée* means here a quantity of different wines blended together in a vat (*cuve*). The origin of this particular *cuvée* was that members of the Bontemps used to donate one cask of their production which was then assembled to make the *cuvée*. This meant that it was composed of wines from all over the Médoc and Haut-Médoc including both Crus Classés and Cru Bourgeois. Then, with the introduction of compulsory château-bottling for the Crus Classés in 1972, this concept was no longer possible, and it was eventually decided to set up *commission de dégustation* to control by means of both analyses and tasting the selection of wines for a Cuvée du Bontemps. They appointed Jean-Paul Gardère to prepare the *cuvée*. He is not only a courtier of long standing and impeccable reputation, but also from 1965 to 1984 the Manager of Château Latour. The Cuvée du

Bontemps is commercialized through a house called Ulysse Cazabonne, belonging to Monsieur Gardère.

The wines of this Cuvée are, as one would expect, classic Médoc, with real depth of flavour and beautifully balanced fruit and tannin. The component parts actually all come from the Haut-Médoc. A *cuvée* is not produced every year, but only when it is considered that one of sufficient quality can be made. Recent vintages have been 83, 82, 81, 79 and 78. All are fine examples of their respective years.

Château Greysac

Cru Grand Bourgeois. Owner: Domaines Codem (Baron François de Gunzburg). 60ha. 35,000 cases. CS and CF 60%, Mer 38%, PV 2%.

Since Baron François de Gunzburg bought this château in 1973 its importance has increased considerably. Fermentation is in stainless steel *cuves* and the wine is aged in cask.

I have found the wines to have an expansive and almost opulent fruity flavour, with a rather overripe style in the best vintages. The wines can be drunk with great pleasure when three to four years old.

Château Loudenne

Cru Grand Bourgeois. Owner: W & A Gilbey Ltd. 50ha. Red: 15,000 cases; CS 53%, Mer 40%, CF 7%. White: 5,000 cases; Sauv 50%, Sém 50%.

The wines of Loudenne tend to be lighter in colour, but with more perfume and finesse than most wines in the Médoc AC. There is a real elegance about them which becomes more noticeable as the wines mature in bottle.

The excellent white wine is fermented in stainless steel at between 17° and 20°C. It is delicious, perfumed and elegant soon after bottling in the spring, but the Sémillon allows for ageing as well.

Château Les Ormes-Sorbet

Cru Grand Bourgeois. Owner: Jean Boivert. 20ha. 10,000 cases. CS 65%, Mer 35%.

The wines here are nicely perfumed and elegant, with a strong assertive Cabernet flavour and plenty of structure. Like many wines in the Bas-Médoc, they have lots of flavour but not a lot of body. Very good wines were made in 83, 82, 81 and 79, with more *goût de terroir* and body than usual. And there was a very classic 78.

About half the crop is sold to Schröder & Schÿler in bulk for their own bottling, and the rest is château-bottled. This is an excellent example of what the Bas-Médoc can do with care and dedication.

Château Patache-d'Aux

Cru Grand Bourgeois. Owner: Société Civile. 38ha. 21,500 cases. CS 70%, Mer 20%, CF 10%.

This *cru* has had a good reputation for many years and belonged to the Delon family (see Léoville-Las-Cases and Potensac) until Claude Lapalu bought it in 1964. The actual château now belongs to the municipality. The fermentation is partly still in wooden *cuves* and partly in concrete and stainless steel vats, but all the wine is matured in cask.

The wines are finely perfumed, with clear overtones of violets and Cabernet, finely flavoured, fruity and supple, quite light in body but with a good backbone.

Château Potensac

Cru Grand Bourgeois. Owner: Mme Paul Delon. Administrator: Michel Delon. 40ha. 20,000 cases. CS 55%, Mer 25%, CF 20%. Secondary labels: Château Gallais-Bellevue, Château Lassalle.

There is a good gravelly outcrop at Potensac lying between St-Yzans and St-Germain-d'Esteuil, where the Delon family (see Léoville-Las-Cases) own three vineyards. Good wines have been made here for years, but in the last decade, under Michel Delon's management, they seem to have gone from strength to strength. The biggest vineyard is Potensac itself, then come Lassalle and Gallais-Bellevue, and the three are effectively run together. The *cuvier* has been re-equipped with stainless steel *cuves*, and the wines enjoy a long, slow fermentation, followed by ageing in casks drawn from Léoville-Las-Cases, with the addition of 20% new casks each year.

The wines are characterized by their depth of colour and a nose full of vigour and very typical of the Médoc, often with spicy or floral overtones. They have a concentrated, complex and powerful flavour, and a rather angular structure. Usually one must wait five or six years for these wines to be at their best for drinking, and they last very well. The vintages of 83,

82 and 81 were very fine. Those of 79 and 78 were good, and 76 was exceptional. The 80 is good in its class. This is certainly one of the best wines today in the Médoc AC.

Château St-Bonnet

Cru Bourgeois 1978. Owner: Michel Solivères. 35ha. 18,000 cases. CS 50%, Mer 50%.

Some excellent wines are made in St-Christoly, and this is one of the most important *crus* there. It is a very traditional Médoc with a very marked character. The wines are deep in colour with a distinctively spicy bouquet and a robust, powerful flavour where tannin and fruit are well balanced. There is a distinct *goût de terroir* which is arresting but attractive.

Cave Coopérative St-Jean

President: René Chaumont. 567ha. 300,000 cases. Mer 50%, CS 24%, CF 24%, PV 2%.

The Cave St-Jean, also referred to as the Cave Coopérative de Bégadan, is by far the largest cooperative in the Médoc AC. Its 170 members come not only from this commune but also from the neighbouring ones of Valeyrac and Civrac. It is also a member of Uni-Médoc, a group of four cooperatives for stocking and maturing the wines of the region. The external buildings have a capacity of more than 60,000 hectolitres. The following châteaux vinify their wines separately at the *cave*: Meilhan, Breuil-Renaissance, Le Barrail, Labadie, Pey-de-By, Lassus, Le Bernet, Le Monge, Bégadanet, Vimenay, Rose-du-Pont, Haut-Condissas.

The produce of this cooperative has a good reputation. Much of it is supplied to négociants for their own generic blends. These wines are characteristic and attractive Médocs.

Cave Coopérative St-Roch

Owner: Société Coopérative de Vinification de Queyrac. 125ha. 50,000 cases.

This cooperative was founded in 1939 and now has 165 members, drawn from the communes of Queyrac, Gaillan, Jau-Dignac-et-Loirac, Vensac, Valeyrac and Vendays. Three individual *crus* are vinified here: Château Laubespin, Château Les Trois-Tétons and Château Pessange. The cooperative is a member of Uni-Médoc, so that, apart from its own marque of St-Roch, much of the wine is sold in bulk to négociants for their own blends, contributing to the good overall standard today of generic Médoc.

Cave Coopérative de St-Yzans-de-Médoc

Owner: Société Coopérative. 200ha. 100,000 cases. Mer 55%, CS and CF 45%.

The cooperative of St-Yzans has 120 members and was founded in 1934. The wines are sold under the name of St-Brice or in bulk to négociants for their own marques. The *cave* has a good reputation for making fine typical Médocs. Apart from those in St-Yzans itself, St-Brice also has members in Blaignan, Couquèques and St-Christoly. Two châteaux, Taffard and Tour-St-Vincent, vinify their grapes here.

Château Sigognac

Cru Grand Bourgeois. Owner: Société Civile Fermière. Administrator: Mme Colette Bonny-Grasset. 44ha. 20,000 cases. CS 33⅓%, CF 33⅓%, Mer 33⅓%.

A Roman villa once stood on this site, and some of the pottery found there may be seen at the Mairie of St-Yzans. This vineyard had been reduced to only 4ha of vines when Paul Grasset bought it in 1969. Now it has been transformed, first by him and then, after his death in 1968, by his wife, now married to M Bonny. The fermentation is in concrete vats, and the wine is matured partly in vat and partly in cask. The wine has a good colour and is full and soft on the nose, with pleasant fruit and tannin on the palate, elegant rather than powerful. If it lacks the finesse of its more illustrious neighbour, Château Loudenne, this is nevertheless very pleasant, honourable Médoc of a good general standard.

Château La Tour-de-By

Cru Grand Bourgeois. Owner: Société Civile (Cailloux, Lapalu, Pagès). Administrator: Marc Pagès. 61ha. 39,000 cases. CS 65%, Mer 32%, CF 3%. Secondary labels: Château La Roque-de-By, Château Moulin-de-la-Roque.

This fine *cru* is situated on one of the highest and very best gravelly ridges in the whole of the Bas-Médoc. There is a very attractive château, and parts of the other buildings are even older and also very pleasing. The tower stands on high ground near the château, and is an old lighthouse. Since buying the property in 1965, Marc Pagès and his partners have made many improvements. They have extended the *chais* and put in some stainless steel, although the old wooden *cuves* are also retained. The wine is matured in cask with a small percentage of new oak.

The wines are deeply coloured and finely scented, and the lively, sappy fruit is often reminiscent of violets. The flavour is very harmonious and attractive. It is also powerful, with real depth, and quite tannic. Other marked characteristics are elegance and length of flavour. This château certainly has a good claim to be considered as the finest wine in the Médoc appellation today.

Château La Tour-St-Bonnet
Cru Bourgeois. Owner: Pierre Lafon. 41ha. 20,000 cases. Mer 50%, CS 28%, CF 22%. Second label: **Château La-Fuie-St-Bonnet.**
This is the largest and probably the best known *cru* in St-Christoly. The vineyard is splendidly placed on the best gravelly ridges of the commune, with its distinctive tower among the vines. The wines, very typical of the Médoc, are highly coloured, vigorous and powerful. They require some ageing to show of their best.

Cave Coopérative du Vieux-Clocher
Owner: Uni-Médoc. 1,200ha.
The newest of the Médoc cooperatives is situated at Gaillan, 2km north of Lesparre. Founded in 1979 this is a grouping of the five cooperatives at Bégadan, Ordonnac, Prignac and Queyrac, as well as joining together the old cooperatives of Prignac and Gaillan. The aim is to hold a maturing stock of around 2 million bottles. The wines are commercialized through the Union des Caves Coopératives Vinicoles Sovicop-Producta. The brand name is Préstige-Médoc. A good standard is maintained.

GRAVES

It is not easy to get to grips with this disparate region. Geographically, it is a continuation of Médoc, but in the north many vineyards have disappeared beneath Bordeaux's urban sprawl, and further south one can motor for miles and see nothing but trees and believe one is already in Les Landes. This used to be a region of many mediocre whites and a few aristocratic reds, but this picture has changed significantly in the past 20 years. The changing pattern can be gauged to an extent from the following table comparing production figures for 1970 and 1982.

	1970	1982	Increase
Graves Rouge	40,958hl	100,869hl	+146%
Graves Blanc	10,095hl	64,043hl }	+51%
Graves Supérieures	45,558hl	20,100hl }	

This demonstrates the two important trends: from white to red, and from alcoholic whites (12% alcohol by volume minimum, plus some residual sugar) to dryer, lighter (11%) ones. The term Graves Supérieures here refers purely to the alcohol level, and such wines usually have some residual sugar as well. The table also shows the revival in the district as a whole, with total production up 91.5% when these two large vintages 12 years apart are compared. In the past decade, the areas under vine have developed as follows:

	1970	1982	Increase
Graves Rouge	1,172ha	1,904ha	+62%
Graves Blanc	1,486ha	763ha	−48%
	2,658ha	2,667	

This shows that the expansion of the red vineyards has been almost wholly at the expense of the whites; yet, in spite of this, as we have seen already, white as well as red wine production has increased. Clearly new vineyards and better husbandry have brought much higher yields.

The 1982 edition of Féret's *Bordeaux et ses Vins* clearly monitors the decline of the vineyards which have been caught up in the expansion of Bordeaux. In the four communes most affected, Gradignan, Merignac, Pessac and Talence, there were 119 wine-making properties in 1908; by 1981 there were only nine. In the whole of Graves in 1981 there were 33 communes where some declarations under the Graves AC were being made (in several others entitled to the appellation, only Bordeaux or Bordeaux Supérieur was declared). But most of the wines are actually being made in eight communes: Léognan and Martillac in the north;

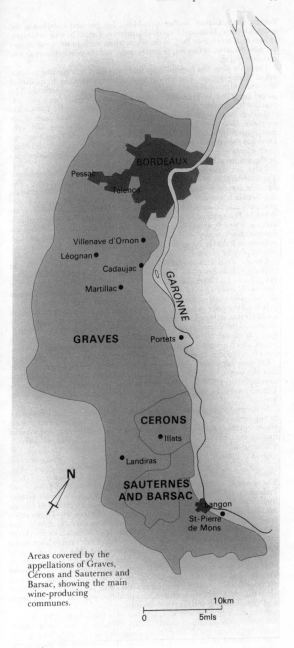

Areas covered by the appellations of Graves, Cérons and Sauternes and Barsac, showing the main wine-producing communes.

Portets, Illats, Cérons, St-Pierre-de-Mons, Langon and Landiras in the south. Of these, Illats and Cérons also produce Cérons as well as Graves. However, it seems that 80% of the white wines made in these communes are now declared as Graves, as are the reds, and the proportion is almost certainly rising.

There are plenty of hopeful signs that the region is beginning to come out of its long decline. There is the general improvement in the quality of dry white Graves through the use of cold fermentation methods. The gospel preached by Professor Peynaud in the 1960s has been put into practice by men like André Lurton and Pierre Coste. André Lurton has reclaimed large tracts of abandoned vineyards in the best parts of the northern Graves. Pierre Coste has made many delicious and very inexpensive white and red wines in the southern Graves. Peter Vinding-Diers has shown what the whole gamut of modern technology, including yeast selection, can do to transform wines coming from quite modest sites in the southern Graves.

There are differing views as to the best *encépagement* for white wines. Traditionally the Sauvignon and the Sémillon are blended together. The Sauvignon gives the initial fruit, on the nose especially, and acidity, while the Sémillon provides the possibility of bottle ageing. Its bouquet gradually takes over as the Sauvignon begins to fade after one to two years in bottle. It also gives the wine body. However, in the search for freshness and fruit for early drinking, some properties have abandoned the Sémillon entirely. Such wines tend to lose their charm rather quickly, and my impression is that many growers are now realizing that the Sémillon has a role to play in giving balance to the wines.

The list of red wine available ranges from some of the greatest wines in Gironde (Haut-Brion, La Mission-Haut-Brion, Domaine de Chevalier, Haut-Bailly and Pape-Clément) to a host of very modestly priced and deliciously vivid wines of individuality. All have the Cabernet Sauvignon as the major variety, assisted by the Merlot and the Cabernet Franc.

It is taking time to bring the wine-drinker back to an appreciation of white Graves, so poor had its image been. But, as more and more fine wines come onto the market at very reasonable prices, their following is bound to grow. With the red wines, the special charm of these Cabernet-based wines, which are quite distinct in character from their Médocain cousins, are bound to win more friends as they become more widely available.

On the quality front, the growers in the north have now won the right to add the names of Pessac and Léognan to Graves on their labels. The developments made by Eschenauer at their properties, added to André Lurton's work, are helping to give new impetus and encouragement in this area.

So the prospects of Graves taking a larger share of Bordeaux's prosperity in the future look bright. The world-wide demand for good dry white wines and the continuously growing market for middle-price red wines of quality must make Graves a happy hunting ground for wine-lovers.

Château d'Archambeau
Owner: Jean-Philippe Dubourdieu. 22ha. Red: 5,000 cases; Mer 50%, CS 40%, CF 10%. White: 6,000 cases; Sem 70%, Musc 20%, Sauv 10%. Second label: Château Mourlet.

The commune of Illats which adjoins Barsac, like those of Cérons and Podensac, can vinify its white wines either as Cérons or as Graves Supérieur. Here at d'Archambeau only very small quantities of Cérons are now made, and the emphasis is on classic dry Graves. The Dubourdieu family have a formidable reputation as wine-makers in Barsac and Graves, and Jean-Philippe, nephew of Pierre Dubourdieu of Doisy-Daene fame, is no exception. The white wines are cold-fermented in lined metal and stainless steel vats, and bottled in the spring. The combination of Sémillon and Sauvignon produces wines of elegance and depth of character which are delicious within months of bottling, but also keep and mature well. The red wine is a more recent development, the first commercialized vintage from young vines being the 82. The wines have vivid fruit and immediate charm, and doubtless will take on more depth and complexity as the vineyard matures.

Château La Blancherie and Château La Blancherie-Peyret
Owner: F.-C. Braud-Coussié. 18ha. White: 10ha; 5,000 cases; Sém 70%, Sauv 30%. Red: 8ha; 4,000 cases; CS 70%, Mer 30%.

The commune of La Brède is famous for its château of the same name, where Montesquieu, the renowned 17th-century philosopher and historian was born and lived. Today this is the most important wine-producing château of the commune. It also has a history of its own, for its proprietors at the time of the Revolution of 1789 were both guillotined! The white wines (sold under the La Blancherie label) are fermented at low temperatures, the red (La Blancherie-Peyret) receive a long maceration and are aged in cask. The whites are fruity and vigorous in style. The reds have a really arresting bouquet, very redolent of tobacco and spice, and lots of flavour and character, but are supple and powerful at the same time, so that they can be drunk young yet can also age. This is an excellent *cru*, with well made wines.

Château Bouscaut

Cru Classé. Owner: Société Anonyme du Château Bouscaut (Jean-Bernard Delmas & Lucien Lurton). Red: 32ha; 11,500 cases; Mer 55%, CS 35%, CF 5%, Malbec 5%. White: 10ha; 2,100 cases; Sém 52%, Sauv 48%.

The only important *cru* in Cadaujac and the Graves Cru Classé closest to the Garonne. Between 1968 and 1980 an American syndicate led by Charles Wohlstetter rescued the property from neglect installing up-to-date equipment and restoring the 18th-century château. During this period, Jean Delmas, *régisseur* of Haut-Brion, acted as *régisseur* here. In 1980 the Americans sold to Lucien Lurton, proprietor of Brane-Cantenac and Durfort-Vivens in Margaux as well as Climens in Barsac. The vineyards, which adjoin the Bordeaux-Toulouse road, are on gravelly ridges on limestone, perfect for natural drainage. Metal vats are used for red and white wines, the latter fermented in stainless steel at 18–20°C (64–68°F). The reds are matured in casks of which a quarter are new, while the whites spend six months in cask.

I must confess to disappointment at the Bauscaut wines of recent vintages. The reds are relatively light in colour and body, supple and pleasant but lacking in personality or any real distinction. To put it in context, there are a number of Crus Bourgeois in the Médoc which make better wine.

The white wines often seem to lack breed and "lift" or projection of flavour, though the 83 seems to have more length and breed than other recent efforts. It will be interesting to see if Lucien Lurton's flair can turn things around.

Château Cabannieux

Owner: René Barrière, Dudignac family. 20ha. Red: 8,000 cases; Mer 55%, CS 35%, CF 10%. White: 4,000 cases; Sém 75%, Sauv 25%.

This property is situated in the highest part of the commune of Portets on well drained, gravelly soil, with some traces of clay. It belongs to the same owners as the well respected négociant firm of A. & R. Barrière. The red wines are given two to three weeks in contact with the skins for maximum extraction. Part of the crop is put in cask, and a small amount of new wood is used. For the white there is a controlled low-temperature fermentation at below 20°C (68°F). The aim is to produce red wines with a pronounced Graves character, full-flavoured but soft and capable of early drinking. The white has a small percentage of Sauvignon to give the early bouquet. Both enjoy a good reputation.

Château Carbonnieux

Cru Classé. Owner: Société des Grandes Graves. Administrator: Antony Perrin. Red: 35ha; 15,000 cases; CS 50%, Mer 30%, CF 10%, PV and Mal 10%. White: 35ha. 15,000 cases; Sauv 65%, Sém 30%, Musc 5%.

This famous old property first had vineyards in the 12th century, which were revived when Benedictine monks took it over in 1741. Marc Perrin bought it in 1956, and his son now administers the property. The white wine is fermented in stainless steel and used to see no wood at all, but recently it has been put in new oak for about three months. The reds are matured in cask, of which a quarter are new oak.

The more famous white Carbonnieux comes from the largest vineyard of the Graves Cru Classés. With its Sauvignon and early bottling it is delicious when very young (9 to 18 months), then often goes through a dull stage as the primal Sauvignon fruit fades, only to emerge again as the Sémillon begins to mature and flower (after about 2½ years). In recent years this has been a most consistent wine, the best of the Crus Classés available in commercial quantities.

The red wine has in the past been rather rustic, and certainly not among the top classified Graves, but determined efforts have been made in recent vintages to improve the quality. The 83, 82, and 81 were all good, with the 81 especially so in the context of the vintage. The 80 is an attractive example of the year.

Château de Chantegrive

Owners: **Henri & Françoise Lévêque**. Red: 28ha; 15,000 cases; CS 60%, Mer 40%. White: 32ha, 17,500 cases; Sém 50%, Sauv 30%, Musc 20%. Secondary labels: **Château Bon-Dieu-des-Vignes; Château Mayne-Lévêque; Château Mayne-d'Anice.**

The Lévêques have steadily built up this property from modest beginnings. When I first visited Chantegrive there were only 15 hectares of vines; now there are 60. The soil is white sand mixed with quartz pebbles. The vinification is carefully controlled at low temperatures for the whites. The reds are aged for six months in oak vats, then for a year in cask, of which 20% is new oak, in an underground cellar.

The white wines are fresh, delicious, fruity, aromatic and easy to drink, without being quite top class. The reds are fruity and supple but with some depth as well, the sort of easy-to-drink wines that deserve more attention than they often get.

Domaine de Chevalier

Cru Classe. Owner: **Société Civile**. Administrators: **Claude Ricard & Olivier Bernard**. Red: 15ha; 5,000 cases; CS 65%, Mer 30%, CF 5%. White: 3ha; Sauv 70%, Sém 30%, 800 cases.

From 1865 to 1983 Chevalier was the property of the Ricard family, and Claude Ricard owned it from 1948. He has been obliged to sell, but the new owners, the Bernard family, have contracted him to manage the *cru* for a further five years and pass on his vast experience to Olivier Bernard, the member of the family deputed to look after the property. Here they ferment the red wine at a slightly higher temperature than is today fashionable, 32°C (90°F), to facilitate the maximum tannin extraction from the grape skins. For the maturation in cask 50% new oak is used. The white wine fermentation takes place entirely in cask at a low temperature. Then it is matured in oak, including a small proportion of new oak, for 18 months – Chevalier is the last of the great Graves to follow this procedure.

The result of this meticulous wine making is exceptional wines. The reds are deep in colour. The bouquet takes time to open out and is then complex with overtones of tobacco, while the flavour is compact and well-structured with great breed, power and length of flavour. This wine in some years can approach the quality of Haut-Brion and La Mission. It is also a slow developer. Outstanding wines were made in 83, 82, 81, 79 and 78, while the 80 and 76 were charming examples of their years.

The white wine has a different style from that of Laville or Haut-Brion perhaps because of its cask ageing. It is perfumed, firm and compact of flavour and only slowly opens out after six to eight years. It has extraordinary delicacy and finesse, and can improve and last for 15 to 20 years.

Château Couhins

Cru Classé. Owner: **Institut National de la Recherche Agronomique**. 7ha. White: 1,500 cases; Sauv 50%, Sém 50%. Red: 1,000 cases.

A curious situation exists at Couhins, which is now divided between the National Agricultural Research Institute, which owns the main part, and André Lurton, who has a smaller section (see Couhins-Lurton). For many years the Gasqueton and Hanappier families were owners and produced only white wines (this is the only property in Graves where only the white wine is classified). Then the INRA bought the property in 1968. It lies on an elevated site in Villenave-d'Ornon, with vineyards near the Garonne. This is, of course, a modern, low-temperature fermentation wine, and is fresh and elegant in style. Unfortunately, with the division of the property and the production of unclassified red wine, the small quantities available mean that this is a wine which is hard to find.

Château Couhins-Lurton

Cru Classé. Owner: **André Lurton**. White: 6ha; 400 cases; Sauv 100%.

André Lurton began as *fermier* here in 1967, just before the INRA bought from Gasqueton-Hanappier, and made the wine for the whole of Couhins during most of the 1970s. The INRA then took a major part of the property into their own control, and André Lurton was able to buy this part. The gravelly soil here has traces of clay in the subsoil, and this gives body to the wine. Unlike the INRA part, which is classically planted with both Sémillon and Sauvignon, this vineyard is 100% Sauvignon. The fermentation is in new casks (since 1982) at 16–18°C (61–64°F) followed by ten months ageing before bottling. The 1982 was very attractive with real length of flavour and beautiful fruit when three years old. I would suspect this wine to be at its most attractive between two and four years, owing to the Sauvignon. There are now plans to plant Cabernet Sauvignon and Merlot to produce red wines, and the white vineyard, already extended from 1.5ha to 6ha, will be further extended.

Château Coutet

Owners: **Marcel & Bertrand Baly.** White: 38ha; 9,000 cases; Sém 80%, Sauv 15%, Musc 5%.

This is a rather confusing wine. Everyone knows that dry wines made in Sauternes and Barsac are only allowed the Bordeaux Blanc AC. In 1977 the Baly family bought the famous Barsac *cru* of Coutet (they are also proprietors in Pujols-sur-Civon, a commune with Sauternes and Barsac on three sides of it). Now they are selling their Pujols *cru*, formerly known as Reverdon, as "Vin Sec du Château Coutet" with the Graves AC. This is a very cold-fermentation wine which I find rather disappointing at present. It has a strong aroma of gooseberries and is surprisingly skeletal for a wine with so much Sémillon.

Château du Cruzeau

Owner: **André Lurton.** Red: 41ha; 18,000 cases; CS 60%, Mer 40%. White: 9ha; Sauv 90%, Sém 10%.

Another outpost of André Lurton's viticultural empire, this is the most important *cru* in the commune of St-Médard-d'Eyrans and lies on the borders of this commune and Martillac, benefiting from the new appellation Graves-Léognan. The property was acquired by André Lurton in 1973 and entirely replanted in 1979. The vineyard is on deep gravel. Harvesting of the red grapes is by machine, while the white ones are hand-picked. The red wine is vinified in lined cement tanks and stainless steel vats at 28–30°C (82–86°F) and then matured for a year in casks of which one-third are new. The white is vinified in stainless steel and glass-lined steel vats at 16–18°C (61–64°F) and sees no new wood before bottling.

The red wine is scented, full-bodied, fruited and supple, with the capacity for ageing while at the same time being pleasant to drink after about three or four years. The white has a subtle aroma of spring blossoms allied to a pleasant fruitiness of flavour. The 83 showed this to be a wine of considerable class and potential.

Château Ferrande

Owner: **Héritiers H. Delnaud.** Administrator: **Marc Teisseire.** Red: 34ha; 15,000 cases; CS 33⅓%, CF 33⅓%, Mer 33⅓%. White: 9ha; 5,000 cases; Sém 60%, Sauv 35%, Musc 5%. Second label: **Château Lognac.**

This is the most important *cru* in the commune of Castres. Since the Delnaud family began their partnership here with Marc Teisseire in 1955 the vineyard has much been expanded and the facilities improved. Concrete and stainless steel vats are used for the vinification, and the red wine is matured in cask, with 10% new oak.

I have found the red very deep in colour with a bouquet which is lively, spicy with tobacco overtones, and a flavour that is frank and fresh, light-textured but full-flavoured and fruity. This is a very enjoyable wine which can be drunk with pleasure when three to four years old – the 81 was perfect in 85.

The white has quite a pronounced Graves flavour. It is powerful and slightly earthy but fruity. It has its admirers, but for me it has less charm and breed than the red.

Château de Fieuzal

Cru Classé. Owner: **SA Château de Fieuzal.** Administrator: **Gérard Grubelin.** 23ha. Red: 8,000 cases; CS 65%, Mer 30%, PV and Mal 5%. White: 600 cases; Sauv 60%, Sém 40%.

In 1945 a Swede, Erik Bocké, took over this property, then in a ruinous condition, and lovingly restored it. In 1974 the present proprietor took over and has continued in the same vein. The wines are fermented in lined steel vats equipped with an electronic temperature control system. The red wine is matured in casks, of which 50% are new.

The red wines here are well made, on the light side, but with elegance and a very marked and vivid fruity character. The Graves character is there, but is not too obtrusive. The reputation of this wine has grown steadily in recent years. Only a very small amount of white wine is made.

Château La Garde.

Owner: Louis Eschenauer & Co. Red: 41ha, 20,000 cases; CS 70%, Mar 30%. White: 66a; 3,000 cases; Sauv 100%.

A substantial programme of development has been undertaken here in recent years. Not only has the red wine vineyard been expanded, but an elegant, pure Sauvignon white wine has now been introduced. The red wine is soft and rather light-textured but with plenty of flavour.

Château Haut-Bailly

Cru Classé. Owner: SCI Sanders. Administrator: Jean Sanders. Red: 25ha; 11,000 cases; CS 60%, Mer 30%, CF 10%. Second label: La Parde de Haut-Bailly.

Today Haut-Bailly is regarded as one of the best red Graves, just behind Chevalier, and on a level with Pape-Clément, and making its wines more consistently today than its rival in Pessac. The soil is abundant in gravel and pebbles, which are mixed with sand and clay.

The wine tends to be lighter in colour and texture than the other leading red Graves, but the great feature is its harmony. There is a richness and vinosity which are reminiscent of La Mission, but less tannin and power, while the bouquet is strikingly similar to Pape-Clément, with more definition and style. Thus the wines often develop quickly at first, yet keep very well. There were great successes in 83, 82, 81 and 79. A pleasant, early-drinking 80 was made. The 78 is good but not up to top form owing to problems at the end of Daniel Sanders' administration, and this affected all the years after 1970 to a greater or lesser extent.

Château Haut-Brion

1e Cru Classé 1855. Owner: Domaine Clarence Dillon. Red: 41ha; 12,000 cases; CS 55%, Mer 30%, CF 15%. White: 3ha; 1,300 cases; Sém 55%, Sauv 45%.

Haut-Brion is the only wine outside the Médoc to feature in the 1855 classification of red wines. In 1935 it was acquired by Clarence Dillon, the American banker. Since 1975, Clarence Dillon's grand-daughter Joan, the Duchesse de Mouchy has been president of the company, with her husband as director-general. The much respected Jean Delmas succeeded his father as *régisseur* in 1961. In 1960 this was the first of the great *crus* to install stainless steel fermentation vats.

The essence of the Haut-Brion style today can be summarized as elegance and harmony. The tannin, new oak (100% each year) and fruit seem to be in balance after the first few months. This can give the wine the appearance of being ready to drink very early. I remember my disbelief at the forwardness of the 75 in 79. But, while this wine is more forward and more enjoyable than most leading wines of 75, there is also no doubting its ability to age well. The great successes here in recent vintages are 83, 82, 81, 80, 79, 76 and 75. Of the 78 I have tasted some superb bottles but also some very disappointing ones. It is hard to fathom the inconsistency.

The very small quantity of white wine produced makes it a rarity, and most of it seems to go to the USA. It seems to show its charm more quickly than the Laville. The 83 was full of charm in May 85 only months after bottling. Then the wine seems to go through a period of change, so that neither 78 nor 79 showed well at this time, but the 76 again was superb.

Château Larrivet-Haut-Brion

Owner: Mme Guillemaud. Red: 15.4ha; 7,600 cases; CS 60%, Mer 35%, Mal and PV 5%. White: 0.76ha; 400 cases; Sauv 60%, Sém 40%.

A famous old property in the central sector of Léognan, adjoining Haut-Bailly. It was once called Haut-Brion-Larrivet, until a law-suit from Haut-Brion compelled a change. The Guillemaud family has owned the property.

This is a very classic Graves, with a fine colour and a spicy delicate bouquet. The wine has both finesse and the ability to age well. Usually they are as good or better than some of the red Crus Classés. The white wine, of which very little is made, is not of the same standard.

Château Laville-Haut-Brion

Cru Classé. Owner: Domaine Clarence Dillon. White: 6ha; 2,000 cases; Sém 60%, Sauv 40%.

The history of this tiny vineyard follows that of Château La Mission-Haut-Brion, where the wine is vinified, matured and bottled. The soil here is richer and less stony than that of La Mission or La Tour-Haut-Brion, and this contributes towards the wines' remarkable keeping powers. The vinification is in cask and not *cuve*, and takes place in an air-conditioned cellar. The new owners plan to keep the wine in cask for 12 months.

This is, with Chevalier, the great example of classic white Graves. It is full-bodied with a complex flavour and character which only gradually evolve. These wines are very consistent, and mostly differ from year to year in weight and power, and therefore in the speed at which they evolve. The 77, for instance, is light but delicious. The 76 is now coming into full maturity, but the 75 is more powerful and concentrated. The 78, 79, 81 and 83 will all be very fine. The 82 has great ripeness and power with acidity to match, a long-term developer, but without the elegance of some years.

Château La Louvière

Owner: André Lurton. Red: 37ha; 16,000 cases; CS 70%, Mer 20%, CF 10%. White: 18ha; 7,500 cases; Sauv 85%, Sem 15%. Secondary labels: Château Cantebeau, Château Coucheray, Château Clos du Roi.

This very old property, which is a historical monument, has been largely restored and reconstructed by the dynamic André Lurton since 1965.

The white wine of Louvière has been notable for its outstanding finesse, delicacy and fruit since the 1970 vintage at least. It certainly deserves to be Cru Classé.

The red has made steady progress. The wines during the 1970s were vivid in colour, quite tannic but light-textured and with a tendency to be rather one-dimensional. However, the balance has recently improved. In 83, for example, the quality was very similar to Carbonnieux, with a very perfumed bouquet, a tobacco aroma and a really lovely flavour.

Château Magence

Owner: Dominique Guillot de Suduiraut. Red: 18ha; 5,800 cases; CS 40%, CF 32%, Mer 27%. White: 12ha; 10,000 cases; Sauv 64%, Sem 36%.

One of the best known properties in St-Pierre de Mons, the most important Graves commune lying to the south-east of Sauternes. It has been in the same family since 1800, in spite of which everything here is most up to date. The fermentation is in stainless steel with careful temperature control. This was one of the early classic modern white Graves, at one time entirely Sauvignon, but now balanced with some Sémillon, producing wines of real finesse and style. The reds are also useful, supple as well as slightly tannic.

Château Malartic-Lagravière

Cru Classé. Owner: Jacques Marly-Ridoret. 14ha. Red: 7,500 cases; CS 44%, CF 31%, Mer 25%. White: 900 cases; Sauv 100%.

This is a very well positioned vineyard on a high platform of gravelly soil, just south-east of the town of Léognan. The red and white wines are vinified in stainless steel vats, the white at a low temperature not exceeding 18°C (64°F). The red wines are matured in casks of which one-third are new, the white in one-year-old casks for about seven months.

The red wines have a very marked Graves character, without a lot of weight or flesh, but with a very clean, fresh flavour and good fruit. In recent years the leanness which afflicted some wines of the 60s seems to have been overcome. They have a good backbone and age well. The 83, 82, 81, 79, 78 and 75 were all very successful examples of their vintages, with charming lighter wines in 80 and 76. This is good Graves at the level of a Cinquième Cru Classé in the Médoc.

The white wine is one of the most attractive of white Graves with an outstanding bouquet and real individuality. With its 100% Sauvignon it develops quickly and for me is at its most attractive in this most youthful phase. A very consistent wine from year to year.

Château Millet

Owners: Henri & Thierry de la Mette. 56ha. 25,000 cases. Red: Mer 60%, CF and CS 40%. White: Sauv 50%, Sem 50%. Second label: Château du Clos Renon.

This is now the largest property in Portets, with a large château to go with it. The red wine, now more important than the white, is matured in cask. Wines not considered up to standard (e.g. the 77 and 80 vintages) are not bottled with the château name. These are decent, fruity, early-maturing wines with a certain reputation.

Château La Mission-Haut-Brion

Cru Classé. Owner: Domaine Clarence Dillon. Red: 17ha; 7,000 cases; CS 60%, Mer 35%, CF 5%.

When the all-too-familiar problems of succession caused the Woltner heirs to put La Mission on the market in 1983 it was logical that their neighbours across the road at Haut-Brion should decide to buy. These two properties now constitute an oasis of vines surrounded by housing, much of it built on former vineyards between the two World Wars. Vinification is in glass-lined vats, a method pioneered by Henri Woltner who master-minded the wine-making here from 1921 until his death in 1974. La Mission was probably the first property in Bordeaux to ferment its red wines at around 28°C (82°F) as a consistent policy. The wine is matured in casks, of which half are new. The gravel in the vineyard is of exceptional depth, and results in low yields and great concentration.

The wine of La Mission is rich and powerful, whereas that of Haut-Brion is all finesse and delicacy. Clearly La Mission is today a Premier Cru in all but name. Its price has yearly been edging closer to that of the Premiers Cru Classés, and since it has belonged to Domaine Clarence Dillon, the opening price has only been 10F a bottle below that of the best of the Médoc. The quality and individuality of this wine is exceptional. Always deep in colour, it is rich and concentrated in flavour, without being uncomfortably tannic. It needs time to evolve and lasts well. It also has a wonderful record for successes in "off" vintages. The vintages of 83, 82 and 81 were all exceptional, there was a fine 80, and splendid wines were made in 79 and 78, with classic 76s and 75s.

Château Olivier

Cru Classé. Owner: Mme P. de Bethmann. Administrator: Jean-Jacques de Bethmann; Red: 18ha; 8,500 cases; CS 65%, Mer 35%. White: 17ha; 9,000 cases; Sém 65%, Sauv 30%, Musc 5%.
For over 70 years this famous old estate was farmed by Eschenauer, the négociants, and was their monopoly. Then in November 1981 the Bethmann family took the management back into their own hands and Jean-Jacques de Bethmann assumed the responsibility for running the property. The distribution remains in Eschenauer's hands until 1987, but only for part of the crop.

The vineyard was radically reconstructed in the early to mid 1970s with a view to increasing the size of the red vineyard, and ensuring that the various grape varieties were planted on the most favourable soils, so much of the vineyard is still immature. A wonderfully scented and complex 82 has been made. The 83 is leaner and the 84 is above average. The red is a wine to watch.

The white wine is what Olivier has always been known for. With the high proportion of Sémillon you must not expect the instant charm the Sauvignon gives in the first months of bottle ageing, but the wines become more interesting with bottle age. The flavour is very marked and individual with plenty of character. Again it will be interesting to see what difference the new management makes.

Château Pape-Clément

Cru Classé. Owner: Montagne family. 29ha. Red: 12,000 cases; CS 60%, Mer 40%. White: 100 cases; Sém 33⅓%, Sauv 33⅓%, Musc 33⅓%.
The vineyard here has the longest continual history of any in Bordeaux, being planted in 1300. This is a red wine château, although a few cases of white are produced and are sometimes to be found in some Bordeaux restaurants. The soil is sand and gravel and there are traces of iron. After traditional vinification, the wine is matured in casks of which 30% to 40% are new, according to the vintage.

The wines of Pape-Clément have a marvellous bouquet, intense with overtones of tobacco, and a supple, rich texture that enables them to be enjoyed relatively young. But after some wonderful vintages in the 60s, I have found Pape Clément disturbingly inconsistent in recent years. The last vintage I found really satisfactory in bottle was 78.

Château Picque-Caillou.

Owner: Alphonse Denis. 17.5ha. 7,500 cases. Mer 35%, CS 35%, CF 30%.
This vineyard lies on gravelly and stony soil, surrounded by the sprawling suburbs of Bordeaux. The wines have a good reputation for being stylish, supple and full-flavoured. They usually evolve fairly quickly and also keep well. Wines of breed.

Château Rahoul

Owner: Lothardt Dahl. Administrator: Peter Vinding-Diers. Red: 11.5ha; 5,000 cases; Mer 60%, CS 40%. White: 2.5ha; 1,000 cases; Sém 100%.
This old property in Portets was bought by an Australian syndicate in 1978. The Australians brought in a young Danish oenologist, Peter

Vinding-Diers, and invested in stainless steel and new oak. In 1982 they sold to the present owner who, like Vinding-Diers, is Danish. Although the vineyard is not in the best position, being low-lying with some drainage problems, the care and expertise of the wine-making have borne fruit. One of Vinding-Diers' important contributions was the isolation of R2, a pure strain of yeast found in the vineyard here. By eliminating the other yeasts and using only this one, he found it was possible to produce cleaner-tasting wines. R2 has since been used as far afield as Australia. A proportion of new oak is used for both red and white wines, after low-temperature fermentations. I find the white wines extremely elegant and long-flavoured, only lacking perhaps the complexity and depth of the best Graves further north. The reds are full of vivid spicy fruit and are at their most delicious when young. This is an example of what investment in expertise and the best equipment can achieve, and makes one realize how much room for improvement there is at many better-known and better-placed vineyards.

Château de Rochemorin

Owner: **André Lurton**. 55ha. Red: 9,000 cases; CS 60%, Mer 40%. White: 2,500 cases; Sauv 90%, Sém 10%.

The name of this château is derived from "Roche-Morine", indicating that it was a fortified place at the time of the Moorish incursions from Spain in the 7th and 8th centuries. The energetic André Lurton bought this old property in 1973 and began replanting the vineyards (which had been replaced by forest) in 1979. The vines are on deep gravel on the highest ridge of Martillac. As at other Lurton properties, harvesting is mechanical for the reds and manual for the whites. Fermentations are controlled at 28°–30°C (82–86°F) for the reds and 16–18°C (61–64°F) for the whites. The reds are matured for a year in cask, with one third new wood, but the whites see no wood at all.

The red wines already show quite a spicy, aromatic Graves bouquet allied to elegance and breed, and lighter and more marked by new oak than nearby Cruzeau. Fine 83, 82 and 81 wines have been made. The white wine is very different from that of Cruzeau. It has a less floral bouquet and more body, but is very elegant, with a finish that is flinty and drier than that of Cruzeau. Again, the white here is of course more evolved than the red, but, as the vineyard develops and the reds acquire more depth and finish, they should become really interesting.

Château de Roquetaillade-La-Grange

Owners: **Pierre & Jean Guignard**. 36ha. Red: 12,000 cases; Mer 40%, CS 25%, CF 25%, Mal 5%, PV 5%. White: 2,200 cases; Sém 80%, Sauv 20%. Second label: Château Roquetaillade-Le-Bernet.

The name of Roquetaillade is famous for the splendid medieval château built by a nephew of Pope Clement V at the beginning of the 14th century. It is regarded as the finest example of military architecture in the whole of southeastern France. But this property, lying on the hillsides to the east of the château, is actually unconnected with the château itself, which has no vineyards of importance. In recent years the owners (also owners of Château Rolland in Barsac) have raised the standard of the wines here to a high level, winning a number of medals in Paris and a deserved reputation for one of the best red wines in southern Graves.

The red wines have real individuality and lovely mellow fruit on nose and palate – sometimes, in years like 79, with an unmistakeable hint of cherries, a fruit flavour most unusual for Bordeaux. The vintages of 78 and 79 were especially successful. The white was pleasantly fruity without being special; but, with new controlled temperature vinification, quality is likely to become more exciting.

Château de St-Pierre

Owner: **Henri Dulac**. 43ha. Red: 6,200 cases; CS 60%, Mer 40%. White: Sém 66⅔%, Sauv 33⅓%. Second label: Clos d'Uza.

This excellent property is run in conjunction with Château Les Queyrats by Henri Dulac. But here red as well as white wines are made. The vineyard is on ridges of clay and limestone in the southeast of the commune of St-Pierre-de-Mons, the most important wine-producing commune south of Sauternes. The wines are very carefully vinified. The whites, like those at Les Queyrats, were some of the first of the new style Graves to emerge and have real finesse and character. The 82 won a gold medal in Paris. The reds are not as distinguished, but are vivid and quite generous, ageing well for wines from this area. The record for consistency over the years here is excellent.

Château Smith-Haut-Lafitte

Cru Classé. Owner: Louis Eschenauer. Red: 45.4ha; 22,000 cases; CS 73%, Mer 16%, CF 11%; White: 5.6ha; 3,000 cases; Sauv 100%.

A proprietor with the splendidly English name of George Smith bought this *cru* in 1720 and added his name to that of the place-name. Now Louis Eschenauer, distributors since 1902 and owners since 1958, are themselves owned by the British company Lonrho. In recent years there has been a major investment here in both vineyards and buildings. In 1960 less than 6ha was planted, and no white wine was made. Now there are 51ha planted, 5.6 devoted to white wines. A large new underground cellar was built in 1974 to hold 2000 casks, and all the vinification equipment was renewed. Half the red wine is matured in new oak.

The wines here have a very pronounced character, aromatic and spicy. Until 83 there was no selection, so big vintages like 82 and 79 tend to be diffuse and quick-developing, although delicious. Now sturdier wines are being made which augur well for the future. The 84 is remarkably good for the year.

A very pleasant perfumed Sauvignon white is being made, which is ideal for early drinking.

Château Toumilon

Owner: Jean Sévenet. 12ha. Red: 3,000 cases; CS 45%, Mer 35%, CF 20%. White: 2,500 cases; Sém 60%, Sauv 40%. Second label: Château Cabanes.

Another excellent *cru* in St-Pierre-de-Mons, the most important commune south of Sauternes. The property has been in the same family since 1783, and the vineyards are on gravelly ridges overlooking the Garonne. Since the 1983 vintage there has been a big improvement in the white wines here, due to new vinification facilities. Previously they were rather pedestrian with a soapy finish; now they have finesse and delicacy. The reds have finesse and personality and a real Graves character, but without the crudeness often found in secondary growths. A very fine 81 was made here, and the 80 was delightful for the year.

Château La Tour-Haut-Brion

Cru Classé. Owner: Domaine Clarence Dillon. Red: 4ha; 1,500 cases; CS 70%, CF 15%, Mer 15%.

This is a small property, adjoining La Mission, which the Woltner brothers purchased in 1933. The wines have been vinified at La Mission since then, and in recent years La Tour-Haut-Brion has been treated as a second wine, using more *vin de presse*. The result is still a very fine wine, certainly better than a number of the other Crus Classés of Graves. It is full-bodied but less intense than La Mission, and matures more quickly. The relationship is very similar to that between Latour and Les Forts, so La Tour-Haut-Brion is an excellent way of enjoying an earlier-drinking La Mission of similar style at a much more accessible price. The intention now is to treat it as a separate *cru* again.

Château La Tour-Martillac

Cru Classé. Owner: Jean Kressman. Red: 20ha; 8,500 cases; CS 60%, Mer 25%, Cf 6%, Mal and PV 9%. White: 4.75ha; 1,500 cases; Sém 55%, Sauv 30%, other varieties 15%. Second label: Château La Grave-Martillac (red, 1,000 cases).

The name comes from a 12th-century tower, once the staircase of a fort, the ruins of which were used in the building of today's farm two centuries ago.

In the 1870s, Edouard Kressmann, the founder of the famous old négociant house, obtained the exclusivity of this *cru*, and the family finally bought it in 1929. Ten hectares of pasture allows the estate to have invaluable cattle manure for the vineyard. The grapes from the older vines are still fermented in the traditional wooden vats at 32°–33°C (90°–91°F), while the production from younger vines goes into lined steel vats which are water-cooled. Maturation is in casks of which one-third are new. The second wine, Château La Grave-Martillac, is made from vines less than ten years old and *vin de presse*. It is not sold through the trade but only at the château direct. The white wine is vinified in stainless steel with automatic water cooling and is bottled after seven or eight months.

I have found the red wine has elegant fruit on the nose and a fine flavour with breed and length, but is rather light-textured. Although the character is different the level of quality is similar to Malartic-Lagravière. The white wine is elegant and fresh with quite an original character. It has delicacy, real breed and a fine finish. This is high-class white Graves.

Château Tourteau-Chollet
Owner: Société Civile. 30ha. Red: 8,000 cases; CS 60%, Mer 40%.
White: 4,000 cases; Sém 50%, Sauv 50%.
This is another part of the Mestrezat empire (see Grand-Puy-Ducasse, Rayne-Vigneau etc). The red wines carry a gold label, and the whites a white label. The commune of Arbanats is immediately to the southeast of Portets, and this is now the most important property there. Since taking over in 1977 the new owners have steadily improved the property, and pleasant, fruity red wnes, and elegant, dry whites are being made. A property to watch.

SAUTERNES AND BARSAC

Sauternes is produced in five communes: Sauternes, Barsac, Fargues-de-Langon, Bommes and Preignac. Barsac is also an appellation in its own right, and producers there can label their wines Barsac or Sauternes or (as many have begun to do) Sauternes-Barsac.

Traditional Sauternes is a luxury wine, and luxury wines have to be sold at luxury prices. If an article becomes unfashionable and can no longer command its former high price, something has to give, and that is likely to be quality. This, in a nutshell, has been the dilemma facing Sauternes since the late 1950s.

The top red growths can expect to make 40hl/ha in a good vintage, sometimes more, and very seldom less than 30. At Yquem, the standard-bearer for Sauternes, over the past 20 years the average yield has been 9hl/ha, as against the 25 allowed by the appellation. On this basis, Yquem's price would need to be around four times that of Lafite or Pétrus to produce the same income, whereas in fact it is in the region of two and half times. Then, costs are much higher because of picking methods (see page 11), and there are years when frosts, hail or rain during the vintage mean that the wine is simply not good enough to go out under the famous label of Yquem.

The result of all this has been that only a few Sauternes properties have been able to continue to make wines in anything approaching the traditional way. Whatever short cuts may be possible with the aid of modern technology, there can be no substitute for botrytis or *pourriture noble* (noble rot). This is what gives Sauternes its distinctive bouquet and flavour, its complex range of fruit, flavours and finesse. The short-cut of picking ripe but unaffected grapes and then chaptalizing can only produce unsubtle sweet wines, which may possibly be quite elegant and fresh but will never develop into anything of interest.

Fortunately, there are signs that there are now enough lovers of the nectar that is true Sauternes to pay the price for a certain quantity of this style of wine, and enough dedicated proprietors with the financial strength to withstand the burdens of the bad years.

One way of helping to cover costs is to produce a certain proportion of dry wine, or even red wine. Unfortunately, however good these may be, such efforts are hampered by the appellation system which will only give a simple Bordeaux AC to such wines (or Bordeaux Supérieur in the case of red wines). Ironically, in neighbouring Cérons, the producers of this sweet wine have been saved by having the right to the Graves AC for their dry whites and reds. This has so far been denied to the growers of Sauternes, quite illogically, so it would seem.

The actual balance sheet between success and failure is at the moment nicely poised. There are now 11 Premiers Crus. Five years or so ago, only five of these were making wines which were up to standard. Since then the new owner of Guiraud has started to turn it around, and the Cordiers have reversed their previous policy at Lafaurie-Peyraguey. At the same time, changes at Coutet now put a question mark against the future there. Most recently of all, Domaines Rothschild have secured the future of one of the best properties, Rieussec.

There are 14 Deuxièmes Crus, and here there are probably eight owners who aim to produce quality wines to some extent. But only half of these make 2,000 cases or more. On the other hand, one of the Deuxièmes Crus, Myrat, was pulled up in 1976. Doisy-Daëne has been the Deuxième Cru most dedicated to quality over the past 20 years. In the 1970s, Nairac was transformed by Tom Heeter, and more recently Pierre Perromat has leased d'Arche and the Guignard brothers have begun promisingly at their part of Lamothe.

There are three unclassified growths which now make wines of classified quality: Bastor-Lamontagne, Raymond-Lafon and Fargues.

Essentially Sauternes is a great dessert wine intended to be drunk at the end of a meal, and this clearly puts it into the special-occasions-only category. Of course it can be drunk as an apéritif, but it is not exactly designed to put an edge on your appetite, and the Bordelais habit of drinking it with a first course of *foie gras* hardly has a wide application. A more likely way forward is through the new devices for keeping open bottles under nitrogen, which make it possible for restaurant diners to order a single glass of Sauternes at the end of a meal. If this practice becomes widespread the future of Sauternes will look brighter. But unless more people are prepared to pay more and drink Sauternes more often, then the future for even a small number of quality *crus* will remain bleak.

Château d'Arche

2ᵉ Cru Classé. Owner: Bastit-St-Martin family. Administrator: Pierre Perromat. 35.5ha. 4,500 cases. Sém 80%, Sauv 15%, Muse 5%. Second label: Château d'Arche-Lafaurie (not used since 1981).

This is an old property, with a château dating from the 16th century and a reputation going back to the 18th century. After a rather undistinguished period, Pierre Perromat, for 30 years president of the INAO, leased the property in 1981 and is determined to make classic Sauternes again. The traditional selections are now made in the vineyard again and, after fermentation in vat, the wine is now matured for at least two years in casks, of which a small percentage are new.

The first wines of the new regime seem well balanced, with nice fruit and sweetness and a certain fineness and breed. A very good 83 was made and a promising 82 and 81.

Château Bastor-Lamontagne

Cru Bourgeois. Owner: Crédit Foncier de France. 36.5ha. 7,500 cases. Sém 70%, Sauv 20%, Musc 10%.

This excellent *cru* is in Preignac, adjoining Suduiraut. It has for many years consistently produced excellent wines and is on the level of the Crus Classés, indeed better than some of them. The wines are very carefully and traditionally made, with three years cask-ageing and a small proportion of new wood. The result is a rich, luscious wine with the aroma and flavour of apricots and all the stylishness of a top-rate Sauternes. Recently 75, 76, 79, 80, 82 and 83 have all been highly successful.

Château Broustet

2ᵉ Cru Classé. Owner: Fournier family. Administrator: Eric Fournier. 16ha. 1,700 cases. Sém 63%, Sauv 25%, Musc 12%.

This very small property is not well known, mainly because its production is very small. But Eric Fournier (who also runs Château Cannon in St-Emilion) is doing everything to produce quality wines here. It has belonged to the family since 1885, although they did not replant the vineyard until 1900. The wine is fermented in vat but matured in casks, of which a small percentage are new. The wines have a fine perfume and are generous and quite rich with a pleasing individuality and breed.

Château Caillou

2ᵉ Cru Classé. Owner: Bravo GFA. 15ha. 4,000 cases. Sém 90%, Sauv 10%.

A little-known property, because the wine is all sold by *vente directe* to private customers. So this is a place to visit if you have your car and room in the boot! The present owner has run the property since 1969 and keeps stocks of old vintages. I have memories of a wonderful bottle of 1920. The wines are carefully made, with fermentation in vat and maturing in cask – of which a small percentage are new – for up to three years. The wines have the reputation of being light, elegant and fruity.

Château Climens

1ᵉ Cru Classé. Owner: Lucien Lurton. 30ha. 4,500 cases. Sém 98%, Sauv 2%.

For many Climens is the best wine of the region after Yquem, not that the two can really be compared. The emphasis here is on elegance, breed and freshness, and Climens does not generally attempt to compete with Yquem's lusciousness. Since 1971 it has belonged to Lucien Lurton (see Brane-Cantenac, Durfort-Vivens etc), but the *régisseuse*, Mme Janin has been here for 30 years, and her family for over 100 years. The soil is red sand and gravel over limestone. After pressing and settling for 24 hours in vat, the juice is fermented in casks, of which 25% are new, and matured for about two years before bottling.

The wines here are remarkably consistent in a region where it is not always easy to make good Sauternes. They are rather closed at first and usually need a minimum of ten years before they begin to give of their best. The great qualities here are balance, freshness, elegance and liquorousness in the great years. This makes it a very long-lived wine. The 82 is no more than average, 81 and 80 are both very fine, 79 lighter but fine and can be drunk now, 78 without botrytis but elegant. The 76, 75 and 71 are all outstanding wines for these vintages. Surprisingly acceptable light wines were also made in 77 and 72, years not noted for Sauternes at all.

Château Coutet

1e Cru Classé. Owner: **Marcel Baly. 36ha. 7,000 cases. Sém 80%, Sauv 20%.**

The name of Coutet is always linked to that of Climens, the other great wine of Barsac. Generally Coutet is less powerful and often a little drier than Climens, which also tends to have more finesse in the great years. For 30 years the property was well run by the Rolland-Guy family, who sold in 1977 to Marcel Baly. The production methods here are traditional, with fermentation in casks, of which a third are new, and two years in cask before bottling.

There must be a slight question mark over Coutet since its change of ownership. The last two vintages of the old regime were superb, the 75 a classic in a year when many wines were clumsy and unbalanced, while the 76 is perfumed and beautifully balanced but lighter. Since then 79 is elegant but rather dry and nothing else stands out. One must await the 83 which promises much. Among earlier vintages, the 71 is very fine and 73 one of the few fine wines in this mixed year.

Château Doisy-Daëne

2e Cru Classé. Owner: Pierre Dubourdieu. 14ha. 4,000 cases. Sém 100%. Secondary labels: Vin Sec de Doisy-Daëne, Château Cantegril.

Once the three Doisys were one, and when they split up in the 19th century the first owner of this part was an Englishman called, improbably, Daene. Its present owner, Pierre Dubourdieu, is a great innovator, being one of the first to make a dry wine in Sauternes in 1962. The vinification methods here have been developed over a number of years and are special to Doisy-Daëne. The juice is fermented in vat at a controlled temperature of not more than 18°C (64°F). Then, after 15 to 21 days when the balance between alcohol and sugar is judged correct, the temperature is lowered to 4°C (39°F) and the wine is sterile-filtered into new casks. Arresting the fermentation in this way much reduces the amount of sulphur needed. The process is repeated for the final assemblage the following March, and the wine is filtered a year later, again sterile-filtered.

All this gives Doisy-Daëne a freshness and elegance which I find delightful. The wines seem light to start with but mature and keep very well, developing great finesse. It certainly paid dividends in the difficult 75 vintage, when this wine is much more elegant than most. Also fine are the 76, 78 (very late picked in November with still no botrytis but very elegant), 79, 80, 81 and 82. An exceptional 83 is promised. This wine is finer than several Premiers Crus today.

Château Doisy-Dubroca

2e Cru Classé. Owner: Lucien Lurton. 3.3ha. 425 cases. Sém 90%, Sauv 10%.

This very small property has been run in conjunction with Climens for nearly 70 years. The vinification and maturation all take place at Climens with exactly the same care as the 1e cru. The distribution is exclusively handled by the aptly-named Louis Dubroca firm.

The wines here, as at Climens, are remarkably consistent. In style they are light and elegant and take time to evolve in bottle, but can be drunk young. The years 71, 75, 76, 79 and 80 all produced good examples.

Château Doisy-Védrines

2e Cru Classé. Owner: Pierre Castéja. 20ha. 2,200 cases. Sém 80%, Sauv 20%. Second label: Château La Tour-Védrines.

This property contains the original Védrines château and chais. Pierre Castéja's family have inherited the property through several marriages since 1840, and he comes from an old family of proprietors. He also runs the négociant firm Roger Joanne. The wines are traditionally made with fermentation and maturation in casks, of which one-third are new.

There is a strong contrast between this and the other Doisys, which both concentrate on elegance and delicacy. Védrines is fuller and richer, but to my mind lacks the breed and stylishness of the others. Curiously enough I found the 75 here better balanced and finer than the 76, while at many properties the reverse is the case. There is a red wine La Tour-Védrines, but another wine, Chevalier Védrines, is a Joanne brand unconnected with this property.

Château de Fargues

Cru Bourgeois. Owner: Comte Alexandre de Lur-Saluces. 10ha. 1,000 cases. Sém 80%, Sauv 20%.

This tiny vineyard lies on the extremity of the commune of Fargues and of the Sauternes AC and has belonged to the Lur-Saluces family for over 500 years. Under the present owner, Comte Alexandre de Lur-Saluces, the production of red wine has been abandoned, and they concentrate on producing the best possible Sauternes. Wine-making is identical to Yquem, with fermentation and maturation in new casks.

The wines, most of which are sold in the USA, combine lusciousness and elegance with great breed and finesse. The 80, 76, 75, 71 and 67 are all great successes here, with the 76 finer than the 75 for me. This wine is of the standard of a top Premier Cru, and the price is correspondingly high, indeed higher than most Premiers Crus, at approximately half that of Yquem.

Château Filhot

2e Cru Classé. Owner: Comte Henri de Vaucelles. 60ha. 9,500 cases. Sém 60%, Sauv 37%, Musc 3%.

There are many beautiful properties in Sauternes, and this is one of the finest, an imposing late-18th-century mansion set among woods and fields. The wine is fermented in glass fibre vats and also matured in them – no wood is used. At its best this is a wine of individuality and great fruit, but not necessarily great sweetness except in exceptional years. The higher than usual proportion of Sauvignon and the practice of keeping in vat help this tendency. Yet I cannot help feeling that the full potential here is not being realized. The 75 and 76 vintages are liquorous but lack style, while the 79 was still masked by sulphur when six years old.

Château Gilette

Owner: Christian Médeville. 3.5ha. 400–900 cases. Sém 83%, Sauv 15%, Musc 2%.

This is a curiosity among the wines of Sauternes. Situated just outside the village of Preignac, it belongs to the Médeville family of Château Respide-Médeville in Graves. The soil here is sandy with a subsoil of rock and clay. Between three and seven pickings are made, with the earliest being of single berries affected by botrytis. Each picking is vinified separately with temperatures controlled at 24–25°C (75–77°F) during the first days of fermentation, and then brought down to 20°C (68°F) for the remainder of the time. The result is several different *cuvées* with differing characteristics, and normally two separate wines are made in each vintage. After the fermentation the wines are kept in small concrete vats for at least 20 years. The theory is that the large volume gives a mature flavour and bouquet while preserving fruit and freshness, so that the maturation process is slower than in a bottle.

In 1985 I was able to taste the 59 and 55 bottled in 1981, and the 50 and 49 bottled only six to seven years after the vintage. I thought the early bottlings were clearly superior to the later ones. In particular the 59 and 55 lack the bouquet and balance of the 50 and 49. In addition the 59 and 55 had great sweetness and concentration but rather lacked complexity. The 49 seemed the finest wine of all, and I preferred the 55 to the 59. So, while this system means you can find an old vintage more easily, it is far from clear that the result is actually as good as those achieved by earlier and more conventional bottlings.

Château Guiraud

1e Cru Classé. Owner: Société Civile Agricole. Administrator: Hamilton Narby. 118ha. Main wine: 7,000 cases; Sém 54%, Sauv 45%, Musc 1%. Dry white: 4,000 cases; Sauv 100%. Red: 8,000 cases; CS 50%, Mer 50%. Secondary labels: Le Dauphin de Lalague (Sauternes), "G" Château Guiraud (Bordeaux Sec), Le Dauphin Château Guiraud (Bordeaux Supérieur, red).

After some years in the doldrums, this famous old property received a shot in the arm when it was bought by Hamilton Narby, a Canadian with a British passport, in 1981. He has shown a determination to impose the highest traditional standards for making classic Sauternes. Because of a shortage of money Guiraud had been reduced to maturing its wines in vat instead of cask after a cask fermentation. Now 50% new wood is used for maturation in cask. A dry white wine and a red wine are also made.

I remember this as a light, elegant wine which was less luscious than most Sauternes, but extremely fine in vintages such as 53, 55 and 62. Part of this distinctive character comes from the higher than usual proportion of Sauvignon. Now signs of this old distinction are returning. The 83 looks enormously promising, while the 81 is elegant and long-flavoured.

Château Haut-Peyraguey

1er Cru Classé. Owner: Jacques Pauly. 15ha. 3,000 cases. Sém 83%, Sauv 15%, Musc 2%.

At the time of the 1855 classification there was a single *cru*, Château Peyraguey, which was divided in two in 1878. This is the smaller part, with just a tower built in the manner of the older, grander one at Lafaurie to remind you of its origin. Jacques Pauly has been in charge since 1948. The fermentation is in vat, and after this the wine spends six months in vat and about 18 months in cask. The wines here are light. They can be rather fine, but can also be inconsistent. There are certainly Deuxièmes Crus which are better today.

Château Les Justices

Owner: Christian Médeville. 14ha. White: 8ha; 1,800 cases; Sém 85%, Sauv 10%, Musc 5%. Red: 6ha; 3,000 cases; Mer 50%, CS and CF 50%.

This property, run in harness with the same owners as Gilette, is marketed in a more conventional manner. It has belonged to the family since 1710. The harvesting and vinification are basically the same as at Gilette, but the wines are bottled after only four years in small vats.

The 71 is superb, with a concentration of sweetness, a strong perfume and a lovely ripe fruitiness. It was perfection at nearly 14 years of age. The 80 and 81 are both promising, with the 81 having more richness, and the 80 very elegant with length and charming fruit.

Château Lafaurie-Peyraguey

1er Cru Classé. Owner: Cordier family. 20ha. 3,500 cases. Sém 90%, Sauv 5%, Musc 5%.

After Yquem, the château here is the most spectacular in Sauternes, with its 13th-century fortifications and 17th-century buildings inside. It has belonged to the Cordiers since 1913 and is most carefully run. Recently the whole policy has changed significantly. The proportion of Sauvignon has been dropped from 30% to 5%, and the Sémillon increased from 70% to 90%. In 1967 a new system was introduced whereby the wines were kept in glass-lined vats under nitrogen after fermentation in cask. The result was that they became light and one-dimensional, quite lacking the distinction expected of a top Sauternes. Now they have returned to more traditional ways and are maturing in casks, of which one third are new. This, combined with the change in the vineyard, promises well for the future.

Much more interesting wines have been made here in 79, 80, 81 and especially 83. They have the honeyed bouquet and elegant fruit and breed that one looks for, and will really be worth waiting for once more.

Château Lamothe

2e Cru Classé. Owner: Jean Despujols. 8ha. 2,000 cases. Sém 70%, Sauv 20%, Musc 10%.

This is another divided property. Lamothe used to belong to the same owners as Château d'Arche. Then in 1961 they sold half the property, including the château and half the cellars, to the Despujols family. They ferment in tank and then mature partly in tank and partly in cask. The result is a rather light and dryish commercial Sauternes, which is decent but no more. There are more interesting wines among the Crus Bourgeois.

Château Lamothe-Guignard

2e Cru Classé. Owners: Philippe & Jacques Guignard. 11ha. 2,000 cases. Sém 85%, Musc 10%, Sauv 5%.

Lamothe as a single property belonged to the owners of d'Arche. In 1961 they sold a part of the property to the Despujols family, and continued to sell the wines from their portion as Lamothe-Bergey. Then in 1981 the Guignards bought Lamothe-Bergey and substituted their name for Bergey. They are members of the same family as own Château Rolland. The first vintage of the new regime, 1981, shows great promise, with elegance and ripeness, length and finesse, delectable fruit and moderate sweetness. Clearly a wine to watch with interest in the future.

Château de Malle

2e Cru Classé. Owner: Comte Pierre de Bournazel. 26ha. 2,700 cases. Sém 75%, Sauv 22%, Musc 3%. Secondary labels: **Château Ste-Hélène**, **Chevalier de Malle** (white Graves, 3,000 cases), **Château du Cardaillan** (red Graves, 6,000 cases).

This beautiful property is interesting to visit for the sake of the 17th-century château as well as the wine. The vineyard is partly in Sauternes and partly in Graves. Fermentation is in cask as well as vat, and the maturation follows a similar pattern. The wines have great elegance and charm, and are of a light style which is only moderately liquorous. It can be drunk young (three or four years old) but in good years gradually opens up in bottle and repays keeping.

Château Nairac

2e Cru Classé. Owners: Thomas & Nicole Heeter-Tari. 15ha. 1,400 cases. Sém 90%, Sauv 6%, Musc 4%.

This is a heartening tale of restoration. Tom Heeter, a young American, came to work at Château Giscours to learn about wine. In the process he carried off the daughter of the house, and his father-in-law Nicolas Tari spotted that Nairac, in the commune of Barsac, was for sale at a reasonable price. They finally took possession in 1972. With Professor Peynaud's guidance, Tom Heeter has set himself to make his Barsac in a very traditional way, using only wood (65% new) to ferment and mature his wines. However, like Pierre Dubourdieu, he wants to reduce the use of sulphur. He has not gone as far as they do at Doisy-Daëne, but by using vitamin B, an anti-oxidant, he has reduced its use.

The care of the wine-making has quickly won admirers for Nairac. The wines are not normally very liquorous, but are quite powerful and rich under the influence of new oak. The most successful years here are 82, 80, 79 and 76. This is certainly a wine to watch out for.

Château Rabaud-Promis

1e Cru Classé. Owner: GFA Rabaud-Promis. Administrator: Mme Michèle Dejean. 32ha. 3,750 cases. Sém 80%, Sauv 18%, Musc 2%. Second label: **Château Jauga**.

Château Rabaud was a single property until 1903 when it was divided (see also Sigalas-Rabaud), and this part was bought by Adrien Promis. The château is 18th-century and is built on a fine hilltop position. This consists of two-thirds of the original property. The properties were reunited in 1929, but divided again in 1952. The Deuxième Cru Château Peixotto is also now incorporated into Rabaud-Promis. The grapes here, contrary to the tradition in Sauternes, are crushed before going into the presses, and the fermentation and maturation are done entirely in cement vats. There is no wood at all. The wines are sold directly and appear to be bottled when there is a sale. Their reputation is undistinguished, which is a pity for anyone fortunate enough to have tasted the lovely wines made before the properties were divided.

Château Raymond-Lafon

Cru Bourgeois. Owners: Pierre & Francine Meslier. 20ha. 2,000 cases. Sém 80%, Sauv 20%.

This property adjoins Yquem and since 1972 has belonged to Yquem's *régisseur*, Pierre Meslier. The vineyard is not only well placed, with Yquem on one side and Sigalas-Rabaud on the other, but Pierre Meslier makes it with the same meticulous care he gives to Yquem. The wine is matured in cask with as much as a third in new oak. The resulting wines are already beginning to carve out a reputation for themselves as being well up to Cru Classé standards, with fine, perfumed, luscious wine. Fine wines were made in 82, 81, 80, 79, 76 and 75. In the difficult 78 harvest, with little or no botrytis, a particularly successful wine was made here.

Château de Rayne-Vigneau

1e Cru Classé. Owner: Société Civile. Administrator: Jean Pierre Angliviel de la Beaumelle. 68ha. 16,500 cases (including 4,000 cases dry). Sém 50%, Sauv 50%. Dry wine: **Rayne Sec**.

The wines of Rayne-Vigneau enjoyed a great reputation in the 19th century and the first part of this century. Until 1961 it belonged to the Pontac family, who still own the actual château. In 1971 it was bought by the group which owns Château Grand-Puy-Ducasse and a number of other châteaux. Their properties are run and distributed by Mestrezat. The Sémillon and Sauvignon are pressed separately here, because some of the Sauvignon is also used for the dry wine, although most of this is of course made from less ripe grapes picked earlier. The fermentation is in vat, then the wine goes into casks for maturation, of which 20% are new. Undoubtedly the property is now well run again, but the yields are high, and the wines tend to be correct but rather dull and uninspired. Certainly not up to the high standards of the past, these are frankly commercial wines. The 76 is the best one I have tasted, but the 75 was poor.

Château Rieussec

1er Cru Classé. Owner: SA Château Rieussec. 66ha. 6,000 cases. Sém 80%, Sauv 18%, Musc 2%. Secondary labels: Clos Labère, "R" (dry).

This is superbly placed on the highest hill in Sauternes after Yquem. The vineyard is in the commune of Sauternes, but the estate buildings are in Fargues. The soil here is particularly gravelly. Rieussec has always been regarded as one of the finest crus in Sauternes, producing wines of great individuality with an outstanding bouquet and great concentration of flavour, but also marked elegance and less lusciousness than some. In 1971 it was acquired by Albert Vuillier who determined to use the most traditional methods and produced some wines which have been adored by some and disliked by others. In 1984 he sold to Domaines Rothschild but remained in charge. The fermentation is in vat, then maturation is partly in large oak foudres (vats) and partly in casks, of which 50% are new.

After making an absolutely classic Rieussec in 71, Albert Vuillier has mostly made heavily botrytized wines, deep in colour, often with that dry nose and aftertaste associated with botrytis which in excess has the effect of cutting the sweetness at the finish owing to high volatile acidity. For this reason I dislike the 75 in spite of its obvious concentration. The 76 is very opulent and attractive but I think slightly unbalanced and therefore at its best when young. My favourite is the 80 which has more elegance than the others, as well as being very rich, and I prefer the 79 to the 81. It will be interesting to see what happens under the new Rothschild regime.

Château de Rolland

Cru Bourgeois. Owners: Jean & Pierre Guignard. 20ha. 4,000 cases. Sém 60%, Sauv 20%, Musc 20%.

This cru in Barsac not only makes wine but is also a good restaurant and hotel, the only place to stay if you want to be in the middle of the Sauternes vineyards. The owners are also the proprietors of the excellent Château Roquetaillade-La-Grange in Graves. The wines enjoy a good reputation at the Cru Bourgeois level. Wines are vinified and matured in casks bought from Yquem.

Château Romer-du-Hayot

2e Cru Classé. Owner: André du Hayot; 15ha. 4,000 cases. Sém 70%, Sauv 25%, Musc 5%.

This cru deserves to be more widely known. The vineyard adjoins de Malle on the edge of the commune of Fargues. For some years the ownership has been divided between the du Hayot and Fargues families, but since 1977 the Fargues portion has been leased to the du Hayots, so that the property is now run as one, although there are two owners. The wine is both fermented and matured in vat, and bottling is done early. André du Hayot clearly knows how to make Sauternes because, both here and at Guiteronde in Barsac (where the wines are actually made), he is making excellent wines, of their sort, with limited resources. There is an emphasis on fruit and freshness. Only in years like 76 is there a lot of sweetness, but the wines always seem well balanced and most attractive. Recently both 80 and 79 are successes, with the 79 fuller and richer.

Château Sigalas-Rabaud

1er Cru Classé. Owners: Héritiers de la Marquise de Lambert des Granges. 14ha. 2,000 cases. Sém 90%, Sauv 10%.

This cru formed part of the old property of Rabaud, which was divided in 1903. From 1929 to 1952 the properties were united again. The yields here are low and the traditional trie (selective picking of the ripest grapes) is made through the vineyard four or five times. The fermentation is in vat, and the maturation is also mostly in vat. I have found the wines usually very perfumed, elegant and quite delicate, yet liquorous and with real breed. For me the best and most typical vintages here have been 81, 75 and 71. The 67 was especially fine and there are excellent reports of the 83.

Château Suau

2e Cru Classé. Owner: Roger Biarnès. 6.5ha. 1,500 cases. Sém 80%, Sauv 10%, Musc 10%.

Probably the least known of the Crus Classés. The vineyard is in Barsac, but the present owners vinify the wine at their other property in Illats.

Much of the wine is sold by *vente directe* in France. The wine is fermented in vats and then in used casks. The reputation is for producing rather ordinary, dull wines with an unbalanced sweetness and lacking breed.

Château Suduiraut

1e Cru Classé. Owner: L. Fonquernie. 70ha. 11,000 cases. Sém 80%, Sauv 20%.

This famous old *cru* adjoins Yquem and is partly in the commune of Sauternes and partly in that of Preignac. The Fonquernie family bought this property, with its lovely 17th-century château, in 1940 and have slowly nursed it back to quality and fame. It is normally the most liquorous and intensely rich wine after Yquem, and when at its best is also one of the very best Sauternes. The juice ferments in vats after a careful selection in the vineyard, and is then matured in casks, of which 35% are new. But one should note that Suduiraut went through a bad patch when there was little or no selection and virtually no cask-ageing. This affected the vintages from 1971 to 1975 inclusive.

The best Suduirauts are pale gold in colour, the bouquet is exquisitely perfumed and penetrating, and the flavour very rich and vigorous, very distinctive, honeyed, with great finesse and breed. In good years the wines usually have 5° Baumé or more. 76 produced a classic wine to stand beside the 67 and 62 and 59, since when there have been good but not outstanding wines in 79 and 80. The 82 looks like being exceptional for the year. The 70 was one of the best examples of this vintage.

Château La Tour-Blanche

1e Cru Classé. Owner: Ministry of Agriculture. Administrator: Jean Pierre Jausserand. 30ha. 5,600 cases. Sém 70%, Sauv 27.5%, Musc 2.5%. Second label: Cru St-Marc.

The *cru* was placed at the head of the Premiers Crus in 1855 and since 1910 has belonged to the state, now being run as an agricultural school. Unfortunately its reputation is nowhere near what it should be, and there are Deuxièmes Crus and indeed unclassified wines which are better. The wine is fermented in vat and then matured in cask with 25% new wood. Considering the care taken in making the wine, it is hard to understand why it should be so uninspired. The most attractive recent vintage I have seen was the 81, which was rich, supple and attractive but rather forward; and there was a well balanced, rich 76.

Château d'Yquem

1er Grand Cru Classé 1855. Owner: Comte Alexandre de Lur-Saluces. 102ha. 5,500 cases. Sém 80%, Sauv 20%. Second label: "Y" (Bordeaux Blanc, 2,000 cases).

In 1855, when the great sweet wines of Sauternes and Barsac were classified, Yquem was placed in a category of its own as the sole Premier Grand Cru, as distinct from the Premiers Crus. Its unique position has remained unassailed ever since. This is not only the greatest Sauternes, it is also the supreme dessert wine in the world. The Lur-Saluces family have owned it since 1785. None have been more dedicated than the present owner Alexandre de Lur-Saluces who succeeded his uncle in 1970. The château is a superb fortress commanding fine views over the region. Everything here is meticulous. The vineyard is carefully rotated, so that, although there are 102ha under vine, only about 80 of these are actually producing the Grand Vin; the rest are young vines. Then the picking is carefully controlled, using only skilled workers, mostly drawn from the 57 full-time estate workers, to go through the vineyard a number of times (anything from four to eleven) to select only overripe and botrytized berries. The aim is to pick at not less than 20° and not more than 22° Baumé. This produces the most balanced wines, which ferment to between 13.5% and 14%, leaving between 4° and 7° Beaumé unfermented sugar. The pressing is traditional and the musts are fermented in new oak, and mature in cask for 3 years prior to bottling. Yquem can never be sampled, even by its burgers, prior to bottling. A dry wine, "Y" or Ygrec, is made in some years. It has quite a honeyed nose, and is full-bodied and quite rich.

This is the quintessential of Sauternes, with its colour turning gradually to pale gold, its intense honeyed bouquet, the wonderful lusciousness and elegance of the flavour itself. It is always a privilege to drink this wine. One should not attempt to drink it before 10 years of age, and it has a special charm of freshness for another decade after that. In the greatest years it can continue almost indefinitely. Wines at their peak now are 73 (a good lesser vintage), 71 (a great wine), 70 (very fine) and 67 (a great year). Years to look forward to are 75 and 76 (exceptional), 80 and 81 (very good).

ST-EMILION

What strikes one about St-Emilion as a district, compared to the other great regions, especially Médoc or Graves, is its smallness and compactness. One can walk straight out of the cramped medieval streets of St-Emilion and find all but one of the Premiers Crus Classés of the *côtes* are but a few minutes walk away.

The area of 5,000ha is divided among 1,000 different *crus*, of which only a small proportion are actually classified, and 1,150 hectares belong to the 330 members of the cooperative known as the Union de Productions. Another notable feature is the small size of the properties themselves. The average size of the 11 Premiers Grands Crus Classés is a bare 20ha; that of the Grands Crus Classés is less than 10ha. Compare this with the vineyard sizes in Médoc. An analysis of the declarations made by growers for the 79 crop showed that out of 1,153 declarations, 843 were made by individuals, 331 by members of the cooperative, and 25 for family consumption.

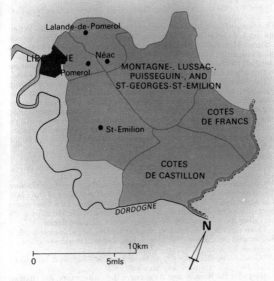

Another fundamental characteristic of St-Emilion is its complex variety of soils. For practical purposes these can be divided into three groups:

First, the limestone plateau (*plateau calcaire*) and the *côtes et pieds de côtes*, the hillsides and lower slopes. Here there is also an important element of clay. This basically covers the area around the town of St-Emilion, and it is here that all but two of the Premiers Grands Crus Classés are to be found.

Second, the *graves et sables anciens*, an area of gravel mixed with sand, but sand of an old windblown variety as distinct from the more recent alluvial kind. This is a small area near the border with Pomerol, where there are a succession of gravelly slopes covering about 60ha, in a sea of sandy soils. The area is dominated by Cheval Blanc and Figeac, and nearly all the other *crus* here are classified.

Third, the *sables anciens*, the area of sandy soils of the type already described. There are a number of good attractive classified *crus* in this category, which basically lies between the first two.

In terms of appellation and geography the region is divided as follows:

1. The Grands Crus Classés, a system of classification under the ultimate control of the INAO which is subject to revision every ten years. In fact the original one of 1954 was revised in 1969, and the second revision came in 1985. This actually reduced the number of classified wines from 12 to 11 in

the Premiers Grands Crus, and from 72 to 63 in the Grands Crus. All the above with two exceptions come from the commune of St-Emilion itself.

2. The Grands Crus, comprising some 200 *crus* that have to submit samples annually for tasting.

3. Wines bearing the simple St-Emilion appellation.

Geographically, although the best wines are to be found in the commune of St-Emilion itself, eight communes which come within the ancient jurisdiction of the Jurade de St-Emilion are also entitled to the appellation. In these communes the best wines come from St-Christophe-des-Bardes, St-Laurent-des-Combes, St-Hippolyte and St-Etienne-des-Lisse. The remaining four – St-Pey-d'Armens, Vignonet, St-Sulpice-de-Faleyrens and Libourne – are mostly on low-lying, sandy soil or on terraces of recent gravel and sand.

There was a time when St-Emilion was said to tend its vines better than anywhere else but not to be so good at making its wines. In the past 20 years there has been a great improvement in this direction with many new *chais* and *cuviers* being built. There remain only the problems involved in commercializing so many small properties.

Château L'Angélus

Grand Cru Classé. Owner: de Bouard de Laforest family. 24ha. 12,000 cases. CF 50%, Mer 45%, CS 5%.

This is one of the most important estates on the St-Emilion *côtes*. Before buying L'Angelus in 1924, the de Bouard de Laforest family owned Château Mazerat, which they later incorporated, together with several other properties, into l'Angelus. The vineyard is on the lower slopes of the *côtes*, to the west of St-Emilion. There is a large modern *chais* and maturing in 100% new oak was introduced in 1980. Before this no wood was used.

The wines are characterized by a marked perfume and easy flattering fruit, but tend to lack depth and concentration. It will be interesting to see what difference the policy of using new oak makes. The best of recent vintages have been 79 which has more body and extract than usual, the 82 which has style and charm although lacking real concentration, and 83 is full of deliciously crunchy fruit. All these wines promise to mature relatively quickly. These are very enjoyable commercial wines, but for me lack real excitement.

Château l'Arrosée

Grand Cru Classé. Owner: François Rodhain. 10ha. 5,000 cases. Mer 50%, CS 35%, CF 15%.

A wine of growing reputation, the vineyard is well sited on the *côtes* above the cooperative and below Tertre-Daugay, just southwest of the town. The name means "watered by springs". The balance of the wine comes from its position. The *haute de côte* giving body and power, the *milieu de côte* providing the richness and the *pied de côte* contributing finesse.

This is very classic St-Emilion, rich and luscious, but with great depth of flavour and personality. Not easy to find, but well worth the effort.

Château Ausone

1er Grand Cru Classé. Owner: Mme Dubois-Challon & Héritiers Vauthier. 7ha. 2,150 cases. Mer 50%, CF 50%.

Named after the Roman poet Ausonius in the 18th century, this château has the remains of a Roman villa of importance nearby, which may well have belonged to the poet. It was only in the 1890s that Ausone was recognized as the first wine on the St-Emilion *côtes*, a position previously held by its larger neighbour, Belair. During the 1950s and 60s the reputation of Ausone was not up to its rank as a Premier Cru, although in 1955 it was placed alongside Cheval Blanc at the head of the new classification by virtue of its undoubted intrinsic merit. Then in 1975 a new *régisseur*, Pascal Delbeck, arrived and took full control in 1976. Since then the reputation of Ausone has soared. Fermentation is now in stainless steel, and 100% new oak is used.

The essence of Ausone is the combination of delicacy and finesse with power, so that the concentration of complex perfumes on the nose is both lively and beautiful, while the sensation of multi-layered flavours on the palate is remarkable. The wines take longer to mature than other St-Emilions and have an ability to age which is unrivalled on this side of the river. Since the massive 75, there has been a fine 76, a great 78, a less monumental but glorious 79, a fine 80, an elegant and rich 81 and exceptional wines in 82 and 83. Everything seems set for Ausone to become the new Pétrus in terms of extraordinary wines produced in very small quantities. Let us hope that wine lovers as well as collectors get a look in.

Château Balestard-la-Tonnelle
Grand Cru Classé. Owner: GFA Capdemourlin. Administrator: Jacques Capdemourlin. 10.6ha. 5,000 cases. Mer 65%, CF 20%, CS 10%, Mal 5%.
This estate lies at the limit of the *plateau calcaire*, to the east of St-Emilion and across the road from Soutard. The maturation is in $\frac{1}{3}$ new wood, $\frac{1}{3}$ in one- or two-year-old wood and the remainder in *cuves*.

The wines here are consistent and most attractive, archetypal St-Emilion which is big, luscious and full-bodied, easy to drink, yet lasting longer than one might expect. The 82 shows real concentration, with a rich meaty structure, but will probably be ready to drink early; 81 is rich and powerful but forward; 80 is soft and full-flavoured and already drinkable by 83; 79 had already developed complex overtones and was a luscious, attractive wine by 83; 78 is soft, ripe and full, ready to drink.

Château Beau-Séjour Bécot
Grand Cru Classé. Owners: Michel, Gérard and Dominique Bécot. 18.5ha. 7,000 cases. Mer 70%, CS 15%, CF 15%.
This *cru* was classified in 1955 as a Premier Grand Cru, and in 1985 was demoted amidst a wealth of controversy. As this is written, Michel Bécot is appealing against the decision. In essence the demotion seems to be because Bécot added the vineyards of La Carte and Trois Moulins on to the original 10ha of Beau Séjour, which he bought in 1970, although the merger was not effected until 1979. The vineyard is on the *plateau calcaire*, and the fermentation is in stainless steel, with fine underground cellars for maturation of the wines in bottle. 90% new wood is used.

The style of the wines here is very different from that at the other Beauséjour, more fleshy and rich, but with less tannin and style. They are very attractive, easy-to-drink wines but do lack distinction. It will be interesting to see what the outcome of it all is.

Château Beauséjour (Duffau-Lagarrosse)
1er Grand Cru Classé B. Owner: Duffau-Lagarrosse. Administrator: Jean-Michel Fernandez. 7ha. 3,000 cases. Mer 50%, CF 25%, CS 25%. Second label: Le Croix de Mazerat.
Today the least known of the Premiers Grands Crus. This is partly because about half of its very small production is sold direct to private customers, rather than through the trade. Beauséjour was a single property until 1869 when it was divided between two daughters. One married a doctor from St-Emilion, and this part now belongs to their heirs.

Long vatting here gives the wine breed and stylish fruit, but perhaps rather too much tannin for wines which are light in body. This is clearly a case of a wine essentially owing its classification to the vineyard site and a long tradition of respectable wines, because the wines are good but not brilliant. Of recent vintages, the 79 had very concentrated fruit, middle richness and quite a lot of tannin – very successful. The 78 is very scented and fine but rather lacking in richness and somewhat tannic. The 76 is very light with an overripe character, for drinking now.

Château Belair
1er Grand Cru Classé B. Owner: Mme Dubois-Challon. 13ha. 4,000 cases. Mer 60%, CF 40%.
Belair immediately adjoins Ausone and is owned by Mme Dubois-Challon, co-owner of Ausone. The two châteaux share the same outstanding régisseur, Pascal Delbeck. The major difference between Belair and Ausone is that, while Ausone is wholly on the *côtes*, the vineyard of Belair is divided between the *côtes* and the plateau above it. Having been made and kept in the Ausone cellars for many years, the wines of Belair returned to their own cellars in 1976, and the old wooden fermentation *cuves* were replaced by stainless steel after the 1980 vintage.

Today Belair is nearly always one of the best of the Premiers Grands Crus B group. The wines tend to be a little richer and more fleshy than Ausone, without quite the same intensity, but with real finesse and great vigour. The wines of 82 and 83 are exceptional. The 81 is fine and typical. There is a good 80, an outstanding 79 and a 78 that gets better all the time. The 76 is a charming lightweight for drinking now, and the 75 firm and backward still.

Château Bellefont-Belcier
Grand Cru. Owner: Jean Labusquière. 13ha. 7,900 cases. Mer 80%, CS 10%, CF 10%.
A good *cru* in St-Laurent des Combes, on the *côte* and its lower slopes. The wines have a reputation for robustness and suppleness.

Château Bellevue

Grand Cru Classé. Owner: **Société Civile M.L. Horeau.** Administrator: René de Coninck. 6ha. 2,500 cases. Mer 70%, CF 15%, CS 15%.
The vineyard lies on the limestone plateau and *côte* just to the west of Beauséjour. It must be one of the least known of the Grand Crus today. It has the misfortune to have one of the commonest names in Bordeaux as there are 23 properties at present using it, several of which are in the St-Emilion region. But it is a very old property and has belonged to the same group of connected families since the 17th century. I have never been able to taste the wine, but it is a *cru* of old repute which was one of the 39 *crus* of St-Emilion that represented the region at the Paris Exhibition of 1867.

Château Bergat

Grand Cru Classé. Owner: **Mme Clause Bertin.** Administrator: Emile Castéja. 4ha. 1,100 cass. Mer 50%, CF 25%, CS 25%.
This is one of the smallest and least known of the Grands Crus Classés. It lies to the east of St-Emilion at the edge of the plateau and *côte*, overlooking the valley of Fougabaud. The property is farmed by Emile Castéja from nearby Trottevieille and distributed by his firm Borie-Manoux.

When I tasted the wine in 1984, the 79 was scented and full on the nose with a very distinctive spicy character on the palate, full-flavoured and still quite tough, promising a good bottle in 1986–87. On this evidence a bottle of Bergat should be worth investigating should one cross your path.

Château Berliquet

Grand Cru Classé. Owners: **Vicomte & Vicomtesse Patrick de Lesqueu.** 7.6ha. 3,200 cases. Mer 75%, CF & CS 25%.
A very old *cru* superbly placed on the *plateau calcaire* of St-Emilion and the *côte*, adjoining Magdelaine, Canon and Tertre Daugay. This *cru* was already regarded as one of the best in the 18th century, but had to wait until 1985 to become a Grand Cru Classé, the only one promoted that year. The reason for this neglect was that as a member of the cooperative its wines were vinified and matured there until the 78 vintage. Then stainless steel fermentation vats were installed, the *chais* restored and the underground *cuves* made ready. Since 78 all the wines have been vinified and matured here using some one-third new oak. All the supervision and work is still in the hands of the Union de Producteurs.

Judging by the wines now being produced, Berliquet well deserves its promotion. The 83 had an intense bouquet of roses and tobacco plants and was rich, complex and powerful with a really lovely flavour. 82 is very dense and rich, powerful and needs time; 81 is very perfumed with verve and finesse and should be ready 88–89; 80 is stylish and pleasant, just ready in 85; 78 is mature and well structured but still taut with more development to come after seven years. This is certainly a *cru* with a growing reputation and considerable potential.

Château Cadet-Bon

Grand Cru. Owner: **François Gratadour.** 4ha. 1,000 cases. Mer 60%, CS 20%, CF 20%.
This small property lies north of the town on the *plateau calcaire* and *côte*. It lost its status as a cru classé in the 1985 revision. Recent tastings had shown that the wines appear rather rustic, with a coarse, stalky flavour suggestive of poor vinification.

Château Cadet-Piola

Grand Cru Classé. Owners: **Jabiol family.** 6.8ha. 3,000 cases. Mer 51%, CS 28%, CF 18%, Mal 3%.
Cadet-Piola lies to the north of St-Emilion on the *plateau calcaire* and *côte* at their culminating northern point. The present owners bought it in 1952 and run it in conjunction with another Grand Cru Classé, Faurie-de-Souchard. Vinification is in glass-lined vats and is carefully controlled. Maturation is in cellars quarried out under the vineyard, and 50% of the wood is new.

The wines are certainly marked by their grape varieties. This is a wine that needs patience compared with many St-Emilions, being tightly knit and austere to start with, but with the structure and style of a wine of some distinction. The 82 has great depth and concentration. The 81 was still very tight and austere after a year in bottle, but with a fine depth of flavour. 80 was pleasantly open-textured and full flavoured at three years old, 79 still firm and austere and very undeveloped when four years old. 78 was a big wine with structure and fruit and a promising future when five years old. 76 is now exceptionally good for the year. This is a wine that needs waiting for, but should be worth it.

Château Canon
1er Grand Cru Classé B. Owner: Eric Fournier. 18ha. 8,000 cases.
Mer 55%, CF 40%, CS 5%.
This is a beautifully placed property, with 13ha of its vineyard in a walled
clos on the plateau just outside the walls of St-Emilion, and a very elegant
little 18th-century château. The remainder of the vineyard is on the *côtes*.
The wines are matured in as much as 40% new wood.

The wines here are very classic, beautifully perfumed, with great length
of flavour, and can be almost silky in texture. There is an inner
concentration of tannin and rich fruit which only slowly opens out. They
always have immense breed, elegance and style. This is usually consistently one of the top St-Emilions, but is a wine you must wait for. The 83
and 82 are both superb – it is hard to say at present which will be the best.
There is a classic 81, the 79 is outstanding, the 78 rather austere and still
backward. The 76 is a charming wine to drink now, and the 75 is another
long-term classic.

Château Canon-la-Gaffelière
Grand Cru Classé. Owner: Comte de Neipperg. 19ha. 10,000 cases.
Mer 60%, CF 35%, CS 5%.
This property lies on the road which runs from the Libourne-Bergerac
road to St-Emilion. It is at the southern foot of the *côtes* and on flat, sandy
soil. The present owner has been there since 1971. Maturation is in cask
and *cuves*, with 50% new wood rotated with wine in vat.

This is a wine that is attractive, quick-maturing and easy to drink. It
makes no pretence of being one of the leading *crus*, but is well made and
dependable. The 78 and 80 are wines for current drinking; the 79 has
something extra in reserve; the 81 is forward and nearly ready. There is a
good 82 with less concentration than the best wines, but robust with plenty
of character. This is a good, attractive, middle-of-the-road St-Emilion to
drink young.

Château Cap-de-Mourlin
Grand Cru Classé. Owner: Mme Jean Capdemourlin. Administrator: Jacques Capdemourlin. 14ha. 6,000 cases. Mer 60%, CF 25%,
CS 12%, Mal 3%.
During the 1970s and until after the 82 vintage this historic property was
divided between two parts of the Capdemourlin family, and its wines were
made and bottled separately, but used identical labels, except that one
bore the name of Mme Jean Capdemourlin, the other that of her nephew
Jacques, who also owns Balestard. Generally I have found the wines
vinified by Jacques Capdemourlin to be superior during this period, and
he is now responsible for the reunited whole. One-third new wood is used
for maturation. The vineyard is north of St-Emilion on the lower *côtes*.

This is a classic St-Emilion, perfumed and fruity on the nose and with a
generous, almost unctuous flavour, supported with a good structure. In
recent years Jacques Capdemourlin made excellent wines in 82, 81, 79 and
78. The future of the reunited property looks promising.

Château Cardinal-Villemaurine
Grand Cru. Owner: Pierre Carille. 18ha. 4,450 cases. Mer 70%,
CF & CS 30%.
A domaine on the *plateau calcaire* just to the east of the town, with extensive
underground cellars. The wines tend to be firm, tannic and a shade
austere. They take time to mature. The years 82, 81, 79, 76, 75 and 70
produced fine examples.

Château Chauvin
Grand Cru Classé. Owner: Henri Ondet. 12ha. 4,200 cases. Mer
60%, CF & CS 40%.
This *cru* lies in what misleadingly used to be called the St-Emilion Graves.
It is the most southeasterly of this group of *crus*, east of Ripeau and south of
Corbin. The soil is sandy. One third of the casks for maturation are new.
The wines are typical of this area near the Pomerol border, rich and dense
in texture, quickly becoming mellow and unctuous in flavour, but with a
touch of coarseness in its makeup. I have always found this to be a very
attractive wine whenever I have come across it.

Château Cheval-Blanc
1er Grand Cru Classé A. Owner: Société Civile du Château Cheval
Blanc. Administrator: Jacques Hébrard. 35ha. 12,000 cases. CF
66%, Mer 33%, Mal 1%.
St-Emilion's two greatest wines, Ausone and Cheval-Blanc, are at
opposite ends of the appellation and on quite different soils. Cheval-Blanc,

the most famous of all St-Emilions, is a large property for the region, right on the border with Pomerol. The modern reputation really goes back to the 1921 vintage, and this was further strengthened by the legendary 47. The soil here is predominantly gravelly and sandy, but clay and sandstone with traces of iron are also present. The high proportion of Cabernet Franc at the expense of Merlot is an unusual feature. In 1956 the vineyard was seriously affected by the notorious February frost and took some time to recover. The vinification is in vat, with refrigeration available to control the temperature. 100% new oak is used for maturation.

The wines of Cheval-Blanc are famous for their powerful enveloping bouquet, which is rich and often spicy, and its very full, mellow, almost unctuous flavour. It is a particular quality of this *cru* that in very ripe years the wines can be drunk very young. This happened with the famous 47, which was delectable when a mere six or seven years old. At this stage the sheer animal vigour and stunning beauty of the wine is matched only by Pétrus, just across the border in Pomerol. Of course the wines keep and develop well according to the individuality of each year, but the early exuberance is not be missed and Cheval-Blanc does not age as well as Ausone and some other wines of the *côtes*, becoming lacy and frail when over 40 years old. Recently the 83 is very fine, 82 probably the best since the 47, then the major years are 81, 79, 78 and 75. 76 is delicious drinking now, and the 79 soon will be. Great vintages worth looking out for are 70, 66 and 64.

Château Clos-des-Jacobins

Grand Cru Classé. Owner: Cordier. 7.5ha. 4,500 cases. Mer 47%, CF 45%, CS 8%.

The wines here have always been consistent and of attractive quality, but I have the impression that recently it has been more concentrated and impressive. The 83, 82 and 81 are all excellent with great richness and opulence. There is a good 80, a delightful 79 and a fine concentrated 78. Certainly this is one of the best *crus* in this section of St-Emilion.

Château La Clotte

Grand Cru Classé. Owner: Heritiers Chailleau. 3.7ha. 1,550 cases. Mer 85%, CF 15%.

This tiny vineyard is beautifully placed on the edge of the *plateau calcaire* and the *côte*, just outside the walls of St-Emilion to the east. It is farmed by Ets J.P. Moueix who take three-quarters of the crop in return for running the vineyard and making the wine. They use 10% new wood. The remainder of the crop is kept by the owners, who sell most of it in their popular restaurant, Logis de la Cadène, in St-Emilion.

The wines have real finesse and delicacy, and are fresh and supple with a lovely bouquet in the best style of the *côtes* wines. Occasionally in vintages such as 70 and 64 the wines have an extra dimension of richness and fleshiness. Owing to the very small quantities involved Ets J.P. Moueix sell the wines on an exclusive basis in the USA and UK.

Château La Clusière

Grand Cru Classé. Owner: Consorte Valette. Administrator: Jean-Paul Valette. 2.8ha. 1,000 cases. Mer 70%, CF 20%, CS 10%.

This tiny vineyard forms a small enclave high up on the Côte de Pavie, among the wines of Pavie and under the same ownership and management. The vinification and *élevage* are carried out in the *chais* and cellars of Pavie, with 25% new wood being used.

The wines are solid, full-bodied and typically St-Emilion. They develop more quickly than those of Pavie-Decesse and are less tannic. There is an excellent 82 full of ripe rich fruit and promising an early developer. The 79 and 78 are both good examples of these contrasting years, with 78 the more stylish. With its tiny production this is not an easy one to find, but well worth it when you do.

Château Corbin

Grand Cru Classé. Owner: Domaines Giraud. 15ha. 5,000 cases. Mer 50%, CF 25%, CS 25%.

A good example of the curse of duplicated names in St-Emilion. In this area of St-Emilion near the Pomerol border there are five adjoining properties, all with Corbin in their names, all Grands Crus Classés, with two of them belonging to the Giraud family, to say nothing of the lesser growths in Montagne-St-Emilion and Graves.

A small amount of new wood is used in the maturation, and the wines have the reputation of being rich and supple, characteristic of this area of sandy soils near Pomerol.

Château Corbin-Michotte
Grand Cru Classé. Owner: Jean-Noël Boidron. 6.7ha. 3,000 cases.
Mer 65%, CF 30%, CS 5%.
There is a double confusion of names here. It is one of five adjoining
properties – all Grands Crus Classés – with the name Corbin and one of
two adjoining Michottes. This one lies immediately to the south of
Croque-Michotte and east of La Dominique. The soil is basically sandy
with some clay in the sub-soil containing iron traces, and some surface
gravel. Since acquiring this property in 1959, Jean-Noël Boidron has
carried out many improvements and entirely rebuilt the *chais* in 1980.
20% of the wine is matured in new wood, rotated with wine held in
stainless steel vats.

I have always been impressed with this wine whenever I have had the
opportunity of tasting it. The rich, plummy texture, fat and very full and
mellow in the mouth, is typical of the best wines from this corner of St-
Emilion near Pomerol. Of recent vintages the 79 is especially good.

Château Cormeil-Figeac
Grand Cru. Owner: Héritiers R. & L. Moreaud. 10ha. 3,500 cases.
Mer 70%, CF 30%.
A good vineyard on the sandy soils southeast of Château Figeac. There is
wood maturation with 15% in new oak. The wines are very scented,
supple and full-flavoured, delicious for early drinking with lots of vibrant
fruit.

Château Côte-Baleau
Grand Cru. Owner: Société des Grandes Murailles. 16ha. 8,500
cases. Mer 70%, CF 15%, CS 15%.
This *cru* was classified in 1969, but then lost its position in 1985. It is on the
lower slope of the *côte* and on sandy soils, north of the town, adjoining
Château Laniote. It is here that the wines of both Grands-Murailles and
Clos St-Martin are actually made and kept. It is hard to say what was
behind the thinking that demoted this *cru* and Grandes-Murailles, but
retained Clos St-Martin. My own comparative tastings suggested that, if
anything, this was the best of the three properties.

The wines have plenty of structure and richness of flavour, and require
some ageing. 82, 81, 79 and 78 are all fine powerful and stylish wines, and
80 is a serious, full flavoured and well structured wine.

Château La Couspaude
Grand Cru. Owner: Aubert. 7ha. 4,000 cases. Mer 60%, CF and CS
40%.
A property on the *plateau calcaire* immediately to the east of the town,
between Villemaurine and Trottevieille. It lost its place in the classification in 1985. The wines are bottled outside the district.

Château Coutet
Grand Cru. Owner: J. David Beaulieu. 11ha. 3,600 cases. Mer 45%,
CF 45%, CS 5%, Mal 5%.
This vineyard is on the *côte* to the west of the town. It lost its classified status
in 1985. The wines seem light but lacking fruit, charm or depth of flavour.

Château Le Couvent
Grand Cru. Owner: Société Civile du Château Le Couvent. 0.4ha.
100 cases. Mer 55%, CF 25%, CS 20%.
This tiny vineyard, actually within the town, changed hands shortly
before the re-classification and did not apply to be considered for the
revised classification. The soil is clay mixed with limestone. The
maturation is in new casks, producing a wine which is supple but rich and
well structured.

Château Couvent-des-Jacobins
Grand Cru Classé. Owner: Mme Joineau-Borde. 9ha. 3,500 cases.
Mer 65%, CF 25%, CS 9%, Mal 1%.
This is a very old property originally belonging to the Dominican friars.
The house and *chais* are in the old town of St-Emilion, while the vineyard
nestles beneath the eastern ramparts of the town on the edge of the *plateau
calcaire* and on sandy soils. Secular owners took over in the 18th century
and the present family have been here since 1902. It was added to the
classification in 1969. This is a traditionally made wine, with 20% new
wood used in the maturation.

In recent vintages I have found the wines to be consistent, well made
with a beautiful flavour and firm finish, quite taut and well structured.
The 81 is more forward than the 79. There is a distinctive blue-black label.
The wine is distributed by Dourthe Frères.

Château Croque-Michotte

Grand Cru Classé. Owner: Mme Rigal. 14ha. 6,700 cases. Mer 90%, Cab 10%.

This *cru* lies on the extreme northwest of St-Emilion where it borders on Pomerol. It has been in the same family since 1890. One-third new wood is used in the maturation.

This seems to be a consistently well made wine. The 81 is tannic and robust with a fine finish; the 80 is full-flavoured with a soft Merlot style, delicious drinking now; 79 is massive and dense with backbone and tannin, a wine with a future; and 78 is ripe and attractive, already drinking well. This is a wine that is certainly above average in terms of quality and consistency.

Château Curé-Bon-La-Madeleine

Grand Cru Classé. Owner: Maurice Landré. 5ha. 2,500 cases. Mer 95%, Mal 5%.

This is a very well placed vineyard on the *plateau calcaire*, a part of which forms the base of an old quarry. Its neighbours are Ausone, Belair and Canon. Maturation is in casks with a small percentage of new wood. The wines have a good reputation and tend to be quite firm in spite of the high proportion of Merlot, but they are also fleshy and generous with a distinctive bouquet denoting breed.

Château Dassault

Grand Cru Classé. Owner: SARL Château Dassault. Administrator: André Vergriette. 23ha. 9,000 cases. Mer 70%, CF 20%, CS 10%.

This was one of eight *crus* added to the classification in 1969. Formerly known as Château Couperie, it was renamed in 1955. Vinification is in stainless steel with maturation in wood, of which a third is new oak.

The style of the wines is uncomplicated, full-flavoured and supple, with charm and breed. They reflect very careful vinification and *élevage* and are most consistent. The 82 has beauty of flavour combined with length and moderate concentration of fruit, probably ready by 87; 81 is full-flavoured and forward; 80 is a pleasing, ready-to-drink lightweight; 79 is lighter and more forward than most wines of this year in St-Emilion; and there is a good 78. There are pleasant middle-of-the-road wines.

Château La Dominique

Grand Cru Classé. Owner: Clément Fayat. 18.5ha. 6,500 cases. Mer 76%, CF 8%, CS 8%, Mal 8%.

This *cru* has always had the capacity to make exceptional wines, but it was not consistent or reliable until the present owner took over in 1969.

The wines here are now an impressive blend of fruit, ripeness and tannin which come together to produce remarkable opulence and power-packed flavour, placing them in the very forefront of the Grands Crus Classés. Those of 83 and 82 are an exceptional pair here; 81 is opulent with softer fruit promising earlier development; 80 is very good for the year, very perfumed, flowery and full of character; 79 is tannic and powerful, with dense fruit and length that demands keeping until around 86–87. The 78 is more open-textured and forward.

Château Faurie-de-Souchard

Grand Cru Classé. Owner: Jabiol family. 11ha. 4,000 cases. Mer 65%, CF 26%, CS 9%.

The name is not to be confused with that of the neighbouring Petit-Faurie-de-Soutard. Previously this property also had had the prefix "Petit", but that has been dropped. The vineyard is on the plateau and *côtes* northeast of the town. Fermentation is in concrete vats, and maturation is by rotating the wine between casks (of which one-third are new) and vats.

Although there is much more Merlot here than at Cadet-Piola, there are some similarities of style, especially a lack of flesh and a tightness of flavour. In recent tastings I found the 79 the most impressive recent vintage, with breed and style. Despite being rather undeveloped, it had a flavour that was very harmonious. The 81 was elegant but closed and lacking flesh after a year in bottle. There seems to be a lack of consistency as well as charm about these wines at present.

Château de Ferrand

Grand Cru. Owner: Baron Marcel Bich. 28ha. 13,500 cases. Mer 66⅔%, CF and CS 33⅓%.

This is the most important property in St-Hippolyte, situated on the *plateau calcaire*. A lot of new wood is used in the maturation, not less than 50% and sometimes 100%. The aim is to produce rich tannic wines that are suitable for ageing.

Château Figeac
1er Grand Cru Classé B. Owner: Thierry de Manoncourt. 40ha.
12,500 cases. CS 35%, CF 35%, Mer 30%.
This fine old property is the remnant of a much larger property, which in
the 18th century included Cheval-Blanc and several other properties
which today incorporate the name of Figeac. As with Cheval-Blanc, some
two-thirds of the vineyard is on gravel and the remaining third on sandy
soil. A fine new *chais* with a large underground section is the latest
improvement here. Under Thierry Manoncourt's direction the consistency
and quality of wine-making has been of a high order. He has been in
charge since 1947.

The similarities and differences between Figeac and Cheval-Blanc are
always fascinating. The size of the vineyards and composition of the soils
are strikingly similar, but the *encépagement* is notably different. Here an
important role is given to Cabernet Sauvignon, while at Cheval-Blanc the
Cabernet Franc reigns supreme. As a result, for all their similarities,
Figeac seldom matches Cheval-Blanc for sheer weight and opulence of
flavour, although it sometimes approaches it and occasionally (as in 1955)
can even surpass it. Superb wines were made in 83, 82, 81, 79, 78 and 75.
The 80 is charming and ready to drink; the 76 rich, opulent and soft, also
at its best.

Château La Fleur
Grand Cru. Owner: Lily Lacoste. 6.5ha. 2,500 cases. Mer 75%,
CF 25%.
A good vineyard northeast of Soutard on sandy soils. The owner is better
known as co-proprietor of Pétrus and owner of Latour-á-Pomerol. The
wines are fleshy and quite rich – full of easy fruit and charm.

Château Fombrauge
Grand Cru. Owner: Bygodt family. 50ha. 25,000 cases. Mer 60%,
CF 30%, CS 10%.
An important *cru* in St-Christophe-des-Bardes, situated partly on the
plateau calcaire, partly on the north-facing *côte* and its lower slopes. The
wines are matured in cask with 25% new oak used. This wine has a long-
established reputation in the UK for consistent, reliable wines.

Château Fonplégade
Grand Cru Classé. Owner: Armand Moueix. 18ha. 7,500 cases. CF
35%, CS 5%, Mer 60%.
These are firm, rather than tannic wines that require time to show their
style and finesse. The 82 promises to be a long-term developer, with a
powerful flavour and tannic undertones. The 80 is stylish and firm,
needing more time to mature than many wines of this year. The 79 shows
maturity and charm already, while 78 was still tough and tannic after six
years. This is consistent and reliable wine, without the richness and charm
of some, but rewarding to keep, solid and dependable if lacking flair.

Château Fonroque
Grand Cru Classé Owner: Ets Jean-Pierre Moueix. 20ha. 6,500
cases. Mer 79%, CF 30%.
The style here tends to be robust, and these are quite firm wines which
need ageing to show at their best – not the sort of flamboyant, early-
drinking style at all. The 83 looks outstanding, with a richness and
concentration of flavour to match the tannin – perhaps better than 82?
The latter is tannic and tough – a wine to wait for. In contrast 81 has a
fullness of flavour and fat but not the usual firmness. The 79 is dense and
powerful, but also has length and complexity – a wine worth waiting for.
The 78 is finely perfumed, with personality and structure, nicely balanced
fruit and tannin. It should be ready around 86.

Clos Fourtet
1er Grand Cru Classé B. Owner: Lurton brothers (André,
Dominique, Lucien, Simone). 17ha. 5,500 cases. Mer 60%, CS 20%,
CF 20%.
The reputation of this château was in decline until 1973 when extensive
improvements were made and the proportion of Merlot increased.

There are distinct similarities of style between Clos Fourtet and its
neighbour Canon. The wines tend to be tightly knit and slow to evolve,
but recently richer and more open-textured than of old. The 83, 82 and 81
are all especially successful, the 81 having more weight than many of that
year. Then 79 and 78 again have great promise. The 75 is good but not
outstanding, and the 76 too overblown to last. This is certainly a château
on its way up, and with the potential to improve its standing further.

Château Franc-Grâce-Dieu

Grand Cru. Owner: Germain Siloret. Administrator: Eric Fournier. 8ha. 3,000 cases. Mer 52%, CF 41%, CS 7%.

Until Eric Fournier from Premier Grand Cru Château Canon took over the farming and management here in 1981, the property was called Guadet-Franc-Grâce-Dieu. Then it was decided that this was rather a mouthful and the Guadet was dropped. Vinification is now in stainless steel with maturation in cask. I found Eric Fournier's first vintage, the 81, had finesse and style with intense, vibrant young fruit – better frankly than some Crus Classés.

Château Franc-Mayne

Grand Cru Classé. Owner: Theillassoubre family. 8ha. 2,700 cases. Mer 75%, CF & CS 25%.

This *cru* lies northwest of St-Emilion, just off the St-Emilion-Pomerol road, and is on the *côte*. In recent years the proportion of Cabernet Franc has been increased at the expense of the Cabernet Sauvignon in order to produce less tannic and more elegant wines. Maturation is in cask, with no new wood used. The reputation of this *cru* is modest.

Château La Gaffelière

1er Grand Cru Classé B. Owner: Comte Léo de Malet-Roquefort. 22ha. 8,000 cases. Mer 65%, CF 25%, CS 10%.

The reputation of La Gaffelière is mixed. It can produce marvellously perfumed, supple, rich and fleshy wines. But in the past there have been inconsistencies and the wines lacked the backbone and breed of some of the best *crus* on the *côtes* and plateau. The signs now are that there is more consistency and a high level of wine-making.

The 83 is particularly successful here, wonderfully rich and complex with real "race" and concentration, while the superb 82 is reminiscent in style of a 47 with its dense almost jammy concentration. Then there is a good 81, an attractive 79 which rather lacks concentration and a rather lightweight if finer 78. The 75 however is most attractive and successful, and an excellent 71 was made. A wine of enormous charm, which perhaps needs a degree of richness to give of its best, and one to watch.

Château La Grâce-Dieu-Les-Menuts

Grand Cru. Owner: Max Pilotte. 13ha. 5,700 cases. Mer 60%, CF 30%, CS 10%.

The name Grâce Dieu comes from a Cistercian grange which was secularized in the 17th century and subsequently divided up. Recently some new casks have been introduced for the maturation in wood, and the reputation of this *cru* is increasing. It lies northwest of St-Emilion on the Libourne road in the sector of sandy soils. The wines tend to be rather light-textured – suitable for young drinking.

Château Grand-Barrail-Lamarzelle–Figeac and Château La Marzelle

Grand Cru Classé. Owner: Association E. Carrère. 34ha. 17,000 cases. Mer 75%, CS and CF 25%.

There are two properties here, each a Grand Cru Classé in its own right, which are run together. They form a very important block of vineyards immediately south of Figeac, on mostly sandy soils, but with some gravel as well. No wood is used in the maturation. The Carrère family bought the properties in the disastrous year of 1956. The wines have the reputation of being supple, fruity and early-maturing. Given the position of the vineyard, one wonders if the full potential is as yet being realized. Château La Marzelle is distributed by Dourthe Frères.

Château Grand Corbin

Grand Cru Classé. Owner: Alain Giraud. 13ha. 6,000 cases. Mer 50%, CF 25%, CS 25%.

The history of this property is the same as that of Château Corbin, as is the ownership. It lies on sandy soils between Corbin and Grand-Corbin-Despagne. Maturation is in casks of which 20% are new. The reputation is for wines which tend to be blander than those of Corbin and are certainly not of the same level as Grand-Corbin-Despagne.

Château Grand-Corbin-Despagne

Grand Cru Classé. Owner: Despagne family. 25ha. 11,000 cases. Mer 70%, CF 25%, CS and Mal 5%.

The wines here have a good reputation, and recent tastings confirm that this is deserved. I found the 81 particularly good, with rich fruit on the nose, a delicious flavour that was ripe and opulent, and more body than many 81s – altogether a very attractive wine with nice firm undertones. In comparison, the 79 looked a shade rustic, an opulent wine with irony undertones, powerful and assertive.

Château Grandes Murailles

Grand Cru. Owner: Société Civile. 2ha. Mer 70%, CF 15%, CS 15%. This tiny vineyard adjoins Clos Fourtet, where the *plateau calcaire* begins to fall away to the *côte*. There is a curious situation here. The wine is made and kept at the cellars of Baleau, the largest of the three properties owned by this company, but Grandes Murailles and Baleau have now lost their classified status as a result of the 1985 revision.

I have found the wines rich and opulent in style, and quick to mature. Delicious wines were made in 82, 81, 79 and 78.

Château Grand-Mayne

Grand Cru Classé. Owner: Jean-Pierre Nony. 17ha. 11,000 cases. Mer 50%, CF 40%, CS 10%. Secondary labels: Château Beau Mazerat, Château Cassevert.

This old domaine lies on the western *côte* and its lower slopes. Stainless steel vats replaced the traditional wooden ones in 1975. Maturation is in casks of which 20% are new.

At a recent tasting the 81 had a complex bouquet, a really long flavour and elegant, crisp fruit – a very stylish and attractive wine. But the 79 had a very dry finish and seemed to lack middle fruit and ripeness – odd in a vintage such as this. If future vintages follow the 81 rather than the 79, this should be a good middle-of-the-road wine to watch.

Château Grand-Pontet

Grand Cru Classé. Owner: Bécot and Pourquet families. 14ha. 6,500 cases. Mer 70%, CF 15%, CS 15%.

This château, at the foot of the *côtes*, lies just outside St-Emilion on the Libourne road. From 1965 to 1980 it belonged to Barton & Guestier, who completely modernized the property. One of the two present partners also owns nearby Beau-Séjour-Bécot.

Under the Barton & Guestier regime sound but unexciting wines were made. It is now said that the quality has improved under the new management, so the wines should be worth watching.

Château Guadet-St-Julien

Grand Cru Classé. Owner: Robert Lignac. 5.5ha. 2,000 cases. Mer 75%, CS and CF 25%.

Generally this is an attractive, supple wine, showing unmistakeable class, which matures quickly. The 81, ready by 86, and the 80 both fall into this category. But 79 was still tough and somewhat astringent after two years in bottle. The 78 is now most attractive with a firm flavour and fruit balanced by structure. It can be enjoyed now or kept.

Château Haut-Corbin

Grand Cru Classé. Owner: Edward Guinaudie. 4.5ha. 2,500 cases. Mer 67%, CS 33%.

This small property, near the border with Montagne-St-Emilion, lies north and east of the other Corbins on sandy soil. It was the only *cru* in this part of the appellation to be upgraded to Grand Cru Classé in 1969. The wines are matured in cask, but no new wood is used.

I found the 81 crisp, clear, simple, straightforward and well balanced, but 79 was hard and edgy – disappointing for the vintage and for a Grand Cru Classé. Whether things are getting better or are just inconsistent, I cannot tell.

Château Haut-Gueyrot

Owner: Jean-Marcel Gombeau. 7ha. 3,500 cases. Mer 85%, CF 15%.

This small vineyard on the lower slopes and the plain of St-Laurent-des-Combes produces consistently attractive rich, fruity, quite luscious and very typical wines, which are usually delicious drinking after three years.

Château Haut-Pontet

Grand Cru. Owner: Limouzin Frères. 5.2ha. 2,500 cases. Mer 75%, CF and CS 25%.

This small *cru* is on the lower slopes of the *côte* north of St-Emilion. This is well made wine, distinctive, rich and full-flavoured with a good backbone. Very consistent.

Château Haut-Sarpe

Grand Cru Classé. Owner: Jean-François Janoueix. 12.5ha. 6,000 cases. Mer 70%, CF 30%.

Tastings of a number of recent vintages have confirmed that this is a wine of character and breed. The 82 promises something special; 81 is stylish and developing slowly; 79 luscious and chewy, very St-Emilion; 78 rather austere and dry.

Château Jean-Faure

Grand Cru. Owner: Michel Amart. 17ha. 5,600 cases. CF 60%, Mer 30%, Mal 10%.

For many years this *cru*, lying on sandy soils between Cheval-Blanc and Ripeau, belonged to Ripeau and the properties were run together, until the present owner bought it in 1976. The wine is distributed by Dourthe Frères. The *cru* lost its classified status in the revision of 1985. The aim is to produce full-bodied wines which are also elegant. Why the wine lost its standing is hard to say.

Château Laniote

Grand Cru Classé. Owner: Freymond-Schneider family. 5ha. 2,200 cases. Mer 80%, CF 15%, CS 5%.

This is not a big beefy St-Emilion but has great finesse. It is very perfumed and intense, with a long, refined and beautiful flavour, and with real "race". It has a most enchanting texture, lush and silky, which makes the wines very exciting. Those of 83, 82, 81 and 79 are all superb.

Château Larcis-Ducasse

Grand Cru Classé. Owner: Mme Hélène Gratiot Alphandéry. 10ha. 5,000 cases. Mer 65%, CF and CS 35%.

The wines here have been noted for their breed and charm, but have sometimes been rather light. Recent vintages have shown a marked improvement in consistency and quality. The 83 has concentration and tannin with the breed shining through. The 82 is exceptional with layers of flavour and real complexity, richness and length. The 81 is finely balanced with depth and length of flavour. There is a light, attractive 80 and a backward 79 with tannin, but still elegant and fine. The 78 has concentration, personality and charm.

Château Larmande

Grand Cru Classé. Owner: Meneret-Capdemourlin family. 18.5ha. 8,000 cases. Mer 65%, CF 30%, CS 5%. Second label: Château des Templiers.

This fine property lies north of St-Emilion looking towards St-Georges. It marks the end of the *côtes* and the beginning of the sandy soils. The last decade has been one of progress here. The vineyard has been enlarged and the proportion of Merlot increased at the expense of Cabernet Franc and, to an even greater extent, the Cabernet Sauvignon. A new *cuvier* equipped with stainless steel fermentation vats was built in 1975.

This is a wine which has won many accolades of late, and consistently does well in blind tastings. The bouquet tends to be perfumed, full and vibrant, the wine rich, full-flavoured, quite spicy and with depth, harmony and style. The 82 is fine and typical of the year; 81 and 79 are both excellent with power and charm, and there is a good 80.

Château Laroque

Grand Cru. Owners: SCA Château Laroque. Distribution: Alexis Lichine & Cie. 45ha. 20,000 cases. Mer 65%, CF and CS 35%.

This large property is in the commune of St-Christophe-des-Bardes where it occupies an exceptional site on the *plateau calcaire* and *côte*. New fermentation *cuves* were installed in 1969. The maturing wine is rotated between vats and casks. The wines have a good reputation.

Château Laroze

Grand Cru Classé. Owner: Georges Meslin. 28ha. 11,000 cases. Mer 50%, CF 40%, CS 10%.

The wines here are characterized by their very fresh, clean, up-front fruit, perfumed, supple and very easy to drink. They mature quite quickly (over three to five years) and are usually at their best at around five to eight years. These are delicious, flattering, fruity wines sold at very reasonable prices. The 83, 82, 81, 80, 79 and 78 are all good examples of these vintages, and all but the 83 and 82 can now be drunk.

Château La Madeleine

Grand Cru Classé. Owner: Hubert Pistouley. 2ha. 800 cases. Mer 50%, CF 50%.

This tiny property is well placed on the southern edge of the plateau of La Madeleine and on the *côte* below it. Most of the production is sold in Belgium. The wines are carefully made and have all the refinement and breed one would expect of this fine site. They are finely perfumed, have charming fruit and are light and easy to drink. The 81 and 79 were both ready to drink in 84 and are good examples of these vintages.

Château Magdelaine

1er Grand Cru Classé B. Owner: Ets Jean-Pierre Moueix. 11ha. 4,000 cases. Mer 80%, CF 20%.

The hallmark of Magdelaine is its great delicacy and breed and refinement of flavour. Very fine wines were made in 83, 82, 81, 79, 78 and an exceptionally attractive 75. The personality of the *cru* is very interesting, because it is more charming than the straight plateau wines such as Canon but less fleshy and more elegant than a lower *côtes* such as La Gaffelière. For me this is one of the most rewarding wines of the St-Emilion *côtes*.

Château Matras

Grand Cru Classé. Owner: Jean Bernard-Lefèbvre. 18ha. 6,000 cases. Mer 33%, CF 33%, CS 33%, Mal 1%.

If you stand on the promontory at Tertre Daugay and look across the *côte* northwards, you will see a battery of tanks standing beside some modest buildings. This is Matras. It is southwest of the town and occupies a hollow on the *côtes* and the lower slope. The proprietor is an oenologist. Maturation is in cask with 25% new wood.

Unfortunately the wines are not as interesting as the history of the property. I found both the 79 and 81 had an unpleasantly marked irony taste and were tough and charmless. The impression is that all is not well with the wine-making, especially since the site is good. Something of a cautionary tale as far as oenologists are concerned!

Château Mauvezin

Grand Cru Classé. Owner: Pierre Cassat. 4ha. 2,000 cases. Mer 40%, CF 50%, CS 10%.

This small vineyard lies east of St-Emilion at the limits of the *plateau calcaire*, between Haut Sarpe and Balestard-La-Tonnelle. Since the present owner took over in 1968 there has been much replanting of the old vineyard, and the yields have increased accordingly. A high percentage of new wood is used in the maturation. The many gold medals won by this *cru* attest to the quality of its wines.

Château Monbousquet

Grand Cru. Owner: Querre family. 30ha. 12,000 cases. Mer 50%, CF 40%, CS 10%.

These are attractive rich supple wines with a distinctive character – sometimes a hint of tobacco on the nose – and a strong rather earthy flavour. It just lacks the ultimate breed of the best St-Emilions, but is nevertheless a highly enjoyable wine for all that.

Château Montlabert

Grand Cru. Owner: Société Civile. Administrator: René Barrière. 11ha. 6,000 cases. Mer 51%, CF 34%, CS 15%.

This property lies on sandy soils northwest of St-Emilion near Figeac. Since 1970 it has belonged to a company of which René Barrière is a member and acts as administrator. The distribution is in the hands of the négociants A & R Barrière. The wines have a good reputation and are widely exported.

Château Moulin du Cadet

Grand Cru Classé. Owner: Ets Jean-Pierre Moueix. 5ha. 1,800 cases. Mer 90%, CF 10%.

A very small property on the *plateau calcaire*, north of St-Emilion and adjoining the Mouix property of Fonroque. The wines bear all the hallmarks of the impeccable care which Ets J.-P. Moueix take of all the properties they own or farm. Recently a small percentage of new wood has been introduced into the cask maturation. The wines are little known because of the very small production, but I have been impressed by their perfume, breed and elegance. They can be rather finer than those at neighbouring Fonroque, but less powerful.

Clos L'Oratoire

Grand Cru Classé. Owner: Société Civile Peyreau. Administrator: Michel Boutet. 9.45ha. 3,700 cases. Mer 70%, CF 30%.

This property lies northeast of the town where the lower slope of the *côte* gives way to the sandy soils, close to the border with St-Christophe-des-Bardes. It is run with the larger Château Peyreau which is an unclassified Grand Cru. 25% new casks are used. in the maturation.

These are rich concentrated wines, very Merlot in style with a good depth of flavour; what one thinks of as a typical St-Emilion. They develop quite quickly. 82 will be an early developer, 81 is excellent, 79 and 78 are both rich and very drinkable. 80 is forward and attractive.

Château Patris
Grand Cru. Owner: Michel Querre. 11ha. 3,000 cases. Mer 70%, CS 20%, CF 10%.
This *cru* lies on sandy soils of the little valley of Mazerat, just at the southwest base of the *côte* of St-Emilion. the property is run with the same care as the same owners' *cru* in Pomerol, Château Mazeyres. Two-thirds of the wine is matured in casks, of which a third are new, the rest in vats. Perfumed, supple wines of good repute are made.

Château Pavie
1er Grand Cru Classé B. Owner: Consorts Valette. Administrator: Jean-Paul Valette. 37.5ha. 12,000 cases. Mer 55%, CF 25%, CS 20%.
This is the largest vineyard on the *côtes*, and is splendidly placed on a long south-facing slope southeast of the town of St-Emilion. In recent years Jean-Paul Valette, the member of the family in charge, has done much to improve the quality of the wines here. It is probable that the land at the foot of the *côtes* on sandy soil reduces the overall quality of the wines, which while full of charm have a tendency to lack concentration.

Recently the 83 was outstandingly successful, and there was a marvellously opulent 82. After a lovely 81, the 79 is soft and easy and 78 rather understated but fine. 76 is rather lightweight and the 75 is less concentrated but more attractive than most. Certainly this is a *cru* to watch now as the wines of the 80s show added depth.

Château Pavie-Decesse
Grand Cru Classé. Owner: Valette family. Administrator: Jean-Paul Valette. 9ha. 4,500 cases. Mer 65%, CF 20%, CS 15%.
This is fine classic "*côtes*" wine, with power and breed. Sometimes one is more conscious of the tannin than with Pavie because the wine has less opulence and fat. Yet sometimes – as in 82 – it can actually have more alcohol. As in Pavie, both 83 and 82 are excellent, as is 81. There is a stylish, delicious 80 and unusually the 78 is better than the 79.

Château Pavie-Macquin
Grand Cru Classé. Owner: Antoine Corre. 10ha. 4,000 cases. Mer 80%, CF 10%, CS 10%.
Named after Albert Macquin who was a pioneer in the grafting of European vines onto American root-stocks to combat the phyloxera. It is on the plateau above the Côte Pavie, and between Pavie, Troplong-Mondot and the town. The wines are elegant and pleasant, of good average quality and sold at very reasonable prices.

Château Pavillon-Cadet
Grand Cru Classé Owner: Anne Llammas. 3.5ha. 750 cases. Mer 50%, CF 50%.
This very small property is on the hill of Cadet, just north of the town. It is one of the least known of Grands Crus Classés. The wines are matured in cask, but I have never tasted the wine and information about it is scant.

Château Petit-Faurie-de-Soutard
Grand Cru Classé. Owner: Mme Françoise Capdemourlin. Administrator: Jacques Capdemourlin. 8ha. 3,500 cases. Mer 60%, CF 30%, CS 10%.
Until 1850 this formed part of Soutard. It lies in a fine position on the *plateau calcaire* and the *côte*.

This is a stylish wine with real breed and finesse. Because of the soil here, with its high limestone element, the wines are less luscious but have more structure and are perhaps finer than at Balestard. The 82 has a very marked character and a fine middle flavour and richness – there is breed but this is not a heavyweight wine. The 81 is more structured and closed with finesse and breed. The 80 is delicious, stylish and ready to drink. The 79 is rich and full, attractive, with real class, but the 78 is surprisingly forward and lightweight, not a keeper.

Château Le Prieuré
Grand Cru Classé. Owner: SCE Baronne Guichard. 5ha. 1,500 cases. Mer 70%, CF 30%.
This property on the *plateau calcaire* is on high ground, on a site set apart, between Trottevieille and Troplong-Mondot. The owners also have an important property in Lalande de Pomerol, Château Siaurac and Château Vrai-Croix-de-Gay in Pomerol. It once belonged to the Franciscan house in St-Emilion, the Cordeliers. A proportion of 25% new wood is used in the maturation. I have found the wines attractive, elegant, on the light side, good breed but not above average. The 79 is very good, the 81 is pretty but lacks depth of flavour.

Château Ripeau

Grand Cru Classé. Owner: Michel Janoueix de Wilde. 20ha. 4,700 cases. Mer 40%, CF 40%, CS 20%.

An important *cru* on the sandy soils near the border with Pomerol, it lies southeast of Cheval-Blanc and La Dominique. Since the present owners took over in 1976 they have considerably expanded the *cuvier* and *chais*.

It is a sure sign of the progress being made here in restoring the reputation of this fine *cru*, that the 81 is better than the 79. I particularly liked its perfumed spicy bouquet, while the wine was better balanced and finer than the 79, with complexity and firm undertones.

Château St-Georges-Côte-Pavie

Grand Cru Classé. Owner: Jacques Masson. 5.5ha. 2,000 cases. Mer 60%, CF 40%.

A small, very well-placed *cru* on the western end of the Côte de Pavie and its lower slope. La Gaffelière is on the other side, and there are views across to Ausone. The fermentation is in stainless steel, and maturation is in cask. The wines are notable for their delicious easy fruit and marked character and breed. They are high toned and flavoured and are delightful to drink when 4 to 7 years old. The 79 is scented and opulent, the 81 more spicy, luscious and stylish. The sort of joyous St-Emilion that is irresistible.

Clos St-Martin

Grand Cru Classé Owner: Société Civile des Grands Murailles. 3.5ha. 1,600 cases. Mer 66%, CF 17%, CS 17%.

The situation here is an odd one. Three *crus* – this one, Grandes Murailles and Côte Baleau – are all managed together, with the wine made and kept at Côte Baleau. Recently the other two *crus* have lost their Grand Cru Classé status. For each vintage 25% of the casks here are new.

The wines I have tasted here have shown a certain unevenness of quality, the best being rich, opulent and well structured. The most impressive were 82 and 79. 81 is attractive but rather lightweight.

Château Sansonnet

Grand Cru Classé. Owner: Francis Robin. 7ha. 4,000 cases. Mer 60%, CF 20%, CS 20%.

This *cru* is on the *plateau calcaire* east of St-Emilion on its eastern culminating point, and just north of Trottevieille. There is clay mixed with limestone here, on rocky sub-soil. The wine is matured in cask. These are firm wines which are not particularly rich or luscious and need time to unfold and develop. The 79 was still firm with an irony flavour, but some balancing fat when five years old, and still needed time. The 81 was lighter and less concentrated with nice fruit which developed and filled out in the glass, indicating that it was still evolving.

Château La Serre

Grand Cru Classé. Owner: Bernard d'Arfeuille. Administrator: Luc d'Arfeuille. 7ha. 3,000 cases. Mer 80%, CF 20%.

This is a wine with structure, depth of flavour and a finely perfumed bouquet, a wine of individuality, typical of the plateau around St-Emilion. This is a solid, reliable Grand Cru Classé of good average quality – not a high flyer but thoroughly worthy.

Château Soutard

Grand Cru Classé. Owners: Comte François & Comtesse Isabelle des Ligneris. 28ha. 8,000 cases. Mer 60%, CF 35%, CS 5%.

The aim at Soutard is to make traditional, long-keeping wines and the result is uncompromising and requires patience. My own feeling is that sometimes the fruit and natural charm of St-Emilion are unnecessarily sacrificed and that often the wines would benefit from earlier bottling and a lighter touch – but these are matters of taste. The stylishness comes through, but the wines often seem lean and ungrateful. This was certainly true of the 79 when six years old. But the 81 was better balanced, rather light but with attractive fruit not crushed by wood.

Château Tertre-Daugay

Grand Cru Classé. Owner: Comte Leo de Malet Roquefort. 16ha. 6,000 cases. Mer 60%, CF 30%, CS 10%.

The property was in an appalling state of neglect when Comte Leo de Malet-Roquefort bought it in 1978. From then until the reconstruction of the *cuvier* and *chais* in 1984 the wines had to be made and kept at La Gaffelière. This property now receives the same care and attention as the Premier Grand Cru, but with one-third new wood used in the maturation.

There can be no doubting the potential of this *cru* to be one of the very best of the Grands Crus Classés. The wines are gloriously perfumed and spicy on the nose, with tannic and rich ripe fruitiness well matched to give a fine powerful complex flavour with stylish breed shining through. The 81, 80 and 78 are all excellent examples of these years, with good keeping qualities. The 78, first year of the new regime, is delicious but forward and lighter. The future here looks to be full of interest and promise.

Château Toinet-Fombrauge
Owner: Bernard Sierra. 8ha. 2,900 cases. Mer 85%, CF and CS 15%.
This *cru* is in St-Christophe-des-Bardes and lies below the north *côte* on mostly sandy soils. It produces rich, full-flavoured, rather soft wines of marked character, usually very drinkable after three or at most four years.

Château La Tonnelle
Owner: Guy Arnaud et fils. 15ha. Mer 65%, CS 30%, CF 5%.
This *cru* is in the commune of Vignonet on the terraces of gravel and sand in the plain of the Dordogne. The wine is vinified and bottled at the cooperative and is compact and firm developing style.

Château La Tour-Figeac
Grand Cru Classé. Owner: Société Civile. Administrator: Michel Boutet. 13.5ha. 6,000 cases. Mer 60%, 40%.
This property lies on the border with Pomerol and was part of Figeac until 1879. Three years later the two La Tour du Pin Figeacs were also hived off.

This is a powerful yet stylish wine, rich and scented on the nose, with real length of flavour and marked by elegant breed. Its recent vintages have consistently done well in blind tastings, placing it with La Tour-du-Pin-Figeac (Moueix) and La Dominique as one of the leaders among the Grands Crus Classés. Excellent wines were made in 82, 81, 80, 79 and 78.

Château La Tour-du-Pin-Figeac
Grand Cru Classé. Owner: Héritiers Marcel Moueix. Administrator: A. Moueix. 9ha. 4,000 cases. Mer 60%, CF 30%, Mar and CS 10%.
These are powerful, robust, full-flavoured wines of style which have consistently come out well in blind tastings in recent years. Together with its neighbour La Tour-Figeac and La Dominique, it is one of the outstanding *crus* in this area adjoining Pomerol, and indeed stands with them among the top of all the Grands Crus Classés today. The 82 is especially fine, and 81, 80, 79 and 78 are all distinguished wines.

Château La Tour-du-Pin-Figeac (Giraud Belivier)
Grand Cru Classé Owner: GFA Giraud Belivier. 10.5ha. 4,000 cases. Mer 75%, CF 25%.
This property is not nearly as well known or as well reputed as its neighbour of the same name owned by the A. Moueix firm of Château Taillefer. They shared a common history until 1882. The Giraud family bought the property from the Beliviers in 1972, but there is no sign that this change of ownership is resulting in wines worthy of its excellent site.

Château Trimoulet
Grand Cru Classé. Owner: Michel Jean. 17ha. 8,000 to 10,000 cases. Mer 60%, CF 20%, CS 15%, Mal 5%.
This property lies north-northeast of St-Emilion, near the boundary with St-Georges. The soils here are sandy mixed with clay and traces of iron. It has belonged to the same family for several generations and 100% new wood is used for the maturation.

Whenever I have drunk mature bottles in France I have found this to be attractive St-Emilion. When young the wines can look rather rustic. Recently I found the 81 had a good fruity flavour and was well structured, but the 79 was disappointing – short and rather coarse and stalky.

Château Troplong-Mondot
Grand Cru Classé. Owner: Claude Valette. 30ha. 13,500 cases. Mer 70%, CF, CS and Mal 30%.
This is one of the most important properties in St-Emilion on the *côte* and plateau. It should be one of the best *crus* in St-Emilion and if sites play a part should be challenging for a position as a Premier Grand Cru. But one feels the full potential is not at present being realized in terms of consistency and quality. At its best this wine can show real breed combined with power and a lovely flavour. There are signs of improvement. The 83 and 82 are both fine; 81 is firm and promising but lacks fat; 80 is meagre and poor. There are fine 79s and 78s. The 70 is exceptional.

Château Trottevieille
1er Grand Cru Classé B. Owner: Philippe Castéja. Administrator: Philippe Castéja. 10ha. 4,500 cases. Mer 60%, CF 25%, CS 15%.
This is the only Premier Grand Cru to be owned by a Bordeaux négociant. The vineyard is apart from the other Premiers on the plateau to the east of

St-Emilion, somewhat below Troplong-Mondot. The soil is a mixture of limestone and clay. The reputation of Trottevieille has been disappointing in recent years, and does not correspond to some of the rich concentrated wines I recall before the 56 frost. Too often the wines are either coarse and dull, or disappointingly diluted. The best of recent efforts seem to be a really rich and tannic 79, a big forceful 75 and a powerful, distinctive 70 with a rich, firm aftertaste showing ripeness and balance. Quite what is wrong is hard to say, since the same proprietors' Batailley is consistently good and getting better.

Union de Producteurs de St-Emilion

Director: **Jacques Baugier.** 1,150ha. 550,000 cases.

There is no other cooperative in Bordeaux which produces so much high-quality wine as this one, lying just at the southern foot of the *côte*, between the town and the Libourne–Bergerac road. In 1985 it saw one of its 330 members, Château Berliquet, become a Grand Cru Classé (see entry).

There are four important wines, all entitled to the Grand Cru status, which are sold under trademarks:

Royal St-Emilion. This is made from properties in the plain. The wines are full, robust and open-textured with a certain coarseness typical of its origins, but attractive.

Côtes Rocheuses. As the name implies, this comes from properties in the *côtes* area. This is a wine which takes longer to develop its richness, and has more power. Some 120,000 cases of the wine are produced annually.

Haut Quercus. Quercus is the Latin for oak. This brand was launched in 1978, and the wine is aged in new oak. At present 2,500 cases, all in numbered bottles, are produced annually. The wines have real intensity and are quite tannic with a very classic flavour. They take time to mature.

Cuvée Gallus. This is a special selection of cask-aged wines. The first vintage was 1982, and it was selected at a blind tasting as one of the 12 best wines for the Trophée des Honneurs in 1984.

The quality of these branded wines is frequently superior to that of many small *crus* made at the property, and certainly more saleable. It is an invaluable source for good, typical, sound St-Emilion.

In addition, a large number of château wines are individually made and bottled under their respective labels. These are labelled as *mis à propriété*.

Château Villemaurine

Grand Cru Classé. Owner: Robert Giraud. 7ha. 3,800 cases. Mer 70%, CS 30%.

The name is derived from Ville Maure meaning Moorish city, the name given to the place where the Saracens camped in the 8th century.

Great efforts are being made to improve the quality here, and there is certainly potential, though whether they are right to have so much Cabernet Sauvignon must be open to question. The 83 is extremely tannic but with rich fat it could do well. The 82 is very perfumed and rich with a very attractive flavour and very long, with a taste of cinnamon, spicy and complex. The 79 was still firm and very young, but had already developed a lovely flavour after five years. If more wines like this can be produced, Villemaurine will soon re-establish its reputation.

Château Yon-Figeac

Grand Cru Classé. Owners: Lussiez brothers. 24ha. 7,500 cases. Mer 33⅓%, CF 33⅓%, CS 33⅓%.

This large vineyard lies northwest of St-Emilion on the road to Pomerol, between Laroze and Grand Barail–Larmarzelle–Figeac on sandy soils. The Lussiez family have been owners here for four generations. The wines only spend about six months in cask, the rest of the time in vat.

The wines here have been noted for their consistency and typical attractive characteristics for many years. They tend to be very scented, soft, rich and full-flavoured, with a nice underlying firmness. The 81 is a good straightforward example, 79 bigger and more typical.

THE ST-EMILION SATELLITES

Outside the St-Emilion appellation to the north and northeast lie the so-called St-Emilion satellites. While they have been excluded from the straightforward St-Emilion AC, they have the right to add the name St-Emilion to their own communal names. Some of these wines are in fact superior to St-Emilions produced from the plain of the Dordogne, and there is a much higher proportion of large domaines than in St-Emilion and Pomerol. Many of the small owners are members of the cooperatives of Montagne and Lussac-Puisseguin. The satellite communes are as follows:

Montagne-St-Emilion. The small communes of St-Georges and Parsac were joined to Montagne in 1972, but some owners in St-Georges continue to exercise their option of using the St-George-St-Emilion appellations. The AC now covers around 1,500ha of vineyard. The soils are *plateau calcaires* and *côtes*, but with more clay than in St-Emilion.

Lussac-St-Emilion. Here there are around 1,100ha of vines. There are *plateau calcaires* of the type found in St-Emilion and St-Christophe. But below these are *côtes* of "sables du Périgord" which are less favourable for viticulture. This is the most northerly of these appellations.

Puisseguin-St-Emilion. This lies northeast of St-Emilion with around 650ha of vines. There is a large *plateau calcaire* and its *côtes*, which provide good viticultural land.

Château Belair-Montaiguillon
Owners: **Nadine Pocci & Yannick le Menn.** 10ha. 4,700 cases. Mer 75%, CF and CS 20%, Mal 5%.
This excellent *cru* is situated on one of the highest points in the commune of St-Georges, facing south towards St-Emilion on limestone and clay soils. Really delicious wines are now being made here. They are full of lovely rich, supple fruit and have marked character. Comparable to the best St-Emilion Grands Crus.

Château Calon
Owner: **Jean-Nöel Boidron.** Montagne vineyard: 35ha; 15,000 cases; Mer 70%, CF 15%, CS 13%, Mal 2%. St-Georges vineyard: 5ha; 2,600 cases; Mer 80%, CF 10%, CS 10%.
Some cause for confusion here! This is basically one property with land in two communes, Montagne and St-Georges. The label is the same, but both appellations are used, although the whole production could now be sold as Montagne. The owner also owns Château Corbin-Michotte. This is well made wine with a good reputation.

Château des Laurets
Owner: **GFA du Domaine des Laurets et de Malengin.** 60ha. 30,000 cases. Mer 70%, CF 15%, CS 15%. Secondary labels: **Château La Rochette, Château Maison-Rose.**
This is the most important property in Puisseguin and one of the largest in the St-Emilion satellites. The vineyards are on the *plateau calcaire* and the *côtes* south of Puisseguin. These are well reputed, robust and attractive wines.

Château du Lyonnat
Owner: **GFA des Vignobles Jean Milhade.** 50ha. 25,000 cases. Mer 50%, CF 50%. Second label: **Château La Rose-Peruchon.**
This is one of the largest and best known domaines in the St-Emilion satellites. It lies in the east of Lussac on the *plateau calcaire*. This is very reliable, fairly light-textured, stylish wine which nevertheless keeps quite well. The standard is comparable to a good Grand Cru of St-Emilion.

Château Maison-Blanche
Owners: **Gérard & Françoise Despagne.** 30ha. 15,000 cases. Mer 40%, CF 30%, CS 30%.
This important domaine is on the *côte* to the west of Montagne. The wines are richly perfumed and very attractive for early drinking.

Château Maquin St-Georges
Owner: **François Corre.** Administrator: **Denis Corre.** 30ha. 15,000 cases. Mer 70%, CF and CS 30%. Second label: **Château Bellonne St-Georges.**
This well known *cru* is on hillside sites near St-Georges. The wines are bottled and distributed by Ets J.-P. Moueix. (See Château Pavie Macquin for information on Macquin.) Fine, attractive, luscious wines are consistently made here. They are up to good St-Emilion Grand Cru standard.

Château Roudier
Owner: **Jacques Capdemourlin.** 30ha. 15,000 cases. Mer 60%, CF 25%, CS 15%.
This fine and important property is on the *côte* (limestone and clay) facing south towards St-Emilion. The proprietor also owns Balestard-la-Tonnelle and manages Capdemourlin. The wines are of a high standard; there is a marvellously rich, gamey flavour. The 79 was ideal drinking when six years old. Easily up to the best St-Emilion Grand Cru standard.

Château St-Georges
Owner: **M. Desbois-Petrus**. 50ha. 22,500 cases. Mer 50%, CS 30%, CF 10%, Mal 10%.
Certainly one of the most spectacular properties in the whole region, with a truly palatial château built in 1774 by Victor Louis, architect of the Grand Theatre in the purest classical style. Its vineyards are on south-facing *côtes* looking towards St-Emilion. These are elegant but well constructed wines that have a considerable life-span. There is 50% new oak used in the maturation. If this was in St-Emilion it is hard to think it would not be a Grand Cru Classé. As it is the wines have a great reputation, especially in France, where much is sold by mail-order.

Château Tour-du-Pas-St-Georges
Owner: **Mme Prot**. Administrator: **Mme Dubois-Challon**. 15ha. 6,500 cases. Mer 50%, CF 35%, CS 15%.
This property lies on south-facing slopes of limestone and clay in St-Georges. It is now farmed by Mme Dubois-Challon, which means that the gifted Pascal Delbeck, *régisseur* of Ausone and Belair, is making the wine. The results look promising. I found the 81, bottled in April 84, deliciously fruity, very easy and evolved after a year in bottle.

Château des Tours
Owner: **GFA Louis Yerlès**. 72ha. 45,000 cases. Mer 33½%, CF and CS 33⅓%, Mal 33⅓%. Second label: **Château La Croix-Blanche**.
This is the largest domaine in Montagne and also has the most imposing 14th-century château. The vineyards are on the *côte* east of Montagne, facing St-Emilion. The *chais* is very modern and well equipped to handle the very large production. There is storage capacity for over 80,000 cases. The wines tend to be rich and quite dense, but soft-centred and charming. For early drinking.

POMEROL

This is easily the smallest of the great red wine districts of Bordeaux. It measures only 4km by 3km and covers an area of only about 730ha producing on average a little less than 30,000hl a year, roughly comparable with St-Julien in the Médoc. But a complexity of soils gives these wines an individuality and originality which sets them apart, enabling them to produce some of Bordeaux's most remarkable wines.

The best Pomerols are more intense, richer, denser and more tannic than most St-Emilions. Although the Merlot is even more predominant here than in St-Emilion, because of the clay and generally cold soils, many wines go through a stage in early maturity when they can look remarkably like Médocs, which shows how soil can change the appearance of grape varieties. The majority of wines become enjoyable to drink when four to seven years old, but a few top growths will take longer. The best vintages keep very well. The 70s, 64s and 55s are still excellent.

There is no classification in Pomerol, nor will there be, since there is no desire for one locally. After Pétrus – universally acknowledged as *hors classe* – the following nine wines are generally recognized as the leading ones, in alphabetical order: La Conseillante, Certan-de-May, l'Evangile, la Fleur-Pétrus, Gazin Lafleur, Latour-à-Pomerol, Petit-Village, Trotanoy, Vieux Château Certan.

Château Beauregard
Owner: **Héritiers Clauzel**. 13ha. 4,500 cases. Mer 48%, CF 44%, CS 6%, Mal 2%. Second label: **Domaine des Douves**.
This counts as a large property by Pomerol standards and has a fine château dating from the 17th and 18th centuries. A replica was erected on Long Island, New York, for the Guggenheims in the 1920s, an unusual compliment for a Bordeaux château, and is called Mille-Fleurs. The vineyard is on the high plateau of Pomerol, with some sand mixed with the gravel. This is a well run and well reputed *cru*; 25% new wood is used in its maturation. While not among the leading dozen *crus* of Pomerol, it is a good wine m the second flight, rich and full-flavoured. It develops quite quickly and has real breed and charm.

Château Le Bon-Pasteur
Owners: **Héritiers Serge Rolland**. 7ha. 2,500 cases. Mer 80%, CF 20%.
This *cru* is right on the Pomerol-St-Emilion border in the northwest of the appellation, between Gazin and Croque-Michotte. Since the present owners took over this property it has established quite a reputation for

itself in the USA. But the wines were rich and enticing before that – I recall a splendid 70. Now 35% new wood is being used in the cask maturation. The wines are very attractive, supple and rich. The most reputed of recent vintages are 83, 82, 81 and 78.

Château Bourgneuf-Vayron
Owners: **Charles and Xavier Vayron.** 10ha. 5,000 cases. Mer 80%, CF 20%.

A property on the western side of the high plateau of Pomerol as it slopes away in that direction. Here the gravelly soils are mixed with sand. This is a good *cru* placed by Alexis Lichine in the third category of Pomerols. The wines tend to become supple and enjoyable quite quickly and lack the concentration of the leading wines, while showing definite breed.

Château Certan-de-May
Owner: **Mme Odette Barreau-Badar.** 5ha. 1,750 cases. Mer 65%, CF 25%, CS and Mal 10%.

This minute vineyard is typical of a number of properties at the heart of Pomerol's high plateau, its very size combined with the devotion of its owners create something very individual and personal. Originally part of Vieux Château Certan, the soil here has clay mixed with the predominant gravel. It lies in the area, close to Cheval-Blanc, where nearly all the best Pomerols are to be found. In recent vintages this *cru* has re-emerged from the shadows and has rapidly taken its place again among the leading wines of the district. A proportion of 25% new oak is used in the maturation. The wines have an opulence, richness and power that are reminiscent of Trotanoy rather than its more compact neighbour, Vieux Château Certan. Splendid wines were made in 83, 82, 81, 79 and 78, with 76 the best drinkable wine. Certainly this is a wine to snatch up when you can.

Château Certan-Giraud
Owner: **Domaines Giraud.** 6ha. 2,000 cases. Mer 70%, CF 30%. Part of crop sold as Certan-Marzelle.

With neighbours like Pétrus and Vieux Château Certan, this small *cru*, situated on the very best gravel mixed with clay in the heart of the Pomerol high plateau, should be among the very top wines of the region. But, while the wines are good, they have yet to rise to the same heights as its illustrious neighbours. Only 10% new wood is used in the maturation. The owners also have Château Corbin just across the border in St-Emilion. These are generous, supple wines which tend to mature quickly. There are encouraging reports of distinct improvements in several recent vintages. A wine to watch.

Château Clinet
Owner: **Georges Audy.** 7ha. 3,000 cases. Mer 60%, CS 25%, CF 15%.
This *cru*, belonging to Libourne négociants Audy, is near the church of Pomerol on the high plateau with its gravelly soil mixed with sand. The unusual feature here is the high proportion of Cabernet Sauvignon, always said to be unsuitable for Pomerol. The result, in my experience, is wines which are hard and lack generosity or charm. One wonders what would happen if the Cabernet Sauvignon were replaced with Merlot. In the maturation 30% new wood is used.

Château La Conseillante
Owners: **Héritiers Louis Nicolas.** Administrator: Bernard Nicolas. 13ha. 5,000 cases. Mer 45%, CF 45%, Mal 10%.
This is always one of the best two or three wines in Pomerol after Pétrus year after year. Added to the consistency is the strong personality of the wine. It combines concentration and breed on the nose with a superb flavour of real originality, unctuous yet firm centred, and great persistence of flavour. Its neighbour L'Evangile is clearly from the same stable, but at present is less consistent and tends to be more massive but less fine. On the other side there are similarities with Petit-Village as the wine improves. The outstanding years here are 83, 82, 81, 79, 76, 75 and 70. Lesser years like 80, 77 and 73 have provided some delicious bottles.

Château La Croix
Owner: **Société Civile J. Janoueix.** 14ha. 6,100 cases. Mer 60%, CF 20%, CS 20%.
These are very well balanced attractive wines that are enjoyable after 4 or 5 years, yet also keep well, acquiring delicacy and a spicy complexity. I found the 79 for instance has lots of fruit and flavour but was already open-textured and forward when 6 years old. But the 71 was keeping well and had fined down, developing a lovely flavour, mellow but with a good backbone when 14 years old. Since then excellent wines have been made

in 83, 82 and 81. If you can sort this out from all the other châteaux of Pomerol with "Croix" in their names, it is a wine worth looking out for.

Château La Croix-de-Gay

Owner: Noel Raynaud. 11.5ha. 6,000 cases. Mer 80%, CS 15%, CF 5%.

This property is on the northern borders of the plateau of Pomerol where the predominantly gravelly soils mingle with sand. In the maturation 30% new wood is used. This is stylish, attractive wine that lacks the richness and concentration of its neighbour, Le Gay, and is made for young drinking. Nevertheless it is the sort of fruity, supple wine that has a wide appeal.

Domaine de l'Eglise

Owners: Philippe Castéja and Mme Peter Preben Hansen. 7ha. 3,500 cases. Mer 85%, CF 10%, CS 5%.

Not surprisingly this vineyard is near the church on the high plateau, and the soil is deep gravel with traces of iron deposit which gives the wines a certain brilliance and depth of colour. The Castéjas bought the property, whose wine they had distributed for many years, in 1972. One-third new oak is used in the cask maturation. The wines tend to be light in style yet fine, perfumed and elegant. This is good second-tier Pomerol.

Clos l'Eglise

Owners: Moreau family. Administrators: Michel and Francis Moreau. 6ha. 1,750 cases. Mer 55%, CF 20%, CS 25%.

This small vineyard lies near the church on the high plateau where the predominantly gravelly soil is mixed with sand. This is a well run property where stainless steel fermentation vats were introduced in 1983. The wines are matured in wood with a small percentage of new oak. The wines here are fine and rather more delicate than some Pomerols, with a particularly lovely bouquet. This fine-textured quality with length and beauty of flavour provides an attractive contrast with some of the heavyweights. It keeps well in spite of its lighter weight. Among recent vintages the 79 is particularly outstanding. A wine to watch.

Château l'Eglise-Clinet

Owner: Mme Durantou, 4.5ha. 1,850 cases. Mer 60%, CF 30%, Mal 10%.

This small vineyard has for many years been farmed by the Lasseire family of Clos Rene. It is near the church on the high plateau. There the soil is mainly gravelly mixed with sand. An important point here is that the vines are older than in most Pomerol domaines because they were not pulled up after the 56 frost, but left to recover, which most of them did. The wines are very carefully made and a small amount of new wood is used in the maturation in cask. The reputation of the wine has long been high amongst its devotees. This is classic Pomerol, rich, supple and very fruity. 83, 82 and 81 are all said to be very fine with the 78 ready to drink. Unfortunately a wine that takes some finding.

Château l'Enclos

Owner: Mme Carteau. Administrator: Mme Marc. 10.5ha. 3,200 cases. Mer 80%, CF 19.75%, Mal 0.25%

This good cru lies on the far side of the N89 Libourne–Périgueux road from the main vineyards of the high plateau of Pomerol. Here the soil is predominantly sandy, but there is an important gravelly outcrop which occurs here and at its neighbour, Clos René, and further away at Moulinet.

The wines here have been well made and are of high quality in the second tier of Pomerol wines. I have memories oa a wonderful 29. Today the style of the wines is rather similar to Close René – dense-textured, succulent and fruity, drinkable quite young but also possessing the capacity to age. This is fine classic Pomerol which is thoroughly reliable and enjoyable.

Château l'Evangile

Owner: Heritiers P. Ducasse. 13ha. 4,500 cases. Mer 65%, CF 35%.

This is one of the leading crus of Pomerol, situated near the edge of the high plateau adjoining La Conseillante and Vieux Château Certan. The predominantly gravelly soil is here mixed with some clay and sand, the feature responsible for the unique quality of Petrus (where the vineyard is almost entirely clay and gravel). The style of the wines most resembles La Conseillante, but has a different emphasis owing to the high proportion of Merlot, the presence of clay in the soil and the fact that only 20% new oak is used here in the maturation. The submerged cap system of vinification is used, which results in high colour extraction. The wines tend to be more massive and chewy in texture, yet sometimes lack the firmness of La Conseillante. There is also a certain inconsistency, so one feels that the full potential is not always realized. But it did produce a delicious 80, and the 83 and 82 are both exotic and massive.

Feytit-Clinet

Owners: Succésseurs Tane-Domergue. Administrator: Ets J.-P. Moueix. 7ha. 3,000 cases. Mer 85%, CF 15%.

A property on the northwestern edge of the plateau where the predominantly gravelly soil is mixed with sand. It is entirely run by the highly efficient Moueix organization presided over by Christian Moueix and his oenologist Jean-Claude Berrouet. While the wine is all plummy fruit on the nose, the flavour is more elegant than one expects, with good length and a firm finish, an excellent second-tier Pomerol. Naturally, from such a stable, the wines are commendably consistent.

Château La Fleur-Pétrus

Owner: Jean-Pierre Moueix. 7.5ha. 2,300 cases. Mer 75%, CF 25%.

One of the leading *crus* of Pomerol, situated just across the road from Petrus, but on quite different soil. Here the soil is very stony with large gravel but no clay or sand. In recent years the reputation of this wine has steadily grown, and this is now one of the flagships of the Moueix empire and almost certainly the finest Pomerol on purely gravelly soil, all the others having some clay in their makeup, save for Latour à Pomerol. One-third new wood is used here in the maturation. The wines are gorgeously perfumed, powerful and elegant on the nose, with great complexity, richness and power of flavour which is so obviously of the highest quality. They are very consistent with lovely examples in 83, 82, 81, 79 and 78. The lovely 71 is not now quite what it was, some of the sheen having gone, and the 70 is now more impressive. Not as massive as most of the other leading *crus*, but there is no doubting the breed and beauty of this wine.

Château Le Gay

Owner: Marie Robin. 8ha. 2,000 cases. Mer 50%, CF and CS 50%.

This *cru* lies on the northern side of the high plateau on gravelly soils, near to the owner's other *cru*, Lafleur. For many years its wines have been exclusively distributed by Ets J.-P. Moueix, but the Robin sisters ran the properties themselves. However, since the death of Thérèse Robin the Moueix team have taken over the management of both properties. Le Gay has always produced big, dense firm-textured wines which age very well, as bottles of 64 and 66 will demonstrate. Now things can only get better and no doubt the wines will be polished up a little and show more consistency. Recent successes have been 83, 82 and 79.

Château Gazin

Owner: Etienne de Bailliencourt. 20ha. 8,300 cases. Mer 80%, CF 15%, CS 5%.

This is the largest of the leading Pomerols, situated on the northeastern corner of the high plateau on gravelly soils. In the late 60s a portion of the vineyard adjoining Petrus, with the same clay in the soil, was sold to Petrus. Only a very small percentage of new oak is used in the maturation in cask. In find Gazin a difficult wine to assess. It is undeniably rich and opulent with an extraordinarily vivid and forceful character when young. There is a touch of coarseness but this perhaps is merely a part of a highly extrovert personality that demands attention. Whether this is something you like or not is something only you can decide, and whether the present management is making the best of it, is another question. It is hard to imagine that any recent vintages will measure up to the 45, which is still full of life and vigour. The 78 is unusually distinctively better than 79.

Château La Grave Trigant de Boisset

Owner: Christian Moueix. 8ha. 2,500 cases. Mer 90%, CF 10%.

This small vineyard has been the personal property of Christian Moueix, of Ets J.-P. Moueix, since 1971. The firm owns many properties, and farms or manages many others with Christian Moueix heading that team. The property is on gravelly soil on the middle plateau in the northwest of Pomerol, just before the Libourne-Périgueux road. The name is something of a handicap, the words "Château La Grave" appearing in large characters on the label, with "Trigant de Boisset" in smaller ones underneath. In the maturation in cask 25% new oak is used. The wine is quite rich, tannic and fine but less spectacular than the leading *crus*, a good second-tier Pomerol. The wines of course are beautifully made and very consistent. The 83, 82, 81, 79 and 78 are all very successful here.

Château Lafleur

Owner: **Marie Robin.** Administrator: Ets J.-P. Moueix. 4ha. 1,500 cases. Mer 50%, CF 50%.

This minute but superb property is on the gravelly high plateau, with some of the precious clay found in the best *crus* in its makeup. It is next to La Fleur-Petrus, but in the patchwork of Pomerol soils, is again different because of the clay missing at La Fleur-Petrus. Since 1981 the Moueix team have moved in to run the property for Mlle Robin and things are going from strength to strength. Unfortunately with so little wine, you have to be lucky as well as rich to find a bottle. The style is all opulent charm with great finesse and a lovely bouquet. 83, 82 and 79 all have a great reputation.

Château Lafleur Gazin

Owner: **Maurice Borderie.** Administrator: Ets J.-P. Moueix. 7.8ha. 3,500 cases. Mer 70%, CF 30%.

A property on the northeastern limits of the plateau next to Gazin. Here the predominantly gravelly soil is mixed with sand. This *cru* has come into great prominence since Ets J.-P. Moueix became "fermiers" here in 1976. It is run with all the usual meticulous care associated with the Moueix team under Christian Moueix and his oenologist Jean-Claude Berrouet. The wine is rich and quite powerful with an underlying firmness. In the 79 I detected a certain coarseness which differentiated it from the best *crus*, but in the very supple and ripe 83 I saw no sign of this. Perhaps an indication of the vintage or of progress. In any case a serious wine worth following.

Château Lagrange

Owner: **Ets Jean-Pierre Moueix.** 8ha. 2,600 cases. Mer 90%, CF 10%.

Another Moueix property on the gravelly high plateau. There is some new wood used in the cask maturation. The wines seem to have a certain originality of flavour, a breeding allied to charm and structure, which marks them out as very fine wines. The 81 is most impressive. A good second-tier Pomerol.

Château Latour-à-Pomerol

Owner: **Mme Lily Lacoste.** Administrator: Ets J.-P. Moueix. 8ha. 2,400 cases. Mer 80%, CF 20%.

This fine property lies on the gravelly high plateau, northwest of the church. Its owner is also co-proprietor of Pétrus, and it is managed and distributed by Ets J.-P. Moueix. 25% new oak is used in the cask maturation. This is a property which has noticeably improved throughout the 70s. In the past there were inconsistencies and fine bottles were interspersed with disappointments. Now the wines are marked by their wonderful perfume, and a delectable beauty of flavour, power and finesse. There is a clear similarity of style with La Fleur-Pétrus now. In 83 I even thought Latour surpassed it. The 82, 81, 79 and 78 were all wonderful wines. This is now indisputably among the leading *crus* of Pomerol.

Château Mazeyres

Owner: **Société Civile (Querre family).** 9ha. 5,000 cases. Mer 70%, CF 30%.

This property lies on the recent gravel and sand lower plateau north of Libourne and at the western extremity of the appellation. Two-thirds of the wine is matured in cask (of which 25% are renewed annually), and one-third in vats. The wines are consistent and well made, with a good colour, quite light textured but full flavoured with lovely easy, attractive fruit. A delicious 80 was made here. A very good lesser *cru*.

Château Moulinet

Owner: **Société Civile.** Administrator: **Armand Moueix.** 17.5ha. 8,000 cases. Mer 50%, CF 40%, CS 10%.

This relatively large property lies beyond the Libourne-Périgueux road on the gravelly sandy soils of the middle plateau. This is one of Armand Moueix's well run properties. One-third new wood is used. The wines are very scented and charming. The 78, for example, is delicious drinking now. A pleasant, widely distributed wine.

Château Nenin

Owner: **François Despujol.** 27ha. 10,000 cases. Mer 50%, CF 30%, Cs 20%.

This is one of the largest and best-known Pomerol properties. It lies on lower ground northwest of the high plateau, on sandy gravelly soils. Unfortunately tastings and a visit have indicated that all is not well here. I suspect the major problem is one of old casks in poor condition, as a result of which the wines often seem coarse and can leave one with a dirty woody after-taste. This is a pity because in cask the raw materials are rich and powerful. 82 is certainly suspect, and 81 tasted very dry and ungrateful before bottling. 79 is most disappointing. A harvesting machine was used here for the first time in 82.

Château Petit-Village

Owner: **Domaines Prats.** Administrator: **Bruno Prats.** 11ha. 3,900 cases. Mer 80%, CF 10%, CS 10%.

A finely placed vineyard on the high plateau with gravelly clay soils, close to La Conseillante and St-Emilion. The management is the same as for Cos d'Estournel. One problem here has been that after the 56 frost the vineyard was largely replanted and the mistake of planting too much Cabernet Sauvignon was then made. This has now been corrected and the wines are getting better and better. A minimum of 50% new wood is used, sometimes more, according to the year. The style is closest to La Conseillante, especially since 78. The wines have a lovely aroma and are very rich and deep, firm centred, with a really lovely flavour of great breed. 83, 82, 81 and 79 are the great recent successes here. On this form Petit Village is back in its rightful place among the leading *crus* of Pomerol.

Château Pétrus

Owners: **Mme L. P. Lacoste and Jean-Pierre Moueix.** Administrator: **Christian Moueix.** 11.4ha. 3,700 cases. Mer 95%, CF 5%.

Forty years ago Pétrus was unknown outside a small circle of wine-lovers in Bordeaux; today it is one of the great names, unfortunately more talked about than drunk, due to its price and rarity.

This is the world's great Merlot wine and shows what can be done with this variety when things are just right. There is an unctuous and almost chewy quality of richness and power which have some similarity with Cheval-Blanc, but Pétrus tends to be more concentrated, firmer and slower to develop. The complexity and nuances of flavour that develop with age are astonishing. Some vintages like 71 and 67 could already be enjoyed when only seven to ten years old, but then go on to surprise one with their further development, while some great years like 64 are still flexing their muscles. Recently 82 is already acquiring legendary status and prices to match, but 81, 79, 78 and 75 are also great wines. The most drinkable today are 76, 73 and the remarkable if controversial 71. Pétrus is a wine which every wine-lover has to find a way of experiencing.

Château Plince

Owner: **Moreau family.** 8.3ha. 3,400 cases. Mer 70%, CF 20%, CS 10%.

A good lesser *cru* situated on the sandy soils in the southwest of Pomerol, behind Nenin. The Moreau family also own the excellent Clos l'Eglise. A small amount of new oak is used in the cask maturation. This property has long had the reputation for producing deliciously fruity supple wines. The marvellous 47 remained fresh and opulent for over 30 years. After some ups and downs, good wines are now being made here and are excellent value for a *cru* on the sand which makes the most of its potential.

Château La Pointe

Owner: **Bernard d'Arfeuille.** 25ha. 9,000 cases. Mer 80%, CF 15%, Mal 5%.

This large property is on the sandy gravelly soils of the middle plateau, opposite Nenin and on slightly lower ground. The property is well known and widely distributed through the d'Arfeuille firm in Libourne. In the maturation 35% new wood is used. A retrospective tasting in 83 confirmed my suspicions that this wine is not as good as it used to be. The splendid 70 cast a shadow over the rest of the decade, making 75 look too tannic and lacking fruit, and 78 and 79 seem only moderate, if charming, lightweights.

A certain lightness, allied to finesse and stylishness, has long been the mark of La Pointe, but they always had a certain balance and flair which somehow seems missing now, even with the 82.

Clos René

Owner: **Pierre Lasserre.** 11ha. 5,500 cases. Mer 60%, CF 30%, Mal 10%. Alternative label: **Château Moulinet-Lasserre.**

This is a wonderfully perfumed, dense, rich, plummy Pomerol which seldom disappoints. The superb 83 is more tannic and alcoholic than the 82 which has a smell of prunes and an incredibly dense, rich but supple flavour. 81 is also extremely fine, very rich with a slightly roasted flavour.

The 78 is better than the 79, which lacks concentration. 76 is delicious drinking now, and 75 is a rich, powerful, tannic wine which is now very harmonious and could be drunk with enjoyment. This is a very good second-tier Pomerol. For fiscal and family reasons, a part of the crop is sold as Moulinet-Lasserre. The wines are the same – this is not a second label but rather an alternative one.

Château Rouget

Owner: François-Jean Brochet. 18ha. 6,000 cases. Mer 90%, CF 10%.

This is an interesting property on sandy and gravelly (with some clay) soils at the northern limit of the high plateau. The wine is very traditionally made and one-third new wood is used in the maturation in cask. An unusual feature is that the proprietor and his uncle before him have kept large stocks of old wines, so you can sometimes see these on restaurant lists in Bordeaux.

This is really a wine that takes time to develop. Even in a ripe flattering vintage like 79 the Rouget has a dense, austere nose and is quite tannic and powerful with lots of fat, a very impressive wine but unlikely to be ready before 87. This is real *vin de garde* wine in all good years.

Château de Sales

Owner: GFA du Château de Sales – les Héritiers de Laage. Administrators: Henri & Bruno de Lambert. 47.5 ha. 22,500 cases. Mer 66%, CF 17%, CS 17%. Second label: Château Chantalouette.

This is the largest property in Pomerol by a comfortable margin and lies on sandy soils with some recent gravel in the northwestern corner of the appellation near the Libourne-Pouis road. There is an impressive château (17th and 18th century) in a park. It has belonged to the same family for 400 years; Henri de Lambert's wife is a de Laage. Their son Bruno is a qualified oenologist.

The wines are alternated between vats and used casks for the maturation. There was a very noticeable improvement in quality here from 1970 onwards. The wines now are scented, rich, plummy and powerful with a pleasant stylishness. They develop quite quickly. Good reliable Pomerol at a reasonable price.

Château du Tailhas

Owner: Société Civile Pierre Nébout & fils. 10.5 ha. 5,000 cases. Mer 70%, CF 15%, CS 15%.

This property is on sandy soils in the extreme southwest corner of the appellation and near to Figeac, just the other side of the stream, which is also called Tailhas. 50% new wood is used in the cask maturation. This is well made and well reputed second-tier Pomerol. The wines have a very full colour, a highlighted bouquet which is most attractive, and lots of young fruit with that slightly earthy taste which occurs in some growths in Pomerol when there are iron deposits in the sub-soil. There is now a pleasing degree of consistency – a very good 80 was made.

Château Trotanoy

Owner: Ets Jean-Pierre Moueix. 7.5ha. 2,300 cases. Mer 85%, CF 15%.

This leading *cru* is on gravel and clay soils at the western edge of the high plateau. Apart from being one of the most illustrious jewels in the Moueix empire, it is also the home of Jean-Jacques Moueix, nephew of the legendary Jean-Pierre Moueix. Of course the care of this *cru* stands very high among the priorities for Christian Moueix and his oenologist Jean-Claude Berrouet. A proportion of 50% new wood is used for the cask maturation.

The reputation of Trotanoy is now higher than ever before, as can be seen from the prices collectors are prepared to pay for its mature vintages at auction. The style of the wine is for me more reminiscent of Pétrus than any other Pomerol, with its dense colour, rich spicy enveloping bouquet, and opulent fleshy body which develops an enchanting flavour of exceptional length. Great and often exceptional wines were made in 83, 82, 81, 79, 78 and 75. Of these 79 is rather soft centred and therefore the only one which is currently really drinkable. The 71 and 70 are both wonderful wines of contrasting style.

Vieux Château Certan

Owner: Héritiers Georges Thienpont. 13.6ha. 5,500 cases. Mer 50%, CF 25%, CS 20%, Mal 5%.

Until the rise of Pétrus, this fine *cru* was long regarded as the leading one in Pomerol. It is splendidly placed on the high plateau with sandy clay mixed with its gravel, and Pétrus, La Conseillante and l'Evangile are neighbours, with Cheval Blanc not far away. The small but aristocratic 17th-century château is the only one of note among these leading Pomerol *crus*; until the end of the 18th century the estate was larger. It has belonged to the Belgian Thienponts since 1924 and Leon Thienpont ran the property from 1943 until his death in 1985. The *chais* and *cuvier* were enlarged and modernized in the early 70s, but Léon Thienpont remained faithful to wooden vats. One-third new wood is used in the cask maturation.

This is a wine of marked individuality. It is very perfumed, less dense in colour than other leading Pomerols, very compact and firm on the palate, with a complexity, finesse and flavour which set it apart. It lacks the opulence of Trotanoy, and while it has something of the structure of La Conseillante, it lacks its unctuousness. Harmony, "race" and finesse are the great hallmarks here. 83 with its unusual power and 82 with its richness are two exceptional vintages, while 81, 79 and 78 are very classic wines for this *cru*. Evolution tends to be slow; the 71 is still at its peak, the 80 needs longer keeping than most from this year. In terms of breed and individuality this is still one of the very best of all Pomerols.

Château Vraye-Croix-de-Gay

Owner: Baronne Guichard. 3.7ha. 1,200 cases. Mer 55%, CF 40%, CS 5%.
This small *cru* is on gravelly soils on the edge of the high plateau near Le Gay and Domaine l'Eglise. Its owner also has the excellent Château Siaurac in Lalande-de-Pomerol. The reputation is for producing rich, dense and tannic wines which can be superb, but are also inconsistent.

LALANDE-DE-POMEROL

This is an appellation of growing importance, covering about 900ha of vines, of which roughly 60% are in the commune of Lalande, and 40% in that of Néac. In Lalande the vineyards are on recent gravel and sand terraces, which are relatively low-lying. However, in Néac there is a high plateau with those *crus* facing south towards Pomerol being on very good gravel. The best wines are close in quality to the lesser Pomerols, but usually with less power and tannin, so they tend to develop more quickly, but are immensely attractive, with finesse and style.

Château des Annereaux

Owner: M. Hessel-Milhade. 22ha. 10,000 cases.
A good *cru* on the gravel and sandy soils of the lower plateau. Very elegant attractive wines are made. There was a delicious 79, but the 82 seems too forward and lacks stuffing.

Château de Bel-Air

Owner: L. & Jean-Pierre Musset. 10ha. 4,500 cases. Mer 60%, CF 15%, Mal 15%, CS 10%.
This well reputed *cru* is on the gravel and sand of the middle plateau, opposite Moulinet (Pomerol). It has long been considered one of the appellation's leading *crus*.

Château Haut-Chaigneau

Owner: André Chatounet. 20ha. 11,000 cases. Mer 60%, CF 20%, CS 20%.
A good *cru* in the commune of Néac. Rich, plummy and attractive wines are being made here. The 83, 82 and 81 are all of a high standard.

Château Les Hauts-Conseillants and Les Hauts-Tuileries

Owner: Leopold Figeac. 8ha. 3,000 cases. Mer 60%, CS 25%, CF 15%.
This very good *cru* is in Néac. The Les Hauts-Conseillants name is used for *vente-direct* in France, the Hauts-Tuileries are for export sales. One-third new wood is used in the maturation in cask. The wines are well made and have a marvellous opulent perfumed bouquet and a seductively silky texture with good concentration worthy of a Pomerol. Very good wines were made in 83, 82, 81 and 79.

Château Moncets

Owner: Baronne de Jerphanion. 16ha. 8,000 cases. Second label: Gardour.
An excellent *cru* on the gravel and sand at the edge of the plateau in the best southern part of Néac. The wines are bottled in Libourne by Ets J.-P. Moueix. The wine is rich and velvety in texture with style and breed which place it in the same category as the good lesser Pomerols.

Château Siaurac
Owner: Baronne Guichard. 23ha. 8,500 cases. Mer 50%, CF 40%, CS 10%.
This important *cru* is in Néac, in the south of the commune on gravel and sand at the edge of the plateau. It is one of the best known *crus* in this appellation, consistently producing firm, fruity wines which are most attractive.

MINOR APPELLATIONS

The following section covers some of the appellations which do not belong to the major league of Bordeaux regions but which contain many wines that are worth investigating. These wines tend to mature earlier than the Grands Crus of the well known appellations, which makes them extremely useful commercially. Among them are wines of great charm and personality which it would be a pity to overlook.

CÔTES DE BOURG

The attractive, hilly and often wooded countryside of the Côtes de Bourg has seen something of a revival in the past decade. There are now 2,900ha of vines, an increase of 30%. The soil is mostly limestone and clay, and gravel and clay on a limestone sub-soil. The traditional encépagement was one-third each of Cabernet Sauvignon, Merlot and Malbec (still to be found at Château Guerry), but in most properties the role of the Malbec has been reduced and that of the Merlot increased. This factor, together with the inability today of many owners to afford casks for maturation, has meant that something of the distinctively rich fruitiness of the Bourg has inevitably been lost. But good and attractive wines are being made here, in increasing quantities, and as the demand for good, reasonably priced red Bordeaux grows, Bourg should prosper.

Château de Barbe
Owner: Savary de Beauregard family. Administrator: Louis Savary de Beauregard. 56ha. 32,000 cases. Mer 70%, CF and CS 25%, Mal 5%.
One of the largest, finest and best reputed properties in the region. There is no wood-ageing, and the wines are light-textured, fruity and charming, with some "race". Essentially for young drinking (after two to four years).

Château Guerry
Owner: Societé Civile. Administrator: Bertrand de Rivoyre. 22ha. 12,000 cases. CS 40%, Mer 30%, Mal 30%.
A *cru* which shows what Bourg is capable of. There are two distinctive features: the position of the Malbec as a major variety is retained, and this is one of the last *crus* in Bourg where all the wines are matured in cask. The result is a wine which combines richness and suppleness, power and finesse. Distribution is exclusively through Ets de Rivoyre-Diprovin and Louis Dubroca.

Château Guionne
Owner: Richard Porcher. 12ha. 6,250 cases. CF and CS 50%, Mer 45%, Mal 5%.
This *cru* is all château-bottled and produces fruity, attractive and quite elegant wines.

Château Mendoce
Owner: Philippe Darricarrère. 15ha. 8,300 cases. CS 57%, Mer 43%.
This is one of the best known and best reputed wines in the region. There is a fine château, parts of which date from the 15th century. The owners are also proprietors of Château Moulin-à-Vent in Moulis. The wines are supple with some richness and mature rapidly.

Château Peychaud
Owner: Jacques & Bernard Germain. 34ha. 16,600 cases. Mer 40%, CF and CS 50%, Mal 10%.
This large and well known property was acquired by the present owners in 1971. It has a good reputation for producing supple, pleasing wines.

Château Rousset
Owner: M & Mme Teisseire. Administrator: Gérard Teisseire. 23ha. 10,000 cases. Mer 45%, Cs 33%, Mal 16%, CF 6%.
Situated in the commune of Samonac, this is certainly one of the best *crus* of

Bourg. The wines have richness and length of flavour which place them above the general run of wines from this area.

Château Tour-de-Tourteau

Owner: GAEC Chagnaud Père & Fils. 13ha. 7,500 cases. Mer 50%, CF and CS 30%, Mal 20%.

This excellent *cru* was once part of Rousset. Today all the wines are château-bottled and distributed by Calvet and Éts de Rivoyre & Diprovin-Louis Dubroca. The wines are unusually rich and powerful, even pungent, making delicious drinking when three to four years old.

PREMIÈRES CÔTES DE BLAYE

This region forms the northward extension of the Côtes de Bourg. Although the region is larger than the Bourg, the parts suited to the vine are smaller. Today there are 2,382ha of vines, which is more than double the area a decade ago. The output consists predominantly of red wine, with only a small and unimportant production of white. The soil here is clay or limestone and clay, and the Merlot is more predominant than in Bourg.

The prices achieved are often no more than for Bordeaux Supérieur, and some growers take advantage of the higher permitted yields for the lesser appellation and declare their wines as Bordeaux Superieur instead of Premières Côtes de Blaye. This is a good source of fruity, easy-to-drink red Bordeaux.

Château Bourdieu

Owner: Jean Kléber Michaud. 33ha. Red: 15,000 cases; Mer 50%, CS 40%, CF 10%. White: 5,000 cases; Sém 80%, Sauv & Col 20%.

A well known and well reputed *cru*, unusual in its high proportion of Cabernet Sauvignon and in using wood maturation. The result is a wine above average in character and quality.

Château Charron

Owner: Marc Doudet-Beaudry. 23ha. Red: 14,000 cases; Mer 80%, CF and CS 20%. White: 1,000 cases; Sém 65%, Sauv 35%.

A well reputed *cru* which uses wood maturation and even some new oak. The result is a wine with more colour and richness than average.

Château l'Escadre

Owners: Georges Carreau & Fils. 32ha. Red: 13,000 cases; Mer 50%, CS 25%, Mal 25%. White: 2,000 cases; Mer Blanc 40%, Sém 30%, Col 20%, Ugni Blanc 10%.

This very good *cru* in the commune of Cars has acquired an excellent reputation for consistency over the last 20 years. Some wood maturation is used, and the wines are charmingly fruity and stylish.

Château Segonzac

Owner: Mme Pierre Dupuy. 30ha. Red: 5,500 cases. White: 1,500 cases.

This *cru* in the commune of St-Genès-de-Blaye produces very fruity, light, supple wines for early drinking.

FRONSAC

In the 18th and early 19th centuries, Fronsac was the most reputed of the Libournais wines, fetching higher prices than those of St-Emilion. Now, after a long period of obscurity, it is slowly re-emerging as a quality region. In total there are about 1,000ha of vines divided between the appellations of Canon-Fronsac (30% of the area) and Fronsac (70%). These vineyards, like those of the St-Emilion *côtes*, are wines of the plateau and *côtes*, only more spectacularly so. The vineyards of the Canon-Fronsac are on a *plateau calcaire* and on outcrops and *côtes* of sandstone, while those of the Fronsac AC are mostly on a *plateau calcaire* covered with red soils, similar to those of St-Christophe.

The vineyards here tend to be small on average, but there are some lovely buildings, such as at La Rivière and La Dauphine. The Merlot now dominates, but the Cabernet Sauvignon also has an important place in some of the best vineyards. There has been a tendency to use too much old wood and keep the wines in them too long, and many château-bottled wines have looked rustic, but now things seem to be improving. With Ets J.-P. Moueix now taking an increasing interest in the region, better quality should lead to better prices and a wider interest. So there could be a brighter future ahead for Fronsac.

Château Dalem
Owner: Michel Rullier. 13ha. 5,500 cases.
An important property on the *côte*, just out of Saillans to the south-east. It produces very perfumed wines with real charm. They develop soft, ripe, fruity flavours when young, but they last well. I was interested to note that, while the 78 was already very pleasing when four years old, 70, 67 and 64 were also still full of fruit and not drying up at all. All the wine is château-bottled.

Château de la Dauphine
Owner: Ets J.-P. Moueix. 9ha. 9,000 cases. Mer 65%, CF 35%.
One of the best known *crus* of Fronsac, and is on the lower *côte* west of the town of Fronsac. The wines are very well made. A proportion of 20% new wood is used, and the wines are bottled at the right time. This all adds up to delicious, fruity wines with character, which can be drunk young.

Château Jeandeman
Owner: M. Roy-Trocard. 30ha. 12,750 cases.
This is the largest vineyard in Fronsac, and is on the *plateau calcaire* with red soil in the commune of St-Aignan. The wines are distinctly perfumed and have a delicious fruitiness on the palate which makes them very drinkable after three to four years.

Château Mayne-Vieil
Owner: Roger Sèze. 25ha. 14,000 cases. Mer 80%, CF 20%.
An important and well distributed *cru*. The vineyard is on sand and clay, producing very attractive wines with a rich middle flavour, good structure and character, usually very drinkable in three to four years.

Château Moulin Haut-Laroque
Owner: Jean-Noël Hervé. 14ha. 6,000 cases. Mer 65%, CF 20%, CS 10%, Mal 5%.
This important Fronsac *cru* is on the *plateau calcaire* and *côte* southwest of Saillans. The wines are very perfumed with more power and structure than many straight Fronsacs. Tannin and fruit are well matched and the wines are slower to develop than some (four to five years).

Château La Rivière
Owner: Jacques Borie. 44ha. 20,000 cases. Mer 60%, CS 30%, CF 5%, Mal 5%.
A very grand château, superbly sited and complete with huge underground cellers. The vineyard is on the *plateau calcaire* and côte. A proportion of 30–40% new wood is used, and the wines are powerful and tannic.

Château La Valade
Owner: Bernard Roux. 15ha. 8,800 cases. Mer 100%.
This *cru* is on the *plateau calcaire* and *côte* of the commune of Fronsac. The wines are perfumed and vigorous, well balanced with lots of character, and quite fine.

Château Villars
Owner: Jean-Claude Gaudric. 25ha. 11,500 cases. Mer 60%, CF 30%, CS 10%.
This *cru* is in the commune of Saillans, on the *plateau calcaire* and *côte*. In the maturation one-third new wood is used. The wines have a lot of fruit but tend to be rather soft and develop quickly (over about three years).

CANON-FRONSAC

The appellation Canon-Fronsac, or Côtes de Canon-Fronsac, is a small island of about 300ha in the middle of the Fronsac appellation and consisting of parts of the communes of Fronsac and St-Michel-de-Fronsac. Although the outstanding *crus* are in Canon-Fronsac rather than Fronsac, the two areas can in practice be treated as one appellation.

Château Canon-de-Brem
Owner: Ets J.-P. Moueix. 20ha. 9,000 cases. Mer 65%, CF 35%.
One of the best known and best reputed of all Fronsacs. The wines have remarkable concentration of fruit and flavour, and are rich and supple, with great style and character. This really shows what the appellation is capable of. The wines need four to five years to show at their best, and will keep well. Recently bought by Ets J.-P. Moueix.

Château Coustolle
Owner: Alain Roux. 16ha. 8,000 cases. Mer 60%, CF 30%, CS and Mal 10%.
A fine *cru* on the *côte* north of Fronsac. In the maturation 20% new wood is

used, and the result is a wine of concentration and richness which holds very well and develops character and some distinction. The 71 was still excellent when 11 years old.

Château du Gaby
Owners: **Yves & Henri de Kermoal. 10ha. 4,250 cases.**
A good *cru* on the *côte* and *plateau calcaire* northwest of Fronsac. The wines are rich and powerful with lots of extract, needing time to develop, and can keep very well. The 62 was still delicious when 20 years old.

Château Jumayne
Owner: **Héritiers de Coninck.** Administrator: **René de Coninck. 16ha. 7,000 cases. Mer 80%, CF and CS 20%.**
This well-known *cru* is on the *côte* of Canon. Its wines are less powerful than the best *crus* today in Canon-Fronsac, but have a wide following.

Château Mausse
Owner: **Guy Janoueix. 10ha. 4,500 cases.**
A good *cru* on the *plateau calcaire* northeast of St-Michel. Produces very perfumed wines with richness and some concentration, which develop a pleasing suppleness after four to five years.

Château Mazeris-Bellevue
Owner: **Jacques Bussier. 11.5ha. 4,500 cases. CS 50%, Mer 40%, Mal 10%.**
A fine *cru* on the *plateau calcaire* and *côte*. Unusually, the Cabernet Sauvignon is in the ascendancy here, and the result is a distinguished and fine flavour with lots of character and style.

Château Pichelèbre.
Owner: **GFA de Brem. 12ha. 5,500 cases.**
Another de Brem wine, not so well known nor such a memorable name as Canon de Brem, but very near it in quality. The vineyard is on the *côte*, west of Fronsac. The wines are deep-coloured, decidedly powerful, tannic, rich and full of character, needing four to five years to show their best and keeping well.

Château Toumalin
Owner: **Bernard d'Arfeuille. 8ha. 4,000 cases. Mer 70%, CF 30%.**
This *cru* is on the *côte* above the valley of the river Isle north of Fronsac, and belongs to the well known Libourne négociants who also have La Pointe (Pomerol) and La Serre (St-Emilion). It produces lovely vivid, fruity wines with the necessary balance to be enjoyed young.

ENTRE-DEUX-MERS

This huge area is the largest source of good dry white wines in Bordeaux today. There are now 2,550ha benefiting from the AC (including the small Haut-Benauge AC), that is 78% more than a decade ago. This is a region of large estates with mechanical harvesting now widely used and cool fermentation the rule. Much good red wine is also made, but this is only entitled to be called Bordeaux or Bordeaux Supérieur.

Château Bonnet
Owner: **André Lurton. Red: 80ha; 45,000 cases; CF and CS 60%, Mer 40%. White: 40ha; 40,000 cases; Sém 60%, Sauv 20%, Musc 20%. Rosé: 1,000 cases.** Secondary labels: **Château Tour-de-Bonnet, Château Gourmin, Château Peyraud.**
One of the most impressive properties in Entre-Deux-Mers, with its elegant 18th-century château and enormous vineyard. It is in Grézillac, due south of St-Emilion. The *chais* and *cuvier* are as well equipped as André Lurton's prestigious Graves properties. The white wine is cold-fermented at 16°–18°C (61°–64°F), and part of the red wine is matured in cask and sold in special numbered bottles. With its interesting mixture of *cépages*, the white wine is very perfumed and full of elegant, fruity flavours. The red grapes are mechanically harvested, and the red wines are thoroughly attractive with quite a bit of character.

Château Launay
Owner: **Rémy Greffier. 105ha. Red: 17,000 cases; CS 50%, Mer 50%. White: 40,500 cases; Sem 33⅓%, Sauv 33⅓%, Musc 33⅓%.** Secondary labels: **White: Château Dubory, Château Braidoire, Château La Vaillante. Red: Château Haut Castenet, Château Haut-Courgeaux.**
This very large property is at Soussac, on the road between Pellegrue and Sauveterre in the eastern Entre-Deux-Mers. All the wine is château-bottled. The wines are well reputed.

Château Moulin-de-Launay
Owners: **Claude & Bernard Greffier.** 75ha. 45,000 cases. Sem 40%, Sauv 30%, Musc 20%, Ugni Blanc 10%. Secondary labels: **Château Tertre-de-Launay, Château Plessis, Château La Vigerie, Château de Tuilerie.**
This large property at Soussac, in eastern Entre-Deux-Mers between Pellegrue and Sauveterre, is entirely consecrated to the production of white wines. The wines are very fruity, with elegance and length.

Château Thieuley
Owner: **Francis Courselle.** Red: 8,000 cases; Mer 60%, CF 20%, CS 20%. White: 4,750 cases; Sauv 100%.
The proprietor here is a professor of viticulture. The property is at La Sauve near Créon in western Entre-Deux-Mers. The white wines, made from 100% Sauvignon, have a most attractive fruit, without exaggerated acidity, and are light and fresh.

Château de Toutigeac
Owner: **René Mazeau.** Red: 100ha; 45,000 cases; CF 70%, CS 25%, Mer 5%. White: 50ha; 25,000 cases; Sém 100%.
One of the best known properties to use the sub-appellation Entre-Deux-Mers-Haut-Benauge. The appellation can be used only for white wines. Both red and white wines here are well reputed and all are château-bottled.

PREMIÈRES CÔTES DE BORDEAUX

This attractive area runs from the suburbs of Bordeaux southwards down the right bank of the Garonne to the sweet wine regions of Loupiac and Ste-Croix-du-Mont. It produces moderately sweet white wines and fruity, vivacious reds for early drinking. A decade ago there was slightly more vineyard area devoted to white than to red wine production, but today the red vineyards have increased by $\frac{2}{3}$ to 1,556ha, and the white vineyards have decreased by 22% to 769ha. The best whites in the south of the area carry the superior AC Cadillac, but the idea has not really caught on. The real future of the region seems to rest more with its very pleasant red wines.

Château Birot
Owner: **Jacques Boireau.** 34.5ha. Red: 5,000 cases. White: 15,000 cases.
This *cru* in the commune of Béguey is best known for its fresh, fruity whites, with well balanced acidity and sweetness and some elegance.

Château Fayau
Owners: **Jean Médeville & fils.** 36ha. Red: 27ha; 13,500 cases; CS 40%, Mer 40%, CF 20%. White: 9ha; 4,500 cases; Sém 48%, Sauv 32%, Musc 20%.
This excellent *cru* in Cadillac is carefully run by the Médeville family who make a particularly good sweet white Cadillac, with fruit and style, which ages well.

Château Le Gardera, Château Laurétan, Château Tanesse
Owners: **Domaines Cordier.**
For many years Domaines Cordier have run these adjoining properties in the Premières Côtes as a single production centre, producing several different appellations. Since 1983 the production of Château Laurétan has ceased, and this has been changed into a brand, Laurétan Rouge and Laurétan Blanc, with the simple Bordeaux appellation. The relevant details on the other two châteaux are as follows:
    Château Le Gardera. 25ha. Red (AC Bordeaux Superieur): 11,500 cases; Mer 60%, CS 40%.
    Château Tanesse. Red (AC Premières Cotes de Bordeaux): 35ha; 12,000 cases; CS 55%, Mer 35%, CF 10%. White (AC Bordeaux Blanc): 20ha; 12,000 cases; Sauv 85%, Sem 15%.
    Le Gardera now produces an attractive, light-bodied Merlot-dominated red wine. Tanesse makes a more Cabernet-dominated red wine, together with a flowery, fresh, Sauvignon-styled white.

Château Reynon
Owner: **Denis & Florence Dubourdieu-David.** 40ha. Red: 9,000 cases; Mer 50%, CS 40%, CF 10%. White: 12,500 cases; Sauv 100%.
This well known and well distributed *cru* is the most important property in the commune of Béguey, very near to Cadillac. Here an excellent red wine is made, possessing the almost startling fruitiness which characterizes the

area. The whites are well regarded and fruity but need drinking very young.

STE-CROIX DU MONT

The two appellations of Ste-Croix-du-Mont and Loupiac are situated on some spectacular hillsides and the plateau, just across the Garonne from Sauternes and Barsac, affording a splendid panorama of the whole Graves-Sauternes region. They also provide the best sweet wines outside Sauternes. In fact the best properties are able to make wines which can be better than the lesser Sauternes, given grapes properly affected by noble rot. They tend to be lighter and less rich than Sauternes, but are very fruity and long-lived. The cooperative at Ste-Croix du Mont produces wines of a good standard. The area under vine is 425ha.

Château Loubens

Owner: Antoine de Sèze. Red: 6ha; 600 cases; Mer 45%. CS 45%; CF10%. White: 15ha; 1,500 cases; Sem 90%. Sauv 10%. Secondary labels: **Château Terfort, Fleuron Blanc de Château Loubens.**
This has long been one of the best *crus* of the appellation. The sweet wines have an elegant fruit and freshness about them and are well made with a well balanced sweetness. The vineyard is finely placed at the top of the *côte*. There is an attractive dry wine, sold under the same of Fleuron Blanc, and another sweet wine, Château Terfort, which also maintains an excellent standard.

Château de Tastes

Owner: **Domaines Prats.** White. 1 ha. 400 cases. Sauv 100%.
This historic domaine with its superbly positioned château and vineyard on the summit of the *côte* commands splendid views across the Garonne and over the Sauternes and Graves. Sadly, terribly little of this very fine wine is made today.

LOUPIAC

Apart from the fact that they lie in different communes, there is in fact no useful distinction to be made between the Loupiac appellation and that of its neighbour, Ste-Croix-du-Mont. Loupiac has 332ha under vine.

Château Loupiac-Gaudiet

Owner: **Marc Ducau.** 45ha. Red: 15ha; 900 cases. White: 30ha; 10,000 cases.
This has been one of the best and most consistent wines of Loupiac for many years. The wines are mostly aged in vat. They have delicacy and finesse with a fruity sweetness, and age very well.

Château de Ricaud

Owner: **Société Civile Garreau-Ricard.** 45ha. Red: 5,750 cases. White: 10,000 cases.
This is the most famous *cru* in Loupiac, and many of the historic vintages (such as 29 and 47) are still superb. Unfortunately in the last years of the previous ownership the property was neglected and run down, but since the new owners from Champagne took over in 1980 there has been steady progress. The Loupiac is finely perfumed with finesse, real elegance and richness. Some new wood is now used in the maturation. Fine examples were made in 81, 82 and 83. There is a rather traditional Sémillon-dominated dry white with the Bordeaux AC, and a very fruity, attractive red wine which has the Premières Côtes AC in the best years (81 and 82) and otherwise the Bordeaux Supérieur AC. Again these wines are matured in cask. It looks as if the property will soon regain its former reputation.

BORDEAUX CÔTES DE CASTILLON

This region lies between the St-Emilionnais and the boundary of the Gironde and Dordogne departments, and used to be included in the St-Emilionnais before the appellations came into force. It produces some of the very best Bordeaux Supérieur, with body and some character, much of it from a very good cave cooperative. With 2,268ha of vines, the area under vine has nearly doubled in a decade.

The following châteaux, among others, are worth looking out for: de Belcier, Castegens (also sold as Fontenay), de Clotte, L'Estang, Haut-Tuquet, Lardit, Moulin-Rouge, Pitray, Puycarpin, Rocher-Bellevue, Ste-Colombe, Thibaud-Bellevue.

INDEX

This does not include names of châteaux, which are listed in the A–Z, pages 39–50